CITY STATUS IN THE BRITISH ISLES, 1830–2002

Historical Urban Studies

Series editors: *Richard Rodger and Jean-Luc Pinol*

Titles in this series include:

City Status in the British Isles, 1830–2002

JOHN BECKETT
University of Nottingham, UK

ASHGATE

Published by
Ashgate Publishing Limited
Gower House
Croft Road
Aldershot
Hants GU11 3HR
England

Ashgate Publishing Company
Suite 420
101 Cherry Street
Burlington, VT 05401-4405
USA

Ashgate website: http://www.ashgate.com

British Library Cataloguing in Publication Data
Beckett, J. V.
City status in the British Isles, 1830-2002.—(Historical urban studies)
1. Cities and towns—Great Britain—History—19th century 2.Cities and towns—Great Britain—History—20th century 3.Civic improvement—Great Britain—History 4.Municipal incorporation—Great Britain—History—19th century 5.Municipal incorporation—Great Britain—History—20th century
I.Title
307.7'6'0941

Library of Congress Cataloging-in-Publication Data
Beckett, J. V.
City status in the British Isles, 1830-2002 / John Beckett.
    p. cm.—(Historical urban studies)
Includes bibliographical references and index.
ISBN 0-7546-5067-7 (alk. paper)
1. Cities and towns—Great Britain—History. 2. City promotion—Great Britain—History. I. Title. II. Series.

HT133.B37 2005
307.76'0941—dc22

2004025740

ISBN 0 7546 5067 7

Printed and bound by Athenaeum Press, Ltd.,
Gateshead, Tyne & Wear.

Contents

Historical Urban Studies
General Editors' Preface

Density and proximity are two of the defining characteristics of the urban dimension. It is these that identify a place as uniquely urban, though the threshold for such pressure points varies from place to place. What is considered an important cluster in one context – may not be considered as urban elsewhere. A third defining characteristic is functionality – the commercial or strategic position of a town or city which conveys an advantage over other places. Over time, these functional advantages may diminish, or the balance of advantage may change within a hierarchy of towns. To understand how the relative importance of towns shifts over time and space is to grasp a set of relationships which is fundamental to the study of urban history.

Towns and cities are products of history, yet have themselves helped to shape history. As the proportion of urban dwellers has increased, so the urban dimension has proved a legitimate unit of analysis through which to understand the spectrum of human experience and to explore the cumulative memory of past generations. Though obscured by layers of economic, social and political change, the study of the urban milieu provides insights into the functioning of human relationships and, if urban historians themselves are not directly concerned with current policy studies, few contemporary concerns can be understood without reference to the historical development of towns and cities.

This longer historical perspective is essential to an understanding of social processes. Crime, housing conditions and property values, health and education, discrimination and deviance, and the formulation of regulations and social policies to deal with them were, and remain, amongst the perennial preoccupations of towns and cities – no historical period has a monopoly of these concerns. They recur in successive generations, albeit in varying mixtures and strengths; the details may differ

The central forces of class, power and authority in the city remain. If this was the case for different periods, so it was for different geographical entities and cultures. Both scientific knowledge and technical information were available across Europe and showed little respect for frontiers. Yet despite common concerns and access to broadly similar knowledge, different solutions to urban problems were proposed and adopted by towns and cities in different parts of Europe. This comparative dimension informs urban historians as to which were systematic factors and which were of a purely local nature: general and particular forces can be distinguished.

These analytical frameworks, considered in a comparative context, inform the books in this series.

Université de Tours   Jean-Luc Pinol
University of Leicester   Richard Rodger

List of Tables

List of Abbreviations

AO	Archive Office
HO	Home Office
NAS	National Archives of Scotland
PRO	Public Record Office, the National Archives
PRONI	Public Record Office of Northern Ireland
RO	Record Office
SCA	Southampton City Archives
VCH	Victoria County History

Note: Place of publication is London unless stated otherwise.

Acknowledgements

I am grateful to many people who have helped me at various stages in the preparation of this book. Many of them are mentioned in individual footnotes, but others include David Crook and Hilary Jones of the Public Record Office, Linda Henshaw and Sylvia Brown of the Home Office, Peter Borsay, Ben Cowell, Graham Dines, Matthew Engel, Simon Fanshawe, Heather Forbes, Philip Goldsmith, Caroline Hallett, David Hayton, John Heath, Sue Jones, Paul Murray, Guy Roberts, James Simpson, David Smith, Kate Thompson, Michael Turner and David Windsor. I am particularly grateful to Janice Avery for help with tracking down obscure websites, and for putting the text in order.

John Beckett
Nottingham

Introduction

What is a city? The term is ubiquitously used, seldom defined, and a subject of tremendous angst today in the town halls of those places which have yet to achieve city status. When, in conjunction with the millennium celebrations in 2000, the government announced a competition to find the town most suited to be raised to a city, thirty-nine candidates came forward from across the United Kingdom. Such was the political infighting at Westminster that the government not only agreed to make three cities rather than one in 2000, it also announced that for the Queen's Golden Jubilee in 2002 it would promote four more towns – rather than the one previously promised – one for each of the four provinces of the United Kingdom. Encouraged by such news, forty-one towns applied for the coveted title, and the government once more capitulated to political pressure by raising five towns to city status, one in each of England, Wales and Scotland, and two in Northern Ireland. Today the government recognizes fifty-one cities in England, six in Scotland, and five each in Wales and Northern Ireland.

To most of us 'city' implies something greater and probably grander than a town. It is certainly less cumbersome than the technically correct and preferred Victorian terminology of 'large towns and populous districts', but is it any more than this? Lord Asa Briggs, in what is widely regarded as a pioneering study of the urban world, *Victorian Cities*, published in 1956, took what he called 'a "common-sense view" of the city', accepting that the term had a legal status, but using it as a shorthand form for a group of towns, including Middlesbrough, which is still not a city.[1] City, in this usage, is merely a convenient shorthand phrase, and few people would dissent from such usage because most of us would be hard pressed to decide whether Chelmsford, Guildford and Reading are cities (they are not), as opposed to Chichester, Ely and St Albans (they are). Few of us would understand why country towns such as Salisbury, Lichfield and Winchester are cities, while industrial and commercial centres such as Blackburn, Bolton and Doncaster are towns; or why some historic English counties have no cities at all, among them Suffolk, Essex and Northamptonshire, while others – notably Yorkshire which can boast Leeds, Sheffield, Hull, Bradford, Ripon, Wakefield and York – are teeming with them.

Few people can spell out the difference between a town and a city. If they hazard any sort of guess it is quite likely to be on the lines of a city being a

---

[1]   A. Briggs, *Victorian Cities* (1968 edn.), 32. H.J. Dyos and S. Wolff, *The Victorian City: Images and Reality* (2 vols. 1977–8) contains no sustained discussion of what defines a city, and R. Dennis, *English Industrial Cities in the Nineteenth Century* (1984), simply ignored the otherwise inconvenient fact that none of the 'industrial cities' from which he drew the majority of his material – Huddersfield, Cardiff, Wolverhampton, Preston and Oldham – was a city in the nineteenth century.

place with a cathedral. When Wolverhampton finally succeeded in becoming a city in 2000 after nearly fifty years of trying, one local person asked 'will we have to choose one of our historic churches to be named as a cathedral?'. Karen Skelton, a Preston office worker, was quoted in the local press after hearing that Preston had been promoted to city in 2002, as asking much the same question: 'will we have to build a cathedral?'.[2] In fact, the link between a city and a cathedral was abolished as long ago as 1888.

The world at large has also shown a similar lack of enthusiasm for other marks of civic status, notably the position of lord mayor as opposed to mayor. Many people believe that a city automatically has a lord mayor, but in practice many do not, and only Cardiff (in 1905) was granted both honours at the same time. Lord mayor is another title closely controlled by Whitehall, and since 1907 granted only to cities and then to large cities (in other words not, usually, those cities which enjoy the status purely through having a cathedral) of many years standing. Among those large and important places which have both city status and a lord mayoralty, there has occasionally been debate about distinguishing themselves from the rest by obtaining the prefix 'right honourable' for their lord mayors. These debates have seldom penetrated the public imagination.

So what is a city? In the United States a city is defined by a charter of incorporation setting out its municipal powers and the framework of local government. While this might proliferate cities, it has the benefit of being clear. In Australia and Canada, city is a term applied to larger units of municipal government under state and provincial authority. In New Zealand the more populous towns are known as boroughs under legislation passed in 1933. But in the United Kingdom this clarity is alien: the whole process of promotion has been and remains obscure. No feedback is offered to unsuccessful candidates. When the millennium city status competition was launched in 1998 aspirant cities had to decide for themselves what would be important in persuading the government to take their claims seriously. For the Queen's Golden Jubilee in 2002 the government added a competition for the status of lord mayor, but it refused to set down any rules of engagement. The Home Office, and since 2001 the Lord Chancellor's Department (now the Department of Constitutional Information), has steadfastly maintained that only places which have been granted letters patent entitling them to city status are officially allowed to use the term, but it has struggled to find a suitable definition of entitlement and does not object if towns without the necessary documentation use the title. The Scottish towns of Dunfermline, Elgin and Perth all believe they have evidence to show that they are entitled to be cities, but the Home Office and Scotland Office refuse to listen, although they do not positively warn them off using the title. Even more bizarre is the way in which Rochester seems accidentally to have lost its city status and is having immense trouble reclaiming the position. Nor has it been made clear why

---

[2]   *Wolverhampton Express and Star*, 19 Dec. 2000;
http://society.guardian.co.uk/regeneration/story, 15 March 2002.

one Welsh diocesan town (St Davids) was restored to city status in 1994, while another (St Asaph) has been left out in the cold.

So does it matter? The problem with adopting Briggs's common sense view is that since the mid-nineteenth century a whole procession of towns has been metaphorically hammering on the doors of the Home Office demanding city status: no fewer than thirty-nine towns took part in the millennium competition and forty-two in the Golden Jubilee competition, with another seventeen applying for a lord mayoralty in 2002. It matters in the town halls, and it matters because city status is perceived to mean something and, just as importantly, to convey something in terms of prestige and standing in the national and international community.

Until the 1880s city status was linked directly to the presence or not of a cathedral. So towns which had cathedrals were cities, and this precedent was maintained when the Anglican church began re-ordering its diocesan geography in the nineteenth century. Unfortunately, the Church of England's priorities were not those of the state. It chose its new cathedral towns on architectural grounds, despite offending some of its own longstanding principles. Consequently, the Victorians recognized that many of their great new industrial centres were unlikely ever to be cities if the qualification remained in place. By the later years of the nineteenth century they came to believe that great commercial centres should have their standing recognized by promotion to city status: a title conferred by a gracious monarch as a confirmation of civic achievement. In the 1840s none of the provincial towns we associate with Victorian industrial and commercial supremacy was a city: Manchester, Birmingham, Liverpool, Sheffield, Leeds, Bradford, Newcastle-upon-Tyne, Nottingham and Hull, were all towns. By the close of Victoria's reign they had all achieved city status.

The problem was to decide which towns ranked as great commercial centres. As one civil servant wrote in 1888 after the link with cathedrals had been abolished, unlimited use of the title 'city' in the United Kingdom – the town under consideration was Birmingham! – would reduce the status 'to a meaningless title: in the United States every village is a "City"'.[3] He was right: too many grants of city status would reduce its elite value, but who should decide the number of grants and the qualification for a grant? The answer to the first question turned out to be the Home Office. It was established in the 1850s that grants should be made by letters patent issued with the consent of the monarch through the Home Secretary. The answer to the second question was much more complex. If the Home Office had the right to determine the number of grants, it also had the power to decide on the qualification for promotion. In 1907 the bottom line, below which a town could not be considered for promotion, was set at a population of 300,000, but with the pace of urban growth slowing in the course of the twentieth century few towns reached this limit. It was lowered to

---

[3]   PRO HO 45/9799/B5306.

250,000 and then to 200,000, although in practice a number of towns promoted to city came nowhere near the minimum.

In any case the Home Office was uneasy with a simple statistical definition. When it laid down the 300,000 rule it added that population was not in itself a sufficient qualification. A city ought to have a 'Metropolitan position from its history or geographical position', because 'its education and refined society would, in most people's eyes, be more worthy of the title than a mere collection of mills and factories and working people without any of these advantages, but with a large population'. Above all, a city could never be 'a mere formless collection of inhabitants, but a place of outstanding importance, with a character and identity of its own, and preferably having the position of a capital in a substantial and well-defined district'.[4] As a working definition this continues to be used, but in the second half of the twentieth century the Home Office (and since 2001 the Lord Chancellor's Department) was careful not to say very much about the guidelines, even to the point of occasionally denying their existence. Grants of city status have patronage implications, and since Whitehall was, and still is, desirous of keeping open its patronage options, and because the Home Office has long been regarded as a particularly secretive department of state, definitions of city status and lord mayoralty have never been published.[5] The fact that city status might add value to the standing of a town, and help in its promotion in the international market place, is only just beginning to be recognized in Whitehall.

The normal excuse for not laying down criteria is that they would make promotion mechanistic; once a town had jumped sufficient hurdles it would qualify automatically. This, as internal Whitehall memoranda have often stressed, might lead to inappropriate candidates being successful. And, of course, 'inappropriate' is a qualitative judgement which civil servants consider themselves best equipped to exercise. Yet necessarily they have always worked to guidelines and yardsticks, to measures and impressions, whether admitted or not. Without criteria there is no objective guide against which to measure a town for city status. What has developed in the United Kingdom today is a compromise which, depending on the perspective adopted, may seem neither fair nor objective: some towns are cities because they have always been so; others cannot be cities because, although they are larger and more 'important' than those that are, they do not fit the image of what a city should be. And what is that image? According to the Lord Chancellor's Department at the time of the Golden Jubilee competition 'the use of specific criteria could lead to a town claiming city status as of right, which in turn might devalue the honour'. In other words only Whitehall has the knowledge and experience to make such decisions, although the Constitutional Unit did offer some rather vague 'guidance' for the 2002 competition suggesting aspirant cities needed to show notable features; historical (including royal) considerations; and 'a forward-looking attitude'.[6]

---

4   PRO HO 45/10163/B24512.

5   K. Theakston, *The Civil Service Since 1945* (Oxford, 1995), 18.

6   http://www.lcd.gov.uk/constitution/city/citygj.htm#part7, 6 Feb. 2002.

So why is there so much desire to be a city or, at least, to have a piece of parchment stating that a place is a city? In the nineteenth century it was about elitism, about standing out from those around and being rewarded for municipal success, but in the course of the twentieth century being a city came to be associated less with civic pride and more with civic promotion. Both imply civic standing, a place at the top of the hierarchy and, as such, they relate to the original Roman idea of *civitas*. Chapter 1 briefly sets out the background against which city status needs to be viewed, notably the earliest link with places of importance and the way this was subtly altered after the Norman Conquest. In the 1540s Henry VIII created a legal precedent by granting city status to the new diocesan sees he set up. This precedent was upheld when the Church of England began making new dioceses in the nineteenth century. Chapter 2 shows how these links were maintained between the creation of the new dioceses of Ripon in 1836 and Wakefield in 1888, but it also reveals growing doubts about the automatic promotion of see towns. When places such as Manchester, Liverpool and Newcastle were involved there was little reason for complaint, but because of a growing sense that cities should be places of importance, civil servants in the Home Office were concerned about promoting St Albans and Truro, when Birmingham and Leeds were still towns. They drew a line under Wakefield, and as Chapter 3 shows, the pre-Conquest concept of *civitas* was effectively restored in order to promote the great industrial and commercial towns of Victorian Britain to city status. Belfast, Birmingham, Leeds, Nottingham and Cardiff were among the towns promoted between 1889 and the First World War. Lord mayoralties – previously restricted to London, York and Dublin – were conferred on several large and important towns. Civic pride and civic status went together in a pecking order now reflecting where a town stood in the hierarchy, a hierarchy which was partially determined by the simple criterion of size.

After the First World War, as we shall see in Chapter 4, the situation began subtly to change. Although the Home Office stubbornly refused numerous claims for city status, notably from new diocesan sees unaware of the 1888 ruling, it worked to some informal guidelines which were never published, but against which it measured applicants. Unfortunately, the population minimum (set at 300,000 in 1907) proved impractical, and had gradually to be lowered to 250,000 and 200,000. But the real issue in these years came increasingly to be seen in terms of promotion conveying status in the national and international arena. Being a city was now seen as good for promoting a place because, as has been argued ever since, being a city means something which town or borough does not. It may be intangible, but it is still something that can be understood. Consequently, many towns have tried to join the queue, convinced that they can promote themselves more effectively by being cities. This has largely been lost on Whitehall, which has been more concerned with limiting numbers and retaining its patronage powers than with the likely benefits which might accrue from city status. For the civil servants, keeping such patronage out of the political arena has been an overriding concern, hence the appalled tone of many of the memoranda written when Salford was promoted in 1926, and the debate which went on across Whitehall in the early 1960s when Southampton came up for promotion.

Southampton, as we show in Chapter 5, was next in line for promotion in the late 1950s, but the final push to see it over the threshold was largely political, a result of one MP's desire to retain his seat at the 1964 election. After that, the civil servants reasserted control, and subsequent grants, including Swansea at the time of the investiture of the Prince of Wales in 1969, have been linked to royal or national events to prevent a recurrence of such a situation. Consequently, as we show in Chapter 6, the demand for honours has come to be linked directly to events such as the Queen's Silver Jubilee in 1977 and her fortieth anniversary in 1992. But the business of selling the post-industrial town, sometimes known as civic boosterism, has had a significant impact on the whole issue. In 1991, when a new wave of marketing-driven urban development was already under way, the Home Office ran for the first time a competition to which it invited entries from towns interested in city status. The idea stuck, and although more recent grants have been linked to a global event (the millennium in 2000) and the Queen's Golden Jubilee in 2002, they have both been the result of competitions.

As Chapters 7 and 8 show, this has politicized the whole business. While interested parties expected the millennium city to be announced on 1 January 2000, politicians were so insistent on interfering, despite claims that as a constitutional matter city status is for the Queen's eyes alone, that the announcement was made only in mid-December 2000. Much of the delay was caused by wrangling within the Cabinet. No such problems beset the Golden Jubilee contest, but both in 2000 and 2002 numerous accusations were voiced as to the link between city status and Labour party loyalty at the ballot box. The personal intervention of the prime minister in 2000 confirmed that civic status was now a political matter as much as a constitutional issue, and the fact that forty-one towns applied for promotion (and seventeen for a lord mayoralty) shows that competition was alive and well. Why? Possibly because Sunderland has consistently maintained since it was promoted in 1992 that the new status made a tremendous difference to its economic standing on the world stage, and to its confidence as a place. So why refuse a status which carries no privileges to towns which believe possessing it would improve their international reputation and competitiveness in a world in which they have no option but to sell themselves?

Most of us understand that a city is an important place. We may not be able to decide the relative status of Chelmsford and Chichester, Blackburn, Bolton and St Albans, but we would be shocked to find that Birmingham, Manchester, Liverpool and Glasgow were anything other than cities. They may not be in the mould of ancient Rome or Athens, but somewhere in our collective consciousness we link city status to major towns even if we perhaps lack any great sense of the city as qualitatively and historically distinct within the urban world. Today we think of a city in terms of size and importance, but we probably do not worry greatly about the legal niceties involved in deciding whether Hereford is a city and Reading is not.[7] Those distinctions are primarily about civic standing, about titles, regalia and robes, orders of precedent, and so forth. To most of us it does not necessarily matter that Milton Keynes calls itself a city even though it does not have a charter. No one greatly objects to Elgin, Perth and Dunfermline calling themselves cities on the grounds that they have been recognized as such for many years, even if they lack the necessary legal documents.

Yet it would be churlish to suggest that these distinctions mean nothing. The simple fact that in 2000 and 2002 so many towns applied for city status, and in 2002 for lord mayoralties, suggests that civic pride is alive and well in the town hall corridors, and also that those people charged with the business of selling towns believe that they would have greater success if they were selling a city. On an international level, cities now compete for eye-catching, high profile events such as the Olympics and other major sports events. They spend large sums of money trying to gain the coveted title of European City of Culture, and they see such events in terms of regeneration and development of the city. Lower down the scale, towns compete for the coveted letters patent which enable them to claim truly to be a city, or perhaps to have a lord mayor taking precedence in civic rank over a mayor. These things still seem to matter, and yet city-making remains a closely guarded part of the government patronage machine.

---

[7]   A list of 'official' cities is given in the appendix.

CHAPTER ONE

The City in British History

To most of us a city is a place which is greater in size or importance than a town. Few of us could draw a realistic distinction between a city, a town, or even a large village, since in terms of function and characteristics there is no obvious difference. Size, area, or density of settlement are not in themselves criteria singling out cities from among the broad range of urban settlements, while cultural and economic functions are also more or less indistinguishable. In terms of government, English cities may or may not be county boroughs, while in civic terms they may or may not be the home of magistrates' courts and assizes. County towns are not by definition cities, and neither today are cathedral towns. In other words, we cannot distinguish a city from a town according to a particular set of criteria. 'The city', wrote Lewis Mumford, 'is not so much a mass of structures as a complex of interrelated and constantly interacting functions – not alone a concentration of power, but polarization of culture'.[1] Perhaps so, but no one doubts that a city is more *important* than a town, even if the measure of importance is in the prejudices of the commentator. We must begin by asking how usage of the word 'city' has evolved, particularly prior to the rapid expansion of the urban population since the eighteenth century.

The word 'city' is just one of many terms to have entered the language of Anglo-Saxon England as an increasing number of settlements exercised functions which were recognizably urban. In Old English these places came to be known as *byrig* (*burg, burga, burh*), *ceaster, port* and *wic*, terms usually translated in Latin as *urbs, civitas* and *portus*. From our perspective, the most significant of these was *civitas*, a title the Romans used for the independent states or tribes of Gaul. Over time it came to be identified as the title used to describe the chief town of these states, and these places were usually the seat of civil government and episcopal authority. In Domesday book (1086) terms such as *byrigan* or *burgi*, loosely meaning borough, and *civitas*, were used more or less interchangeably to describe places that in modern English we would probably call towns. More than 100 places were designated as *burgi*, and thirteen as *civitas*.[2] *Civitas* was applied to the more important *byri, bures* or boroughs, places which were the centres of districts and in some cases had municipal authority. What does not seem to have been established by Domesday was a clear link between a bishopric and a city.

---

[1]   Lewis Mumford, *The City in History* (1961), 103. Even in Whitehall there has long been considerable confusion surrounding the definition of cities: PRO HLG 120/57.

[2]   S. Reynolds, *Ideas and Solidarities in the Medieval Laity* (Aldershot, 1995), VII, 4; VIII, 297, 299–300.

Places described as *civitas* included Oxford, Gloucester, Leicester, Shrewsbury and Colchester, none of which were episcopal sees.[3] This was subsequently to change, and the link with episcopal sees was strengthened after the Norman Conquest.

Bishoprics in England date from the Anglo-Saxon period. Pope Gregory sent Augustine to England with a scheme that involved dividing the country into two provinces or archbishoprics, London and York, with twelve bishops in each. Augustine founded Canterbury Cathedral but he spent only a relatively short time in England, and the grand plan was never implemented. Most dioceses were very large and reflected the political realities of the day, although the fact that there were more kingdoms in the south of England than in the north affected ecclesiastical geography for a millennium. The Church of England still officially dates many of its dioceses from the seventh century, but given the conditions at the time it is hardly surprising to find that bishoprics came and went. Leicester claimed to have been a bishopric as early as 679, with eleven successive bishops appointed to the see before it moved to Dorchester.[4] By 1066 there were thirteen bishoprics in the south, but only York and Durham in the north.[5] By contrast, in Wales, Ireland and Scotland, where the church's organization was not based on the territories of powerful kings, there were more bishops controlling small tribal areas.

The fourth-century Council of Sardica established the principle that bishoprics should be established only in important towns. Given that in the later Saxon period urban functions were difficult to distinguish in north-west Europe,[6] it is hardly surprisingly that this did not always occur. Cathedrals were built at Rochester and London (St Paul's) in the early seventh century. In other cases, the seat, or throne of a bishop (*cathedra*) was placed in a church, which in turn became a cathedral church or, colloquially, a cathedral in a rural area.

The Normans, used to a situation in which episcopal sees were traditionally found in the chief borough or 'city' of a diocese, looked to change this situation. They had little time for cathedrals in rural locations, and bishops were encouraged to move to larger towns. The Bishop for Sussex moved from Selsey to Chichester, and the Bishop of Sherbourne to Salisbury. Leofric, Bishop of Crediton, asked for and obtained leave to move his see to Exeter, and the Bishop of Dorchester

---

[3]   F.W. Maitland, *Township and Borough* (Cambridge, 1898), 42; E.A. Freeman, 'City and Borough', *Macmillan's Magazine*, 60 (1889), 32.

[4]   Leicestershire RO CM 1/23, 17 July 1889.

[5]   Foundation dates are a matter of dispute, but the Church of England's own list (of those still surviving) is London (314), Sodor and Man (447), Canterbury (597), Lichfield and Rochester (604), York (627), Durham (635), Hereford and Winchester (676), Worcester (679), Bath & Wells (909), Exeter (1050), Chichester (1070), Lincoln (1072), Salisbury (1075), Norwich (1094), Ely (1109) and Carlisle (1133): *The Church of England Year Book 1996* (112th edn., 1996).

[6]   Adriaan Verhulst, *The Rise of Cities in North-West Europe* (Cambridge, 1999), 24.

(Oxfordshire) moved in 1072–3 to the thriving commercial town of Lincoln.[7] The Bishop of Wells moved to Bath, and the Bishop of the East Angles to Thetford and then to Norwich. At the Synod of London in 1075 it was agreed that only the larger towns should be see towns. That same year, Bishop Peter of Lichfield moved his see from Lichfield, which at the time was a village, to Chester, the seat of the Norman earls. His successor, Robert de Limesey, finding himself overshadowed by the earls, moved the see to Coventry about 1095, claiming a *cathedra* in both Coventry and Lichfield.[8] These relatively mobile bishops often built new cathedrals, with strong defences, Lincoln being an obvious example. The key point is that the assumed link between cathedral and town was a return to the principles established at Sardica, while implying that towns were distinctive places clearly understood to be separate from and more 'important' than the countryside.

While Norman bishops were happy to move their sees to places of importance, little was attempted by way of diocesan division. Only two new bishoprics were created: the small diocese of Ely for the county of Cambridge in 1108–9, reducing slightly the huge diocese of Lincoln, and Carlisle in 1133. Nor were bishops able to translate their ecclesiastical power into civil authority, as happened in some parts of western Europe. Church and state remained largely separate, although some bishops, notably the Bishops of Durham, exercised civil powers.

From our perspective the key point is that the post-Conquest changes ensured that bishoprics were now located in what were perceived to be important towns, and that *civitas* came to be synonymous with episcopal see.[9] The word *cite* was used in English by the thirteenth century, by which time it was applied not only to ancient cities but to important English boroughs such as London and Lincoln. Yet for a long time, despite significant urban growth, there was no obvious distinction between city, borough, or a number of other contemporary terms.[10] Middle English words such as *boru*, *borwe*, *burowe* and *borogh* are often seen as the origin of the modern term 'borough', although originally they probably meant fortified places. By the twelfth century some towns were beginning to acquire formal liberties, and those referred to as 'borough' had rights and privileges. Between the thirteenth and seventeenth centuries towns grew in importance and acquired further privileges, usually as a result of the merchant elites seeking to free their communities from the influence of local lords. In this process 'borough'

---

[7]   William Hunt, *The English Church: From its Foundation to the Norman Conquest (597–1066)* (New York, 1899), 317, 403.
[8]   VCH, *Warwickshire*, VIII (1969), 316.
[9]   Hunt, *English Church*, 38. According to Henri Pirenne, *Medieval Cities* (1925), 63–4, *civitas* became synonymous with bishopric in the ninth century, but while this may be true of Europe it was clearly not the case in England.
[10]   Reynolds, *Ideas and Solidarities*, VI, 12. Pirenne argued that European cities truly emerged in conjunction with trade in the twelfth century: Pirenne, *Medieval Cities*, 101, 103–4, 212.

emerged as a corporate town with privileges granted by royal charter, and often, although not invariably, the right to return MPs to Parliament.

The link which developed in the early medieval period between cathedral and towns of importance established a prima facie case to later generations for the sees of dioceses to be cities. Since no charters or other official documentation were involved, cathedral towns have generally been accepted as cities with the technical status: 'by ancient prescriptive right' (table 1). In other words, their claim to city status is accepted because they can show that for many centuries they have been the seat of a bishop, not because anyone, at any particular time, declared they should be cities. As a result of Norman policy, bishops were usually found only in important places. London, the capital city, was by far the largest town in the kingdom over many centuries; York, the capital of the northern province, and in the Middle Ages Lincoln and Durham were important administrative and economic centres. Other cathedrals, including Exeter, Worcester and Hereford were located in county towns. The majority, of course, were in southern England: Bath, Canterbury, Chichester, Ely, Exeter, Norwich, Rochester, Salisbury, Wells and Winchester represented the south and East Anglia; Lincoln, Lichfield, Worcester, Hereford and Coventry represented the Midlands; and York, Durham and Carlisle the north.

Table 1   English Cities by Ancient Prescriptive Right 1927

Bath	Exeter	Salisbury
Canterbury	Hereford	Wells
Carlisle	Lichfield	Winchester
Chichester	Lincoln	Worcester
Coventry	London	York
Durham	Norwich	
Ely	Rochester	

Source: PRO HO 286/40.

Outside of England only Bangor (Wales) holds the title by ancient prescriptive right.

Distinctions between towns were, for the most part, unclear. Medieval towns are usually defined in terms of function and social definition, rather than being grouped in league tables.[11] Most towns, London excepted, were small and relatively undistinguished. They were often dominated by a major church, although the growing status of elites through time saw the development of civic architecture in the form of town halls and guildhalls. Some of these began life as timber-framed buildings which were little more than adaptations of domestic

---

[11]   D.M. Palliser, ed., *The Cambridge Urban History of Britain, vol 1, 600–1540* (Cambridge, 2000), 5, adopts a definition proposed by Susan Reynolds stresses these points.

houses, and it was only larger towns in eastern England that by the fifteenth century could finance stone-built guildhalls comparable with many European towns at the time.[12] The major urban distinction in England was still between chartered boroughs and other places which clearly had urban functions but did not possess independent powers of government. The term 'city', in other words, with its derivation from the Latin *civitas*, offered no legal or constitutional powers, and was used only of those places which were the seats of bishops. 'What is the city but the people?', Shakespeare had Sicinius ask in *Coriolanus*, to which the citizens answered 'True, the people are the City',[13] a view subsequently echoed by Rousseau: 'houses make a town, but citizens make a city'.[14] In England, no legal distinction was recognized: 'city' described a particular type of town with a cathedral, just as 'borough' described a town with a charter. In a society which saw little need for towns to enhance their reputations and positions by adopting particular titles, no one seems to have been particularly troubled by the absence of clearer definitions.

It was only in the sixteenth century that the loose but acknowledged relationship between cathedral and city was formalized, and then it occurred in a context which would leave an awkward legacy for the future. Henry VIII's plan, following the Dissolution of the Monasteries, was to create thirteen bishoprics, to be funded from the income of twenty large (dissolved) abbeys. However, the vested interests of existing bishops were affected, and in the end only six dioceses were established, with endowments rather less generous than had originally been intended.[15] The process was described by the eighteenth-century historian-bishop, Gilbert Burnet:

> In the end of this year [1540] were the new Bishopricks founded. For in December was the Abbey of Westminster converted into a Bishoprick and a Deanery, and six Prebends, with the officers for a Cathedral and a Quire. And in the year following on the 4th of August the King erected out of the Monastery of St Werburg at Chester, a Bishoprick, a Deanery, and six Prebends. In September out of the monastery of St Peters at Gloucester the King endowed a Bishoprick, Deanery and six Prebendaries. And in the same Month, the Abbey of Peterborough was converted to a Bishop's seat, a Deanery and six Prebendaries. And the monastery of St Austins in Bristol was changed into the same use.[16]

As a result of these alterations, the very large dioceses of Lincoln and York were reduced a little in size, although Chester was as unwieldy as any of the older dioceses because it contained Lancashire, Cheshire, and the Archdeaconry of Richmond in Yorkshire. Colleges of secular canons were created to support the

[12]   Ibid., 3–4, 168, 378–9.
[13]   *Coriolanus*, Act 3, Scene 1, line 198.
[14]   Quoted Mumford, *City in History*, 113.
[15]   J.J. Scarisbrick, *Henry VIII* (1968), 662.
[16]   Gilbert Burnet, *The History of the Reformation of the Church of England* (1679), I, 300.

new cathedrals, and the old cathedrals whose monasteries had been closed were re-founded as secular colleges.

The new cathedral towns were clearly intended to have city status. Gloucester (1541) had been the shire town of Gloucestershire since the late Anglo-Saxon period, and it was sometimes styled *civitas* in the eleventh and twelfth centuries. In the charter of 3 September 1541 it was nominated as the see of a bishop and given the status of 'City of Gloucester', thus giving legal backing to the view that must by then have been current that cathedral and city went hand in hand.[17] Also in 1541 the charter confirming Chester as the see of a new diocese stated that it was to become a city.[18] The see of Oxford was founded in 1542 at Oseney Abbey, and Oxford was deemed to be a city. When in 1546 the cathedral was moved to Christ Church, the grant included retention of city status.[19] Peterborough (1541) and Bristol (1542) also became cities. Westminster survived only ten years as a diocesan see, but it continued to use the appellation of city, and this usage was confirmed by the issue of letters patent in 1900, although this later grant was for a wider area than the original 'city'.[20]

Henry VIII also authorized the appointment of suffragan bishops, assistant bishops with responsibility for part of a diocese or for functions within a diocese. Again, the link with towns was quite specific, since he named twenty-six towns from which they were permitted to take their titles. It was under this dispensation that Richard Barnes was consecrated suffragan Bishop of Nottingham on 9 March 1567. He held the position until he was translated to Carlisle in 1570, when he was not replaced. William Camden, the great antiquary, argued that during those years Nottingham enjoyed the status of a city, and John Blackner, the early nineteenth-century historian, noted that when the bishopric lapsed so did the title of city: 'it resumed its ancient title of borough, which it holds by prescription, that is, antecedently to the existence of its charters'.[21] The last suffragans to be consecrated under Henry VIII's legislation were Richard Rogers at Dover (1569), and John Sterne at Colchester (1592), but with the decline of the suffragan the issue of city status, insofar as it had ever raised much passion in the sixteenth century, disappeared from view.

The link between city and bishop created by Henry VIII in the charters of the 1540s established two significant precedents as far as legal opinion was concerned. The first was the right of the monarch to grant city status. Consequently, towns which desired city status could petition the Crown directly. Both Kilkenny in 1609 and Londonderry in 1613 applied directly to James I for a grant of city status, and both were promoted. Cambridge, however, was turned

---

[17]   W.H. Stevenson, *Calendar of the Records of the Corporation of Gloucester* (Gloucester, 1893), 10; VCH, *Gloucestershire*, IV (1988), 2, 13.
[18]   Rymer's *Foedera*, XIV, 718; PRO HO 45/13142.
[19]   VCH, *Oxfordshire*, IV (1979), 1, 74, 121; H. Ogle, *Royal Letters Addressed to Oxford* (1892), 158–68.
[20]   PRO LCO2/2013, M.W. Ridley to Clerk of the Crown in Chancery, 20 July 1899.
[21]   John Blackner, *History of Nottingham* (1816), 252.

down. In 1616, the burgesses of Cambridge petitioned for a city charter. The university, fearing that enhanced status for the town would menace its own privileges, opposed the grant. The King assured the university that he would not grant titles of honour which might disturb or endanger the university, and the petition made no progress.[22] Cambridge had to wait another 300 years to become a city. Although no further grants of city status were made directly by royal prerogative until 1994, the precedent established by Henry VIII has been observed in that the issue has always been regarded subsequently as a constitutional matter requiring the personal attention of the monarch.

The second legal precedent established in the 1540s was that while the foundation of a bishopric did not make the see town a city, it did give it a prima facie case for promotion. The link between cathedral and city operated in such a manner that lawyers regarded it as immutable. In the seventeenth century Sir Edward Coke wrote that 'A city is a borough incorporated which hath, or hath had, a Bishop, and though the Bishoprick be dissolved, yet the city remaineth', while according to the eighteenth-century writer on common law, Sir William Blackstone, 'A city is a town incorporated, which is or has been the see of a Bishop, and though the Bishoprick be dissolved, as at Westminster, yet still it remains a city'. Jacob's *Law Dictionary,* taking its lead from the Latin *civitas,* defined a city as 'a town corporate, which hath a bishop and cathedral church, which is called *civitas,* oppidium, and urbs; *civitas,* in regard it is governed by justice and order of magistracy; oppidium, for that it contains a great number of inhabitants; and *urbs,* because it is in due form begirt about with walls'.[23] Some commentators were less certain. Coleridge noted in the 1825 edition of Blackstone that

> It is curious that the name of Westminster did not suggest to the author a doubt of the accuracy of his definition of a city; because it is not incorporate, nor did it become a city as being the See of a Bishop, being expressly so created by the letters patent of Henry VIII, by which it was also created into a Bishoprick. The fact is that every city in England is or has been the See of a Bishop, but it is not true that every place which has been the See of a Bishop [is] or was a city.[24]

Although Westminster was often cited as an exception to the rule, it was also the case that Thetford, Sherborne and Dorchester might have been called cities, because they had once been sees. By the definition found in Coke and Blackstone, they were presumably entitled to use the status, but do not seem ever to have done so.[25] Leicester subsequently claimed to have been the seat of an Anglo-Saxon bishop in order to argue its case for reclaiming city status.

---

[22]   VCH, *Cambridgeshire,* III (City of Cambridge) (1959), 33, 192; Maitland, *Township and Borough,* 91.
[23]   Jacob's *Law Dictionary* (10th edn., 1782).
[24]   Quoted in *Royal Cornish Gazette,* 9 Feb. 1877.
[25]   A. Briggs, *Victorian Cities* (1968 edn.), 31.

So far we have looked primarily at England. Similar principles do not necessarily apply elsewhere in the United Kingdom. Wales was traditionally divided into four dioceses based on Bangor, St Davids, St Asaph, and Llandaff cathedrals. Bangor is accepted as a city by 'ancient prescriptive right' in the manner of English diocesan towns. St Davids, as we shall see, was given city status in 1994 on the grounds that it had lost the title in the nineteenth century. However, St Asaph's similar claims have not been recognized, and it was unsuccessful in the millennium and Golden Jubilee competitions. It continues to claim the right to use the term city because it has a cathedral. Llandaff is little more than a village within the Cardiff complex. In Ireland, probably most of the places which have had bishops have been styled *civitas* at some point in time. 'City' is applied only to a few of them, which are ancient and important boroughs. Dublin, Cork, Limerick, Kilkenny and Waterford are usually regarded as cities. Other, more doubtful, cases include Galway.

The most complicated position is in Scotland. The Scottish town was the burgh, but the burgh was a settlement deliberately created with specific legal rights. It did not necessarily have the ecclesiastical linkage associated with the old Roman *civitas*. The style *civitas* was probably introduced from England, but it bore no relation to the size, civil importance or municipal standing of a particular place. Many Scottish settlements were little more than villages, and it was a long time before they were raised to the rank of burghs. *Civitas* was eventually used of Perth and Edinburgh, which were ancient royal burghs and seats of royalty. The vernacular form 'city' was applied by the fifteenth century to some of the burghs which were *civitas* and consequently the link between town, cathedral and city status found in England did not occur. In many cases, the existence of a cathedral was the governing factor in the development of a burgh; indeed, eleven of the Scottish cathedral sites attracted urban settlements, but the automatic link to city status assumed south of the border did not take place. Consequently, Scotland has no equivalent of ancient prescriptive right, and it lacks the diocesan structure found in England and Wales. It had just four great towns in the Middle Ages and sixteenth century – Edinburgh, Aberdeen, Perth and Dundee. Edinburgh and Aberdeen were cities by long usage.[26] After the sixteenth century, the major urban development in Scotland was the rise of Glasgow, which also came to be accepted as a city by long usage.[27]

---

[26]   PRO PC 1/13, no 80. This list of 'Royal Warrants in matters of election granted to Cities and Royal Burghs in Scotland since the Union in 1707', attributes city status to Aberdeen and Edinburgh in 1746, but not to any of the other towns listed, which include Perth (1746), Dundee, Elgin, Inverness and Stirling, among others.

[27]   Glasgow is accepted as a city by long usage, but contributors to the recent multi-volume history have used the terms city and town interchangeably. At the time of the Glorious Revolution in 1688 it was recognized as a city, but with a town council (I, 67). In discussing local government, Irene Maver was careful to write of the town council down to the reforms of 1833, but others referred to it as a city council as early as 1811 (I, 222). There was a city chamberlain as early as 1755, (I, 244) and a city hall

When Dundee was created a city by letters patent in 1889, doubts were raised about the status of other Scottish towns which argue that they are cities but do not have any documentary evidence. Burghs such as Perth and Elgin, which can show *civitas* in early charters, have claimed the style of city although they are not officially regarded as such.[28] Dunfermline has claimed city status on the basis of long usage. In 1855, Dr Ebenezer Henderson, a native of the town, began researching the background to its claim to city status. He approached the Lord Chief Justice of England, who, on 'carefully perusing your letter', came to the view that Dunfermline was entitled to be called a city. Dr Henderson thought Dunfermline needed a rather firmer base from which to work, and he wrote to a number of other authorities on the subject, including Lieutenant Colonel Sir Henry James, head of the Ordnance Survey Map Department. James, after consulting the Solicitor to the War Department, told Henderson that 'we have decided on designating Dunfermline as a City'.[29] Consequently, the subsequent *Ordnance Gazetteer of Scotland* noted that Dunfermline became a royal burgh in 1588, 'but long previous to that it was the ancient royal city of the Celtic kings'. Dr Henderson's findings were presented to the town council in 1856, and it unanimously agreed to use the title of city in legal documents for the future. It also agreed to give Dr Henderson, who lived in St Helens, the freedom of the city when he next visited Dunfermline, as a reward for his researches.[30] The problem is that while Dunfermline might claim long historic tradition as grounds for calling itself a city, it does not have a charter. Although this serves mainly to confirm that there is no direct comparison between Scotland and England as to the manner in which city status has been acquired,[31] it has certainly led to confusion: even the Home Office has been uncertain in recent years as to which Scottish towns should be considered as cities.[32]

by 1842 (II, 3, 247). The confusion of terminology is perhaps not surprising; certainly there seems to have been no single point at which city replaced town in common terminology. T.M. Devine and G. Jackson, eds., *Glasgow, Volume I: Beginnings to 1830* (Manchester, 1995); W. Hamish Fraser and Irene Maver, eds. *Glasgow, Volume II: 1830–1912* (Manchester, 1996).

[28]   http://visit.elginscotland.org/history_of_elgin/index.html, The City and Royal Burgh of Elgin; http://www.perthshire-scotland.co.uk/perth2.htm, 'About Perth City'.

[29]   NAS, B20/20/29.

[30]   F.H. Groome, *Ordnance Gazetteer of Scotland II* (1882).

[31]   Private Communication from John Reid, Secretary of State, Scotland Office, to Councillor James Simpson, 16 Dec. 1999.

[32]   The government today accepts as Scottish cities the following: Aberdeen, Glasgow and Edinburgh by ancient usage; Dundee (1889), Inverness (2000) and Stirling (2002) by letters patent. On this evidence, in 1969 it recognized only Aberdeen, Glasgow, Edinburgh and Dundee, yet during negotiations over conferring city status on Swansea the Home Secretary, James Callaghan, told Anthony Greenwood at the Department of Housing and Local Government that there were six cities in Scotland: PRO HO 286/66. Unfortunately he did not list the six cities.

The concept of the city as the home of a cathedral became established in England in the course of the Middle Ages, and was confirmed in the sixteenth century. However, no new dioceses were created between the 1550s and the 1830s, and because the main urban distinction which emerged was between towns with borough status and those without, there is little evidence of much demand for city status. As a result, in tracing the history of cities before the nineteenth century we are confronted with a term which was regarded as related only marginally to urban size. The key linkage was with the church, and this was widely accepted in practice as well as in theory: it was, in other words, a distinction, not a status, a title which went with a cathedral, not a definition of position in the urban pecking order.

In these circumstances, if a corporate town wanted to improve its image rather than seek a title it was more likely to rebuild its civic premises. Between 1500 and 1640 at least 178 towns acquired 202 civic buildings. This is probably an underestimate because many were timber-framed and consequently only a few survive, including the sixteenth-century Titchfield market hall in West Sussex. They gave way in later generations to stone and brick buildings, and also to larger buildings to meet the increased number of functions they began to handle.[33]

It was not until the industrial revolution, and with it the growth of towns on a scale and to a size never before imagined in the British Isles that marks of status began to take on a greater meaning and definition. The urban renaissance of the post-Restoration period was partly about town living and town improvement, and partly about status and standing. Newly-resident urban gentry rebuilt their houses in brick to the latest fashion, and they wanted to see civic buildings which would bolster rather than detract from the image of their towns. A further wave of town hall building took place between the late seventeenth and late eighteenth centuries, during which time at least forty were constructed, rebuilt or substantially modified. This period saw the introduction of non-arcaded halls built to classical principles, and including merchants' exchanges, based on the model of the Royal Exchange in London, completed in 1671. Perhaps the finest provincial examples were in Liverpool and Bristol.[34] Less impressive, but still a monument to civic pride, was Nottingham's Exchange, built 1723–6 at the eastern end of the market place, with a classical façade including a straight parapet roof broken by a central semi-circular pediment enclosing a public clock.[35]

In the second half of the eighteenth century urban growth took hold in England in a manner that was unprecedented. Within a few years, the old

---

[33]   Robert Tittler, *Architecture and Power: the Town Hall and the English Urban Community, c.1500–1640* (Oxford, 1991), esp. pp. 11, 161–8.
[34]   P. Borsay, *The English Urban Renaissance: Culture and Society in the Provincial Town, 1660–1770* (Cambridge, 1989), 104–6, 325–8.
[35]   John Beckett, ed., *A Centenary History of Nottingham* (Manchester, 1997), 124–5.

hierarchy, such as it was, fell apart, and a new order replaced it, with urban giants such as Birmingham, Liverpool and Manchester leapfrogging some of the traditionally larger provincial towns such as Norwich, Exeter and Bristol. Almost overnight, or so it seemed, a new urban order arose, and by the time the industrial revolution had come to maturity in the mid-nineteenth century an urban-industrial system had evolved which was to persist for more than a century.[36] Observers could see with their own eyes what had happened, and the decennial census offered proof positive not only that the country was turning its back on rural society to become an urban world, but also just how gigantic some of these great new conglomerations were. As they grew, they spread, and as they spread through boundary extensions, they became yet larger.

By the late nineteenth century the British Isles were increasingly urbanized, but how were towns to be distinguished? Why were Norwich, Exeter and Bristol still cities, when Birmingham, Liverpool, Manchester and Belfast, all of them great provincial industrial and commercial giants, were not? For the first time, the concept of city status came to be associated with size and importance, and in this reordering of the urban hierarchy status definitions began to count. They could build greater town halls, and more civic buildings, but the major towns wanted to be cities, cities wanted to have lord mayors, and the status of city, which had once been a definition connected with cathedrals, was annexed by the largest towns in their search for marks of social and civic esteem. Initially, this demand for status seemed to reach its apogee in the 1890s, but it has never gone away. Today, the search for city status is if anything more cut-throat than ever before, hence the enormous interest generated by the millennium and Golden Jubilee competitions of 2000 and 2002.

Since the mid-nineteenth century, city status has been transformed from a distinction attached to a town with a cathedral, to a mark of civic esteem in the eyes not just of this country, but of the world. Towns today fight for a status which carries no privileges, because they believe it raises their status in the eyes of the world at large. It is this transformation of a status once associated primarily with cathedrals, into a much sought after title by larger towns, that we seek to unravel in the chapters which follow. At the same time we show how a prerogative claimed by Henry VIII on the grounds of little more than complicit acceptance by a parliament which had little obvious concern one way or the other, has become a political tool to be wielded by prime ministers on behalf of unsuspecting and, in any case, powerless monarchs.

---

[36]   H. Carter and C.R. Lewis, eds., *An Urban Geography of England and Wales in the Nineteenth Century* (1990), 42–66.

CHAPTER TWO

Civic Rivalry: Manchester and the Quest for City Status, 1836–88

In 1851, the year of the Great Exhibition, Queen Victoria visited Manchester. For the town's corporation this was an opportunity to show off their municipality to the world. They planned a mass pageant, which was to be performed in front of vast crowds, and to be laced with ritual – even if the ritual was invented for the occasion. After the Queen had visited Salford, the royal party, led by the mayor and high sheriff, both wearing ceremonial dress for the first time, passed through the central streets. 'The streets were immensely full', the Queen later recorded in her journal, 'and the cheering and enthusiasm most gratifying'.[1] At the Exchange she was seated on a throne, and surrounded by the town council in front of an audience of 2,000 notables. This was little short of a provincial repetition of her Coronation ceremony, but it was just one event in a visit which was deliberately designed as a spectacle, a civic occasion to which the urban community at large was summoned as witnesses. As a sign of her gratitude, the Queen knighted the mayor, John Potter.[2] Behind the scenes she was also being canvassed for something more. The corporation saw the visit not just as an opportunity to project Manchester to the nation, it saw part of this glorification as the raising of Manchester to city status. Manchester had good reason for thinking it should have the status, but coming as this did at the beginning of two decades or so which saw civic rivalry blossom on a scale never previously witnessed in England, the events of 1851–3 – when a grant of city status was finally made – came to symbolize the growth of civic pride more generally. The transformation of city from a term designating a town with a cathedral, to a symbol of status within the urban hierarchy began in Manchester with Queen Victoria's visit in 1851.

The question of city status was hardly an issue between the 1540s and the 1830s. In that time, no new Anglican dioceses were created, so the precedent established by Henry VIII was not tested. The key urban distinction remained the right or absence of right to self-government: in other words, borough versus town. This distinction was, if anything, emphasized by the reform of the

---

[1] A. Briggs, *Victorian Cities* (1968 edn.), 112.
[2] Simon Gunn, 'Ritual and civic culture in the English industrial city, c.1835–1914', in R.J. Morris and R.H. Trainor, eds., *Urban Governance: Britain and Beyond Since 1750* (Aldershot, 2000), 228–9.

municipal corporations in 1835, which singled out towns considered worthy of independence and laid down the ground rules for others to make a case in the future. Borough status was now a reward for civic achievement, and successful access to the group brought with it self-government and urban status. But the more towns which crossed the barrier – sixty-two between 1835–76 and another twenty-five between 1876–82 – the greater the likelihood that an elite would want to separate themselves off from the rest. Even so, the claim to city status might not have been the means of separation but for the impact of Anglican diocesan subdivision.

Having slumbered peacefully through the early decades of the industrial revolution, the Anglican church started catching up with the new reality of urban-industrial England in the 1830s. It began building churches, splitting parishes, and overhauling its infrastructure, as well as fighting over its doctrine. It also looked carefully at its diocesan structure. Population and urbanization were leaving some of its bishops hopelessly overstretched by developments outside their control. In particular, the Bishop of Chester was trying to exercise episcopal oversight across territory covering 4,100 square miles. If this had been barren wasteland, the task might have been manageable, but his diocese included not only Cheshire, but Lancashire and parts of the industrializing West Riding of Yorkshire. As a result of industrialization he was supposedly looking after the spiritual and pastoral needs of nearly two million people. This was clearly not what had been intended by the early Christian fathers when they established a diocesan structure.

In the sixteenth century Henry VIII had set the precedent that new dioceses should be created by the government – this was, after all, the Church of England – and that the new cathedral towns were entitled to the status of city. Although there had been no subsequent creations, the principle had been upheld by the constitutional lawyers Coke and Blackstone, who had argued that an English city was an incorporated town which was also the see of a bishop. Consequently, the Anglican church required government intervention to form new dioceses, but by the nineteenth century the government was – unlike Henry VIII – largely prepared to let the church make its own decisions about where new dioceses should be, and what cathedrals they should have. The churchmen had little or no interest in the city status issue: they were far too busy falling out over the cathedral question.

When, under the Normans, bishops had moved from villages and hamlets into *civitas* in conformity with the principles established at the Council of Sardica, and in line with Norman expectations in respect of bishoprics, they had as a rule set about building new cathedrals. It was this relocation which produced some of the great buildings which survive to this day, such as Lincoln. In the nineteenth century this was hardly practical. The Church of England recognized a duty to provide accommodation for the new working classes, and its budget was fully employed in erecting new churches and paying their clergymen. It simply could not afford to think in terms of a new wave of cathedral building on the grand scale of earlier centuries. So how was it to form new dioceses? Two viewpoints emerged in the 1830s: those who championed nominating towns which should be diocesan sees, and then selecting an appropriate church for the cathedral; and those who argued in favour of locating appropriate parish churches which could be redesignated cathedrals, and naming whatever town they happened to be in as the see.

Among those in favour of selecting the appropriate town and then nominating a church was Thomas Arnold who argued in 1833 that 'every large town should necessarily be the seat of a Bishop ... and the addition of such an element into the society of a commercial or manufacturing place would be itself a great advantage'.[3] What, asked the Rev. Christopher Wordsworth, a member of the cathedrals commission in the 1850s, would the early Church fathers have said 'to our Liverpools and Birminghams, to our Leeds, Nottingham, Sheffield, Derby, Newcastle, Plymouth, left without bishops?'. They would, he suggested in answer to his own rhetorical question, accuse the contemporary church of abandoning 'the very first principles of missionary labour'.[4] Wordsworth's view was that towns of this stature were bound to have an appropriate 'cathedral':

> there is scarcely a large district, or any populous town in England, which does not possess some noble ancient church, distinguished by architectural beauty, which might soon become a Cathedral. If the inhabitants of a district or a town are desirous of such a result, and if the desire is right, let them be enabled to attain it.[5]

F.H. Dickinson wrote to the high church *Guardian* in June 1876 proposing bishoprics for Liverpool, Birmingham and the Black Country, Leeds, Sheffield, Halifax or Bradford, Rochdale, Blackburn or Preston, Newcastle, Suffolk, Nottingham, The Potteries and Shrewsbury. This was not a random list: Dickinson was careful to point out that the places he named had 'important churches in public patronage which perhaps might be made available' as cathedrals.[6]

If this viewpoint had prevailed, new diocesan sees would have been established only in major towns, and the principle of city status following cathedral nomination would not have been offended, but the Anglican church did not stick to these principles: rather, it tended to choose the cathedral first and scarcely to concern itself with location. As a writer in the *Church Quarterly Review* reflected in 1876, 'we may generally say that the schemes of some twenty or thirty years back were rather more solicitous as to a sufficient cathedral than more modern reforms'.[7] This was amply demonstrated with the first two new dioceses to be created since the sixteenth century, Ripon and Manchester. The view from Canterbury and York was that since cathedral building on a medieval scale was unlikely to meet with public support, the correct course of action was to select as see towns places with appropriate buildings: in other words, existing

---

[3]   Thomas Arnold, *Principles of Church Reform* (4th edn., 1833), 48.
[4]   Christopher Wordsworth, *On a Proposed Subdivision of Dioceses* (1860), 28.
[5]   Ibid., 40.
[6]   *Guardian*, 14 June 1876, 775–6.
[7]   *Church Quarterly Review* (Oct. 1876), 210.

churches suitable for upgrading to cathedrals, especially churches with the necessary trappings of a chapter.

Given this background, it is hardly surprising to find that the Established Church Act of 1836, which authorized two new dioceses to be carved out of the existing diocese of Chester in order to relieve the hard-pressed bishop, designated as cathedrals Ripon and Manchester.[8] Both towns had capitular parish churches. Not only were these large and venerable buildings, most importantly they were served not by a single clergyman but by a chapter of clergy led by a dean, and with a corporate endowment. They were, in all but name, ready-made cathedrals.[9] As the *Church Quarterly Review* writer added in 1876, 'the choice [of Ripon and Manchester] no doubt was determined by the presence of the two collegiate churches, with their surviving chapters; though in the case of Manchester, the place itself had irresistible claims'.[10] Here was a recognition that size ought to matter, but it was not something with which the Anglican hierarchy seemed particularly concerned.

The Diocese of Ripon was established within a few months of the 1836 legislation, with the twelfth-century parish church as the cathedral. Ripon lay on the eastern edge of the newly-created diocese that bore its name, distant from the main centres of West Riding industry, and it was much smaller in 1841 (population 12,368) than Leeds (151,874) and Halifax (130,743), both of which lay within the diocesan boundaries. Ripon seemed, in other words, flatly to contradict the dictum of the Council of Sardica that sees should be established in towns of importance. Manchester was less controversial, but it took rather longer to set up. In 1840, the Warden and Fellows of the Collegiate Church were transformed into Dean and Canons, and after several setbacks the diocese was finally brought into being by the Manchester Bishopric Act of 1847. With a population in 1841 of 243,000, Manchester was one of the largest provincial towns in the country and unquestionably suitable to be the see town of a diocese.

What the 1836 legislation did not do was to mention city status. Henry VIII's charters had established the see and set down the entitlement to city status in a single document. Similar principles were employed in the nineteenth century by the Colonial Office, where 'the older cities were all created by letters patent at the time of the appointment of the first bishop'. When the first bishop of Georgetown (British Guyana) was appointed in 1842, the letters patent issued by the Crown on 22 August constituted the church of St George as the cathedral 'and do ordain that the whole town of Georgetown aforesaid shall henceforth be a city and be called "The City of Georgetown"'. This practice was followed for Gibraltar, Bridgetown

---

[8]   6&7 William IV c.77. The extensive church reforms of these years are discussed in Geoffrey Best, *Temporal Pillars* (1964).

[9]   P.S. Morrish, 'County and Urban Dioceses', *Journal of Ecclesiastical History*, 26 (1975), 279–300; idem., 'Leeds and the Dismemberment of the Diocese of Ripon', *Proceedings of the Thoresby Society*, 2nd ser., 4 (1994), 62–97; 'Parish-Church Cathedrals, 1836–1921: Some Problems and their Solution', *Journal of Ecclesiastical History* 49 (1998), 438–9.

[10]   *Church Quarterly Review* (Oct. 1876), 210.

(Barbados) and St John's (Antigua) in 1842, Victoria (Hong Kong) in 1849, and Nassau (Bahamas) in 1861. It ceased after 1865 when the power of the Crown to create bishoprics in the crown colonies fell into disuse.[11]

Given this background, it is perhaps surprising that Ripon and Manchester were established by legislation which said nothing about city status. The question soon arose as to whether the new cathedral towns automatically became cities, or needed to apply for the status. If they needed to apply, what was the process? Ripon assumed that as a diocesan see it was also a city. When its corporation met on 9 November 1836, the first meeting to be held after the diocese was established and the bishop enthroned, the minutes were simply headed 'This Council of the said City and Borough'. The Corporation sent a congratulatory address to the Bishop (C.T. Longley), who replied to the 'Corporation of the City of Ripon', and sent 'sincere wishes for the prosperity of your city'.[12] Although no questions seem to have been asked in Ripon, the adoption of 'city' in this way was anomalous because Henry VIII had set a precedent followed in the Colonial Office of granting letters patent. Manchester also anticipated being a city. Even while diocesan negotiations were still under way in 1844, the borough council was assured that with the establishment of the bishopric 'Manchester will be entitled to the denomination, and will become, a City'. As a result, the title was used informally from 1847, in much the same way that it was employed by Ripon. Unfortunately, such usage offended the legal profession, and matters came to a head in 1849 when a judge, Mr Justice Maule, refused to accept an affidavit because it was claimed to have been sworn in the 'city' of Manchester, and he knew of no such legally constituted city.[13] Perhaps this was nit-picking, but it raised a genuine issue as to Manchester's entitlement to city status, and the basis on which it was claimed.

It clearly made sense to have the position resolved, and the question of Manchester's status was raised when Queen Victoria visited in October 1851. For the corporation, projecting Manchester to the nation and the Empire also meant raising it to city status, but the government was uncertain as to how it should proceed. Lord John Russell, the prime minister, thought Manchester was entitled to the status, but he insisted that further enquiries needed to be made. These were still apparently incomplete when his government fell four months later, to be replaced by the short-lived first ministry of the Earl of Derby. The mayor of Manchester pursued the city status matter with the new Home Secretary, Spencer Walpole, but he opposed any move to confer city status for fear of creating a precedent. This was in spite of legal advice given by Lord Chelmsford, the Lord Baron, whose opinion was that:

[11]   PRO CO 1032/31, R.1909, 'Colonial Cities'.
[12]   North Yorkshire RO, North Allerton, DC/RIC II 1/1/6, Ripon Corporation Minute Book 1835–47, 9 Nov. 1836.
[13]   A. Redford, *The History of Local Government in Manchester, vol II, Borough and City* (1940), 205.

> It is competent to the Queen to constitute the Borough of Manchester a City if Her Majesty shall be so advised, by Letters Patent. We know of no Civil or political advantages or privileges beyond the mere titular distinction which the grant of such a Charter would confer. 25 October 1852.[14]

In December 1852 Derby's government resigned. He was succeeded as premier by Lord Aberdeen, with Palmerston taking the Home Office. Chelmsford's opinion, together with the mayor of Manchester's letter to Walpole, and other papers relevant to the case, was quickly brought to his attention. Palmerston told the mayor he saw no reason to prevent Manchester from becoming a city, and in April 1853 the Home Office issued letters patent granting to Manchester the status of a city with 'all such rank, liberties, privileges, and immunities'.[15] Manchester now had the civic status to go with its claims to rank and standing as a major industrial town.

Manchester was made a city by letters patent on the authority of the monarch, but this created a new precedent. The establishment of the diocese and the grant of city status were now regarded as separate events. The government had accepted that the principles established by Henry VIII held good, and that diocesan status could carry with it city status, but it had not accepted it as a right: it had to be applied for separately rather than being part of the package. In the longer term, the decision to separate the two events would turn out to have significant implications, but in the immediate aftermath of the Manchester grant it was the position of Ripon which became anomalous.

Initially, Ripon simply continued to call itself a city, but there was unease about using a term for which a form of government sanction was needed. An opportunity to clarify the position arose when in November 1864 Ripon corporation resolved to sponsor legislation to buy the gasworks from a private company. The petition to Parliament was discussed when the corporation met in December, and the town clerk was commissioned to try to persuade the Parliamentary Committee to remove the words 'The Mayor, Aldermen, and Burgesses of the City and Borough of Ripon', and replace them with 'The Mayor, Aldermen and Citizens of the City of Ripon'. Although the proposed change of heading was not granted, a clause was added to the gasworks bill which was designed 'to preclude questions as to the style of the City and Borough and the Name of the Corporation'.[16] The bill received the royal assent on 19 June 1865,

---

[14]   PRO HO 45/24657, copy of document relating to Manchester, 25 Oct. 1852. The file relates to Chelmsford. The Lord Baron's 1852 ruling was referred to in a number of subsequent cases, including St Albans.
[15]   *Manchester Guardian*, 2 April 1853. The charter, dated 29 March 1853, is in Manchester City Archives, M116/6/3. I am grateful to Katharine Taylor for help on this point.
[16]   North Yorkshire RO, DC/RIC II 1/1/8, 14 Nov., 19 Dec. 1864, 20 June 1865. Unfortunately, the local newspaper, the *Ripon and Richmond Gazette*, reported town council meetings only haphazardly in these years. Its edition of 24 June, the first

and was known as the City of Ripon Act.[17] The additional clause was added, to quote from the act's preamble, 'for the purpose of removing doubts'.[18] Ripon did not receive a grant of letters patent.

The government had accepted the principle that new diocesan sees could be created cities. Of course, these were new *Anglican* sees: there was apparently no question of towns designated as Roman Catholic sees becoming cities after the restoration of the episcopate in 1850. The delay in awarding the status to Manchester, and the need to write the title into legislation for Ripon, arose from uncertainty, even some lack of understanding on the part of government, as to the legal position of a city. But the link between diocese and city had been confirmed one way or another, and the right of the monarch to make grants of city status by letters patent upheld. These decisions were significant because the Church of England was locked in debate as to the desirability of further diocesan subdivision. If additional dioceses were created, where would the cathedrals be? In the short term this was a sterile debate because no new dioceses were in contemplation, but the issue returned to the political agenda in the 1870s.[19]

Despite Manchester, the issue of city status generated relatively little passion in the 1850s and 1860s. Manchester had qualified for city status by virtue of being a cathedral town, but the application for letters patent in 1851 had been linked to the civic pageantry which surrounded Queen Victoria's visit. In provincial towns during subsequent decades, civic pride came to be linked to ceremonial, pageantry, and grand iconic gestures such as new town halls. Not only were towns becoming more competitive in the pursuit of a civilizing agenda through public provision of libraries, museums, concert halls and other socially desirable innovations, they were also increasingly concerned with ritual, ceremony and civic status. Processions and parades, the opening of parks and public buildings, the unveiling of memorials and statues, all became opportunities for civic pageantry with the urban community as witness. Civic buildings pointed even more substantially and long lastingly to success. Financial independence, a growing civic consciousness, and the need to house the burgeoning services which became part of town government, produced a

---

following the council meeting of 20 June, made no reference to the legislation, or the implications for Ripon's status.

[17]   28 & 29 Victoria c.cxxvi (1865). 'An Act to authorize the Mayor, Aldermen and Burgesses of the City and Borough of Ripon to purchase the Gasworks of the Ripon Gaslight Company, and to supply Gas within the said City, and Borough and the Neighbourhood thereof, in the West and North Ridings of the County of York; and to preclude Questions as to the Style of the City and Borough and the Name of the Corporation; and for other purposes.' Section 54 of the act dealt with the question of city status.

[18]   PRO HO 286/40. City status files in the PRO do not start until the 1870s.

[19]   Arthur Burns, *The Diocesan Revival in the Church of England, c.1800–1870* (Oxford, 1999), 192–205, summarizes the debate on diocesan subdivision during these years.

powerful mixture which found its outworking in a great rebuilding of the British town hall.

Nothing symbolized this demand for civic recognition more than Leeds town hall. The initial idea was to build a public hall via a joint stock company, but this was quickly superseded by a scheme for a new town hall built from the rates. It was designed in classical style by Cuthbert Brodrick and built 1851–8. The motive driving the corporation was pride: the building was seen as improving public taste, and it was, in short, all about architectural display.[20] In this the dome was particularly important. It was not included in Brodrick's early designs, but was added at the suggestion of Sir Charles Barry, assessor for the architectural competition. Asa Briggs has commented that it represented 'a magnificent case-study of Victorian civic pride and its place in the life of provincial communities'.[21] The building cost far more than anticipated, partly because of numerous additions while it was under construction. Queen Victoria and Prince Albert agreed to attend its opening in 1858 and the corporation sought guidance from their counterparts in Manchester on ceremonial practice. Barry himself wrote in 1859 that in his view a town hall should be 'the most dominant and important of the Municipal Buildings of the City in which it is placed. It should be the means of giving the expression to public feeling upon all national and municipal events of importance.'[22]

The town hall, together with the display involved in its opening, reflected the search for civic celebration, expressed through civic ritual centred on identifying the corporation with the town. Other industrial towns followed suit, often seriously overspending their budgets in the search for grander and greater civic premises. And a pecking order was appearing. When Manchester commissioned Alfred Waterhouse to design a new town hall (completed in 1877) it wanted a building which would be equal, if not superior, to any similar building in the country, and consequently it was prepared to pay – even if the final cost was well above the estimate.[23]

Eventually, city status would become part of this quest for civic recognition, but little could be done in the middle decades of the nineteenth century because no new dioceses were formed. In addition, no one was quite sure what benefits, if any, city status conveyed. The idea that a city was greater than a town was apparent in the case of Manchester, but the related idea that the title conveyed some form of civic prestige had yet to develop. The situation began to change with the return in 1874 of a Conservative government led by Benjamin Disraeli with a Home Secretary, R.A. Cross, who was willing to sponsor legislation to create new dioceses.

---

[20] C. Cunningham, *Victorian and Edwardian Town Halls* (1981), 38–41, 90–4.
[21] Briggs, *Victorian Cities*, 159.
[22] Ibid., 157–80; Cunningham, *Victorian*, 89, 216.
[23] Cunningham, *Victorian*, 46–7.

Initially, Cross supported the case for new dioceses based on St Albans and Truro. St Albans arose from an anomaly. The Established Church Act of 1836, in addition to promoting the new dioceses of Ripon and Manchester, had also contained provision for alterations to the boundaries of other dioceses. One of these had been the slightly bizarre decision to place much of Hertfordshire in the diocese of Rochester. Rochester cathedral, despite being in a state of dilapidation, was named as the see for what was a large and scattered diocese. By the 1850s money was being pledged in Hertfordshire for the purpose of creating a new diocese with the Norman abbey at St Albans as the cathedral. The legislation received the royal assent on 29 June 1875, and the new see, which included both Hertfordshire and Essex, was founded on 4 May 1877. Thomas Claughton, Bishop of Rochester, was formally enthroned at St Albans on 12 June 1877.[24]

Having sponsored the St Albans legislation, in 1876 Home Secretary Cross brought forward a bill to found a see of Truro to serve the county of Cornwall. The finance was relatively straightforward because Lady Rolle, a Cornishwoman living in Exmouth, offered £40,000 towards the endowment. Cornwall had been lobbying for a separate diocese since at least the 1840s, but there was no outstanding candidate for the cathedral. After much debate, St Mary's, the parish church of Truro, was named as the cathedral, and the see was officially founded on 15 December 1876. Subsequently, because St Mary's was considered inadequate, funding was raised to build a new cathedral. The Prince of Wales laid the foundation stone of the new cathedral in May 1880, although it took another thirty years to build, at a cost of £120,000. It incorporated the existing St Mary's church within its south aisle.[25]

Although the St Albans and Truro legislation was passed in 1875 and 1876 respectively, the two dioceses were actually founded in reverse order, but in both cases the question arose as to whether the see town was now a city. It was assumed in Cornwall that the Order in Council establishing the diocese 'virtually created Truro a City, ecclesiastical and historical evidence are alike in favour of this deduction'.[26] The town clerk of Truro, Mr Cock, even referred at a meeting of the corporation to the 'City of Truro', but one of the aldermen, Mr Heard, admitted to being so uncertain as to whether Truro really was a city that 'he had taken some little trouble to look into the matter, and he found that Manchester was not made a city until six years after the See was created, and then by a special order in Council'.[27] To clarify the situation, the town clerk approached Colonel Sir J. McGarell Hogg, one of the borough's MPs and he in turn wrote to the Home Office on 5 March 1877 asking what steps needed to be taken 'so that

---

[24]   Owen Chadwick, 'The Victorian Diocese of St Albans', in Robert Runcie, ed., *Cathedral and City: St Albans Ancient and Modern* (1977), 71–82.

[25]   M. Brown, '*A Century for Cornwall': the Diocese of Truro 1877–1977* (Truro, 1976), 18–20; H.M. Brown, *The Story of Truro Cathedral* (Redruth, 1977); John Beckett and David Windsor, 'Truro: Diocese and City', *Cornish Studies*, 11 (2003), 220–7.

[26]   *Royal Cornwall Gazette*, 16, 23 Dec. 1876.

[27]   Ibid., 23 Dec 1876.

Truro may be designated a City?'. Hogg reflected the uncertainty in Truro: 'Some think that the Bishop being appointed, the name of City follows as a matter of course, but the precedent of the City of Manchester shows that a petition must be presented. Will you kindly let me know what is to be done.' The Home Office informed Hogg that the town council needed to petition the Queen.[28] Hogg passed the information to the town clerk, and on 3 April the mayor read out a letter at a meeting of the corporation 'relative to the conversion of Truro into a City'. Nothing further was done immediately because the corporation became embroiled in a dispute about the likely cost, and how it would be defrayed. The town clerk was commissioned to make enquiries as to the potential outlay via the borough MPs, and the mayor wrote to his opposite number in Manchester.[29]

City status was again debated when the town council met on 8 May 1877. As a result of their enquiries the town clerk and the mayor projected an outlay of £150. In the debate which followed, Alderman Smith argued that although Truro 'might practically be a City now', it was his view that they should do whatever was necessary to have the town 'erected into a City', and consequently he was 'happy to move that an Order in Council be applied for'. He did not believe the corporation would consider the cost excessive, and consequently he moved that 'such steps as were necessary should be taken to make Truro a City', and that a committee should be appointed to raise the required £150. The motion was seconded by Alderman Clyma, who thought that 'if the Corporation were to neglect this opportunity of making Truro a City, they would become the laughing-stock of the whole county'. The motion was passed unanimously, and Alderman Smith joined the mayor (J.G. Chilcott), two other aldermen and four councillors, on the fundraising committee. Their brief was to take 'the necessary steps' in order have Truro made a city.[30] A petition was submitted to the Home Office on 22 June.[31]

The petition from Truro requesting city status arrived at the Home Office almost simultaneously with a similar petition from St Albans. On 18 June 1877 the town clerk of St Albans, I.N. Edwards, asked the Home Office for advice on how city status might be acquired. The Home Office told him that it had no information on the subject – an astonishing claim given that they had so recently been dealing with Truro – but eventually he was informed that a short petition was required. He returned to St Albans, drafted a petition and, two days later on 20 June, convened a special session of the corporation at which the mayor moved that it should be approved. The councillors found much to debate. Why was St Albans not automatically a city now that it was a diocese? What advantages would accrue to the town from city status? How much would it cost? Councillor Hurlock thought it would be 'an empty honour', but went

28   PRO HO 45/9432/62565.
29   Cornwall RO, B/TRU/99/3, Corporation of Truro Minute Books, 1862–1878.
30   *Royal Cornwall Gazette*, 11 May 1877.
31   Cornwall RO B/TRU/99/3, Corporation of Truro Minute Books, 1862–1878; *Royal Cornwall Gazette*, 22 June 1877; PRO HO 45/9432/62565.

along with the general view that the title was worth having, although he thought the expense should be underwritten by a public subscription. In the end the proposal was carried, and the petition sent to the Home Office.[32]

The arrival of the petitions at the Home Office created something of a stir. There was clearly disquiet among the civil servants faced with two simultaneous claims for city status, and particularly over the application from St Albans. A civil servant expressed this unease with an endorsement on the file: 'I don't see why because they have got a Bishop they should be made a City, when it is only a fourth or fifth rate market town, in point of population'. What the people of St Albans would have thought of this slur is not known, but the file was passed to another civil servant to find out the population at the 1871 census. The answer was 8,298, but since other cathedral cities including Ely and Lichfield had smaller populations it was decided simply to 'follow precedent of Manchester'.[33] Queen Victoria approved grants of city status to Truro and St Albans on 6 August 1877.

Truro had taken the trouble to find out the likely costs in advance, but in St Albans there was outrage when a Home Office official wrote to the town clerk on 20 August asking for a cheque for £100 before the letters patent could be drawn up. When the deputy town clerk replied that no cheque could be sent in the absence of the town clerk, who was on holiday in Scotland, the Home Office responded demanding the money to pay the stamp duty. The correspondence was brought to the council meeting on 7 September when several members vociferously opposed the Home Office's claims, arguing that the cost was extortionate, and that they had better things on which to spend their resources. In the end, the matter was dropped when the town clerk offered to pay for the charter himself if the councillors were unwilling.[34] Letters patent for both St Albans and Truro were dated 28 August 1877.[35]

Both new cities had revealed all the concerns of small town politicians trying to understand the importance of a civic honour. Their fear of the cost outshone their pride at receiving a status they did not really appreciate. Of course they celebrated their elevation, but they did so in markedly different styles. St Albans regarded this as a civic honour worthy of public display. The mayor went to London on 11 September to receive the letters patent at the Home Office, and two days later a public proclamation was made from a platform erected in front of the town hall. The mayor, town clerk, and other members of the council wearing their robes of office gathered on the platform, and a crowd assembled to hear the reading of the letters patent. The mayor

[32]   Hertfordshire RO, Off Acc 1162/889, fos. 234–5; *The Herts. Advertiser*, 23 June 1877; PRO HO 45/9439/65472.
[33]   PRO HO 45/9439/65472.
[34]   *The Herts Advertiser*, 8 Sept. 1877. Hertfordshire RO, Off Acc 1162/632 for the Charter. Possibly the town clerk took the matter up again with the Home Office, since the final bill was £90 3s. 6d.
[35]   PRO HO 45/9432/62565.

then proposed three cheers for St Albans, and the Rifle Volunteer Band played the national anthem. The platform party retired to the mayor's parlour for refreshments and toasts, the Union Jack was flown from church towers, and the bells of the abbey were rung.[36]

Truro, by contrast, regarded city status as a civic honour to be celebrated within the confines of the town council. When the new Truro City Council met on 19 September 'the mayor placed on the table the Letters Patent constituting this Borough a City'. Although in his view 'outside Truro it would be said that this was not of much importance.... He certainly thought it was a matter on which they ought greatly to congratulate themselves.' That was it: they then proceeded to business, and no further celebrations were organized. Truro acquired a new coat of arms by November 1877, and a new common seal early in 1878, but that was the limit of indulgence.[37] The new city council was still acting like a closed corporation, with little desire to involve local people in public celebration.[38]

The grants of city status to St Albans and Truro raised a number of issues. Rightly or wrongly, the unease felt in the Home Office suggested that some civil servants understood 'city' to be a distinctive title applying to a place of importance. It was possible to argue that St Albans had been a new diocese designed to sort out an anomaly established by the legislation of 1836, and that there were few large towns in the proposed new diocese which could rival it in size and significance. It was virtually the largest town in Hertfordshire in the 1871 census and outside of the London conurbation in Essex only Colchester (26,343) was a town significantly larger. Similarly, it was possible to argue that although Truro was hardly a major provincial town, it was a county capital and the largest settlement in the area. Yet, to award it simply because the Anglican church chose to nominate a particular town as a see was a questionable practice, both because it was the Church which was making the running and because unless the Church nominated only large and important towns as sees the principles accepted since the Norman Conquest were in danger of being eroded.

Unfortunately, no time was available for these issues to be considered, because long before the letters patent for Truro and St Albans were issued in August 1877, Home Secretary Cross had moved the proverbial goalposts. In February 1876 he announced his intention to bring forward a government bill in the forthcoming parliamentary session to expand the episcopate.[39] Cross set the political agenda by refusing to contemplate creating more than four new dioceses, while Lambeth Palace was left to decide the Anglican agenda in the form of the

---

[36] *The Herts Advertiser,* 15 Sept. 1877.

[37] *Royal Cornwall Gazette,* 21 Sept., 16 Nov. 1877; Cornwall RO B/TRU/99/3, Corporation of Truro Minute Books, 1862–1878; Beckett and Windsor, 'Truro', 220–7.

[38] The reaction of the town council is reflective of civic celebration in Colchester in this period: David Cannadine, 'Civic Ritual and the Colchester Oyster Feast', *Past and Present,* 94 (1982), 109–13.

[39] *Hansard,* 3rd ser., ccxxvii, 369–70, 16 Feb. 1876.

geography and sees of the new dioceses. Cross could not resist intervening in the discussion, but it was soon clear that he and Lambeth Palace disagreed about the location of the new dioceses. In the end, he introduced a bill into the House of Commons in May 1877 with a great deal of fudging about the see towns, and it was lost on a technicality.[40]

Cross was determined to push ahead, and he reintroduced the bill on 18 March 1878. By now, both St Albans and Truro had received their letters patent, so it is perhaps surprising that the issue of city status was not discussed during the passage of the bill through Parliament. Much greater concern was expressed over the issue of whether the bishops of newly-founded sees should automatically command a seat in the House of Lords. Cross announced that the four new bishoprics would have their sees in Liverpool, Newcastle, Southwell and Wakefield. The bill received the royal assent on 15 August 1878.[41]

Liverpool and Newcastle were among the great commercial centres of Victorian England, and both played a major role within their own regions. Perhaps not surprisingly, setting up these two bishoprics proved relatively straightforward. Before any of the new bishoprics could be established, a substantial capital sum had to be raised to provide an endowment for the bishop's salary. In Liverpool this proved relatively straightforward because devout Anglicans who saw their town as Godless were willing to come up with the necessary funding. Within four months of the legislation passing, £71,000 was subscribed, and £80,500 of the £93,000 raised by the end of 1880 came from only forty-seven people, each of whom gave £500 or more. The new diocese was founded in March 1880.[42] Liverpool also understood the importance of grand civic gestures. As long ago as 1789, and already grown fat on the profits of the Atlantic trade, it had sponsored a magnificent hall, which was remodelled to designs by James Wyatt. Nor was the town content: St George's hall, designed in 1840 by H.L. Elmes, was built 1841–54. It was a grand gesture, a monument to romantic classicism, built from revenue, and constructed on a scale that was designed to be larger than Birmingham's new town hall built in the 1830s.[43] Consequently, the absence of a suitable cathedral for the new diocese was not considered a problem. St Luke's was nominated in the Home Secretary's abortive 1877 bill. No potential cathedral was named in the 1878 legislation, but in 1880 a local committee decided that the cathedral should be St Peter's, although – perhaps with the Truro precedent in mind – it was subsequently argued that 'the building of a cathedral would be popular even upon secular grounds, just

[40]   Lambeth Palace Library, Tait Papers 96, fos. 256–8, 302–3; *Church Quarterly Review* (Oct. 1876), 208–24; *Official Yearbook of the Church of England* (1883), 304–5.
[41]   *Guardian*, 1 Aug. 1877; 41 & 42 Victoria c. xxx 1878; *Hansard*, 3rd ser., ccxxxix, 1862–3 passim.
[42]   P.S. Morrish, 'The Creation of the Anglican Diocese of Liverpool', *Northern History*, XXXII (1996), 173–94.
[43]   Cunningham, *Victorian*, 36–8.

as that of a magnificent town hall, exchange or assize court has proved to be in our larger towns'.[44] The new cathedral was completed in 1900.

Liverpool, having watched events in St Albans and Truro (both of which supplied it with copies of their memorials to the Crown requesting city status), had no hesitation in requesting city status. At its meeting on 7 April 1880 the town council approved a draft memorial to the Queen asking that in conjunction with the founding of the bishopric the title of city should be conferred on Liverpool. The petition was sent immediately to the Home Office,[45] and submitted by the Home Secretary to the Queen on 14 April. Five days later she had given her consent, and news of the successful outcome of the petition was sent to the corporation on 22 April – together with a bill for 100 guineas (£105) to cover the Home Office's costs for drawing up the letters patent.[46] Surprisingly, no civic celebrations seem to have been organized, but this may have been because the news arrived almost simultaneously with the foundation of the bishopric, and at a time when preparations were in hand for the enthronement of the first bishop, Rev. John Charles Ryle, on 1 July. Doubtless the Home Office civil servants were relieved that with a population of 552,000 in 1881 there could be no question of Liverpool's suitability for city status.

The second of the four 1878 bishoprics to be founded was Newcastle-upon-Tyne. Fundraising proved more difficult than in Liverpool, and the endowment capital took time to raise. Eventually, the fund was completed with a number of substantial donations and the transfer of £1,000 a year of the Bishop of Durham's salary to the new bishop. The see was founded on 17 May 1882, with St Nicholas's, Newcastle, as the cathedral.[47] Three weeks later, at a meeting of the town council on 7 June, the deputy mayor moved a memorial to the Queen requesting that Newcastle-upon-Tyne be raised to the status of a city.[48] The council adopted the memorial, after the town clerk had assured members that being a city would not make any difference to the rights and privileges of Newcastle.[49] He then dispatched the memorial to the Home Office, the request was passed formally to the Queen for approval, and the letters patent were issued before the end of June. The cost, as at Liverpool, was 100 guineas.[50]

The charter was received in Newcastle on 1 July, and at the next meeting of the town (now city) council on 5 July the mayor announced the good news. Councillors and aldermen alike rose to their feet while the town clerk read aloud

---

[44]   Quoted Morrish, 'Creation', 189.

[45]   Liverpool RO, 283 BIS/10–12; *Liverpool Daily Post*, 8 April 1880. Significantly, the draft memorials seeking city status are listed in the numerous papers relating to the establishment of the bishopric.

[46]   PRO HO 45/9539/51214E.

[47]   Peter J. Jagger, 'The Formation of the Diocese of Newcastle', in W.S.F. Pickering, *A Social History of the Diocese of Newcastle, 1882–1982* (Stocksfield, 1981), 24–52.

[48]   *Newcastle City Minutes 1881–2*, 280.

[49]   *Newcastle Daily Journal*, 8 June 1882.

[50]   PRO HO 45/9622/A17364.

the letters patent. When he had finished many of them said 'God Save the Queen'. Clearly they regarded this as a civic event of some moment, and after they had sat down the mayor gave a speech in which he referred to the benefits of the new status. It was, he began:

> an honour and dignity.... I trust that the occasion which has led to this change will be fraught with benefit and blessings to this city and district.... I trust that fresh energy will be infused into all of us who have the conducting of the public affairs of the city, in order that its best interests may be advanced both morally and commercially. I have no doubt whatever that every member of this council will feel it his duty to maintain the dignity of the office which he holds, by the promotion of all the interests so very closely identified with this important city. I trust it will be a pleasure to every one of us to see the commerce of this city advancing at a very rapid rate.

Clearly there was little of substance in this, but it contained a significant point about the perceived meaning of the new status. The mayor made clear that while 'city' might be only a title, he expected the new city of Newcastle-upon-Tyne to thrive commercially. Links with God in the form of the new diocese may have been responsible for the title in the first place, but improved links with Mammon were immediately seen as a likely spin-off.[51] This was a new interpretation of city status, and one which came to be heard more frequently in future. By contrast, the *Newcastle Daily Journal* was still reflecting the older values highlighted in Manchester's claim for city status in the 1850s when it called to account Councillor Stephens for objecting to the expense: 'it is not every day that the corporation of Newcastle obtains a new charter and is promoted to the dignity of a City ... we are not so unsentimental as not to appreciate the formal and ceremonial dignity'.[52]

Celebrations in Newcastle were muted. The civic ceremony was brief but formal. After the mayor's speech, the whole council immediately adjourned to an adjoining committee room for a celebratory drink. The mayor (Alderman Angus) toasted the Queen; Alderman Cail, the deputy mayor, toasted the mayor; and the mayor proposed the health of the sheriff. They then returned to the council chamber to continue with business. Beyond the council chamber the good news was conveyed to the people of Newcastle with the ringing of the bells of St Nicholas's, the new cathedral, a gesture organized by the town clerk.[53]

Liverpool and Truro had evoked memories of the medieval bishops who had built themselves cathedrals, while Newcastle and St Albans had ecclesiastical property highly suitable for cathedral status. In addition, Liverpool and Newcastle were great centres of Victorian population, and Truro at least had the benefit of being a county town in an area where urbanization had not taken hold. Newcastle, with a population in 1881 of 145,000, was, like Liverpool, a major Victorian

51   *Newcastle City Minutes 1881–2*, 306–7.
52   *Newcastle Daily Journal*, 6 July 1882.
53   *Newcastle City Minutes 1881–2*, 306–7.

commercial centre, and entitlement to city status, which had been queried in the Home Office in the case of St Albans, was hardly an issue. The other two foundations under the 1878 legislation, Southwell and Wakefield, were always likely to be more contentious; indeed, the process of founding these dioceses revived the debate about St Albans and led directly to the abandonment of the link between diocesan creation and city status.

If the Church of England had wanted to provoke the government over city status, the nomination of Southwell to be the see for a new diocese consisting of the counties of Derbyshire and Nottinghamshire could not have been more timely. Unfortunately, the motives were rather more mundane. Home Secretary Cross would agree only to four new dioceses under the legislation of 1878, and the Anglican church, desperate to balance competing needs and claims, could spare only one of these for the Midlands. The compromise reached was to take the archdeaconry of Derby from Lichfield diocese, and the Archdeaconry of Nottingham from Lincoln diocese – more or less the historic counties of Derbyshire and Nottinghamshire – and to create a single diocese. Since the two counties proved quite incapable of working together in church matters, this turned out to be a serious mistake, but it was compounded by the choice of cathedral.[54] No one seriously doubted that the finest church in the two counties was the collegiate church of St Mary the Virgin, Southwell, better known as Southwell Minster. Unfortunately, Southwell itself was little more than a village, with a population of just 2,897 in 1881. It was not even an incorporated borough.

Clearly, the only serious option if the Church of England was to maintain any semblance of its principle of establishing sees in important towns was for the cathedral to be in Nottingham. With a population of 186,575 in 1881 it was far and away the largest place in the two counties, several times greater than Derby with 58,568. Nor did it lack a suitable cathedral, because the fifteenth-century church of St Mary the Virgin had been the seat of a suffragan bishop since 1870.[55] Bishop Christopher Wordsworth of Lincoln admitted when he installed Henry Mackenzie as the first suffragan bishop of Nottingham since the sixteenth century that 'the appointment of a bishop suffragan, with a title derived from it, may be expected to lead to ... a bishop of its own'.[56] So what went wrong? Wordsworth, who in his Cathedral Commission days in the 1850s had been a passionate supporter of having bishops in large towns, was still bishop in 1878, and his written words from the 1850s and spoken words from 1870 must have come home to haunt him given what subsequently happened. The Derbyshire

---

[54]   John Beckett, 'Edward Trollope, the Archbishop's Palace, and the Founding of the Diocese of Southwell in 1884', in John Beckett, ed., *Nottinghamshire Past* (Nottingham, 2003), 137–54.

[55]   The position of suffragan bishop introduced by Henry VIII was revived in 1869 by reactivating unrepealed legislation from his reign.

[56]   BL Additional MSS, 44,346, f. 384; John Henry Overton and Elizabeth Wordsworth, *Christopher Wordsworth, Bishop of Lincoln, 1807–1885* (1888), 302; Laura Ridding, *George Ridding: Schoolmaster and Bishop* (1908), 164.

churchmen refused to be governed in Anglican affairs from Nottingham.[57] They were able to make common cause with the architectural purists of the Church of England who saw Southwell Minster as a cathedral in all but name. A.J. Beresford Hope, MP, a leading ecclesiologist and supporter of diocesan subdivision, 'approved the church of Southwell ... a suitable cathedral ... [it] would not compromise the rivalry of the two county towns, Nottingham and Derby'.[58]

Funding for the diocese was completed by the end of 1883, but the cathedral remained an issue. On 1 January 1884 an unsigned letter appeared in *The Times* pointing out that with the imminent founding of the new diocese 'the little insignificant village' of Southwell would be entitled to city status, while 'the two important manufacturing centres of Nottingham and Derby will simply remain a town'.[59] This was red rag to a bull as far as the Oxford constitutional historian Professor E.A. Freeman was concerned. He fired off a furious response which appeared in *The Times* a few days later:

it is a grotesque absurdity, when a Bishop is wanted for Nottinghamshire, to plant his bishopstool in the village – it is hardly more – of Southwell, while the great town of Nottingham stands ready as the natural centre. The practical minds of the bishops of the 11th and 12th centuries, who shifted their sees from Crediton to Exeter, from Dorchester to Lincoln, would assuredly have been moved to scorn at such a scheme as this.[60]

Altering the cathedral-designate may have been too late at this juncture, but another correspondent of *The Times* suggested that the new bishopric should be called 'Nottingham and Derby', thereby enabling both places to be cities. The same theme was echoed in the local press. In the words of the *Derby Mercury*:

Might not the members for Derby and Nottingham be induced to urge upon the Premier, before it is too late, the justice and the advantage of entitling the new See as *The Bishopric of Nottingham and Derby* instead of the Bishopric of Southwell? The former appellation will most certainly create a far more extensive and hearty sympathy throughout the new diocese. What do the majority of the inhabitants know about Southwell? What endearing associations will the name excite in the hearts of the working classes? Southwell may have some advantages in its history and its grand old church, in its quiet seclusion from the stormy billows of his see, to be the Sedes Episcopi, but that it should monopolize the title of the diocese and prevent two large and important towns from being cities is an unintelligible paradox.[61]

---

57 John Beckett, 'Derbyshire and the Establishment of the Diocese of Southwell in 1884', forthcoming.
58 *Hansard*, 3rd ser., 234 (1877), 180–3; PRO HO 45/9539/51214G, Memorandum, 8 May 1877.
59 *The Times*, 1 Jan. 1884.
60 Ibid., 16 Jan. 1884.
61 *Derby Mercury*, 16 Jan. 1884.

The *Nottingham Journal* weighed in with an editorial criticizing the decision to fix the bishopric in a 'squalid village' just because it had a fine church.[62] Colonel Seely, one of Nottingham's MPs, enquired of the Home Office as to whether a change of title might be considered, but the response was negative: no change could be made because the title had been settled in the 1878 legislation.[63]

The parallel here was with Ripon, where Leeds and Halifax had been overlooked in favour of a much smaller town which happened to have the appropriate buildings. What the newspaper correspondence highlighted was the concern that insignificant little Southwell should be promoted to a city, while Nottingham and Derby 'will be for ever debarred from attaining the dignity of a city'. The unwritten agenda was that a pecking order existed, that a city should be a place of importance: 'It will be a disgrace to the Churchmen of Nottingham and Derby', wrote one infuriated correspondent:

> and a permanent scandal to the Church of England itself if the locale of the new see is fixed at Southwell, and the supreme title of city is conferred upon a dilapidated village which has not even yet begun to set its pigsties in order, and will probably not be brought under an efficient system of municipal government for half a century. With proper representations from the local authorities, I am convinced Her Majesty could be induced to alter the title to 'The See of Nottingham and Derby', and to constitute each of those places a city.[64]

Yet not everyone thought in this way. A debate on the issue was initiated at a meeting of Nottingham Town Council on 4 February 1884. Councillor Jacoby proposed 'that a memorial be presented to the Secretary of State for the Home Department asking that the new Bishopric to be constituted for the Midland Counties should include in its title the name of the town of Nottingham so that this town may be henceforth styled a city'. Jacoby referred to the correspondence in the national press, and to suggestions that 'by a blunder the village of Southwell had been fixed upon as the seat of the new bishopric'. There was some discussion, but he could muster little support for the proposal. Councillor Brewster 'contended that Nottingham, being a town and county in itself, had quite as high a title as could be conferred if it were made a city'. The proposal was lost 'by a considerable majority'. Jacoby recognized that the nonconformist majority on Nottingham Corporation had little enthusiasm for a title it regarded not so much as a sign of status as an indication of Anglican approval. This fundamental difference of view ensured that his hope that religious differences could be put aside in pursuit of a common cause proved mistaken.[65]

Southwell Minster became the cathedral of the new diocese and Professor Freeman feared the worst: 'I looked carefully for some time to see whether a

---

62   *Nottingham Journal*, 17 Jan. 1884.
63   Ibid., 22 Jan. 1884.
64   Ibid., 15 Jan. 1884.
65   *Nottingham Daily Express*, 5 Feb. 1884; *Nottingham Journal*, 5 Feb. 1884.

proclamation would come making Southwell into a city; but I have not seen it yet'.[66] This was not because the Home Office listened to and approved of his argument. As a civil servant noted when Chelmsford put in an application in 1914, Southwell 'which is not a municipal borough, does not seem to have applied'. In the absence of a corporation, nobody in the town had the authority to apply and, in the end, no one did.[67] Southwell became the first new English Anglican diocesan see *not* to become a city, but it did so by default rather than on a point of principle.

The fourth new diocese named in the 1878 legislation was Wakefield, which provoked similar disquiet, both locally and in the Home Office. At the time of the abortive 1877 bill, the Home Secretary had referred only to a new diocese in the West Riding, without naming a see town. This was simply a mechanism to paper over a fierce debate which was taking place in Yorkshire. The initial choice for the see had been Halifax (population 65,000 in 1871), although both Wakefield (28,000) and Huddersfield (70,000) also had claims to a bishopric. Huddersfield, for various reasons, later dropped out of the competition, but by the summer of 1877 Wakefield and Halifax were locked in conflict over the issue. Leeds, which might have been expected to participate in these disputes, chose to stand aloof, largely on the grounds that Leeds parish church and the authority of its vicar were equivalent to any bishop and diocese.

In the end, Wakefield was named as the see in the 1878 legislation. As with Southwell, the town was considered to have a church suitable for upgrading to cathedral status. While Wakefield was rather more substantial as a town than Southwell, it still encountered the same ambivalence when it came to funding; indeed, it took ten years to raise the required capital to set up the diocese, and dissatisfaction with the way the new diocese had been carved out of Ripon, and the new cathedral chosen, was certainly a contributory factor. Many Leeds people, it was claimed, were indignant when the honour went to Wakefield, and this made fundraising difficult. By early 1884, £20,000–£30,000 had been promised and £4,000–£5,000 given, but the diocese was not founded until 17 May 1888.[68] All Saints, Wakefield, was the cathedral church, and Bishop William Walsham How was the first bishop.

Wakefield, unlike Southwell, immediately sought city status. A special meeting of the corporation on 12 June 1888 approved the wording of a petition, with only one dissenting voice, Councillor Lupton, who was following well-worn

---

[66]   E.A. Freeman, 'City and Borough', *Macmillan's Magazine*, 60 (1889), 34.

[67]   PRO HO 45/24657; John Beckett, 'City Status in the Nineteenth Century: Southwell and Nottingham, 1884–97', *Transactions of the Thoroton Society*, 103 (1999), 149–58.

[68]   Arthur Elton, 'Becoming a City: Leeds, 1893', *Publications of the Thoresby Society*, 2nd ser., III (1993), 71; P.S. Morrish, 'Leeds and the Dismemberment of the Diocese of Ripon', *Publications of the Thoresby Society*, 2nd ser., IV (1994), 76–82; *Guardian*, 5 March 1884. In recent years 'Leeds' has been added to the diocesan title of the old Diocese of Ripon.

tracks when he asked how much it would cost.[69] The following day, the town clerk submitted the petition to the Home Office, where it raised the same hackles as had St Albans. A civil servant annotated the Wakefield file on 18 June 'What is the population of Wakefield and are the precedents uniform as to making a borough a City when it is the seat of a Bishopric?'. The most recent population estimate was just 30,854. As with St Albans, the issue was avoided: after some internal discussion at the Home Office it was agreed on the basis of the Manchester and St Albans cases that 'the precedents are uniform as to making a Borough a City when it becomes the seat of a Bishopric'. On 27 June the Home Secretary, Henry Matthews, passed the petition to the Queen, and the town clerk and mayor of Wakefield were told that the title of city was to be granted. The fee was £110. The letters patent were dated 11 July.[70]

Wakefield Corporation formally acknowledged receipt of the letters patent when it met on 14 August: the minutes refer to the City of Wakefield. Alderman MacGirr complained that 'there is not very much for the money', and no celebrations were suggested. The chairman thought it unnecessary to read the letters patent publicly, and simply commented – echoing the discussion in Newcastle – that 'I hope great prosperity may attend the change' of status. No one apparently asked what advantages they were to anticipate.[71]

Southwell had demonstrated the ill-logic of maintaining the bishopric-city link, and Wakefield was to be the last town promoted purely on this basis. The disquiet first expressed in the Home Office over St Albans was increasingly pertinent as time went on. Why, if the status of city offered not just prestige but also perhaps prosperity to the towns which enjoyed it (and this was the implication of the acceptance speeches made by the mayors of Newcastle and Wakefield), was it so carefully limited to the sees of Anglican bishops, especially as those sees were nominated by the Church of England rather than the government? Professor Freeman had summed up the dilemma in his letter to *The Times* in January 1884 when he argued that by tradition bishops should be located in *important* centres of population, not just in places which happened to have the appropriate church architecture. It had also been clear since Manchester was raised to city status in 1853 that the link between city and bishop was accepted as a result of precedent, and was not enshrined in law.

Once 'city' seemed to represent something significant in respect to a differentiation *between* towns, it was almost inevitable that the informal rules would collapse. As towns became increasingly concerned with their status by the

---

[69]   West Yorkshire Archives, Wakefield, WW1/9, fos 306, 308. We know from the report in the *Wakefield Express*, 16 June 1888, that the background work for the charter was undertaken by the borough's General Purposes Committee. The papers of this committee have not survived at this date.

[70]   PRO HO 45/16841/B4371; HO 45/9774/B1512, note from the Home Office to Sir W. Kaye, 8 Aug. 1888.

[71]   *Wakefield Express*, 18 Aug. 1888.

closing years of the century,[72] the implied suggestion that a city was somehow more important than a town was bound to raise the stakes. Although Wakefield jumped the hurdle, it was the last new diocesan see to be promoted to city simply on the grounds of having a cathedral. In the course of the twentieth century a number of Anglican see towns became cities, but there has been no specific link between the two honours, and several sees remained towns. When Wakefield approached the Home Office in 1937 petitioning to have its mayor raised to the status of lord mayor it was turned down because 'under present practice Wakefield would certainly not be made a City. In former times it was considered that a town which became the seat of a Bishopric was entitled to become a City, but Wakefield itself was the last borough to become a City on these grounds.'[73] The achievement of city status, which had motivated Manchester's corporation in the 1850s, finally came by the 1890s to be seen as a necessary accessory for the great provincial towns of industrial Britain.

---

[72]   D. Cannadine, *The Decline and Fall of the British Aristocracy* (1990), 718–20; Gunn, 'Ritual', 230.
[73]   PRO HO 45/16841/B4371/3.

CHAPTER THREE

Civic Pride:
Towns into Cities, 1888–1914

In May 1887 F.D. Ward, President of the Belfast Chamber of Commerce, proposed that Belfast should make a case for city status in conjunction with celebrations of Queen Victoria's Golden Jubilee:

> The matter is one rather of a sentimental character than as being likely to lead to practical advantages.... Belfast need not be ashamed of being inspired by the example of Liverpool and Manchester, which were not content until commercial and manufacturing eminence was marked by the bestowal of that dignity to which this town is now aspiring with a right that may be looked upon as not inferior in certain respects to that recognized in the case of the great seaport on the Mersey and the great centre of the cotton manufacture of England. [It will] raise the status of our town and port to a higher level among the other great cities of the British Empire, [and] increase the importance of Belfast in its mercantile relations with foreign countries.[1]

Mr Ward had his facts a little confused because both Liverpool and Manchester had been promoted to city status in conjunction with the formation of Anglican dioceses. He may also have had hidden motives, since requesting a grant from the Crown would demonstrate Belfast's loyalty in the ongoing Home Rule debates. But he also had a point: just as Newcastle corporation had celebrated the likely commercial benefits it expected to arise from city status, so Mr Ward believed Belfast could expect to enjoy 'practical advantages' because a city meant more than a town to the international commercial community in which Belfast wished to trade.

Where Belfast led, others followed. Before the First World War, Dundee, Birmingham, Leeds, Sheffield, Bradford, Nottingham, Hull and Cardiff had all achieved city status: none were the sees of Anglican bishoprics. But while Belfast blazed a trail because it set a precedent, the commercial argument so eloquently elucidated by Mr Ward had few echoes elsewhere. The search for city status in these years was all to do with civic pride. It was viewed as a reward for successful municipal achievement, a process of rubber stamping which spurred on corporate bodies to demand new titles and to invent new ceremonials. They could create grandiose images through civic buildings, civic robes, parades, ceremonial and, to cap it all, royal visits if Queen Victoria obliged, but they could achieve city status only if the Home Office – as the arbiter of civic status – accepted their claims.

[1]   PRO HO 45/9774/B1512.

The Home Office found itself in difficulties over Belfast's claim. Since Manchester's success in 1853 the rules had been clear: city status could be granted by letters patent, on receipt of an appropriate petition (and fee) from towns which had become the sees of Anglican dioceses. Fearing that any movement away from this position would create unwelcome precedents, the Home Office put up fierce resistance. When it lost the battle, it was forced to make policy on the hoof, but in doing so it gradually created a new precedent: that only towns of importance – most easily measured through population – could be considered worthy of the title city. Since this was not enough, almost by accident in 1897 it introduced a further qualification, a link with royal events. The potent mix of civic pride and Home Office conservatism brought obfuscation and annoyance, and not much has changed since, with towns seeking the status of city as a perceived promotion in the urban hierarchy, and the Home Office successfully if inadvertently stoking demand by limiting supply.

Belfast broke the mould on city status. Mr Ward's proposal in May 1887 was passed by the town clerk to the corporation's law committee to investigate. Subsequently, the town clerk reported to a meeting of the town council on 13 June that no legal objections had been uncovered. Since promotion did not seem likely to cost a great deal, he suggested that a petition should be prepared, which the lord lieutenant would be asked to submit to Westminster. The town councillors were of much the same view. Mr Ewart, in seconding the motion, noted that 'they were asking only a recognition of the advancement in position and dignity to which they thought they were fairly entitled'. In putting the proposal, the mayor argued that 'there could be no question that beyond the immediate surroundings of Belfast this would carry considerable weight, and, therefore, it was not an empty title'. Those who contributed to the discussion did so primarily in terms of regarding the title as recognition of Belfast's economic success. The resolution was carried unanimously, and the memorial was subsequently drawn up and presented to the lord lieutenant in July 1887. It stressed Belfast's long history, its population (at 230,000 second only in Ireland to Dublin), the importance of the town's commerce and manufacture – particularly the linen industry – and its status, reflected in having four MPs.[2]

At Westminster this request for city status was an unwelcome development. As the Home Office saw it, here was a dam waiting to burst: let one non-diocesan town become a city and who knew how many others would come rushing through the floodgates? And, if they did, how was the case for promotion to be assessed? What criteria could now be used to decide how a city was 'made', and who should do the deciding? How clear should the criteria be? In the corridors of power in 1887 the only obvious thing to do was to stall, to play for time in the hope that either the Belfast request would conveniently go away, or at least that the civil servants would have an opportunity to find good reasons for refusing city status. Initially they succeeded in stalling, and Queen Victoria's Golden Jubilee

[2]   *Belfast News-Letter*, 14 June 1887; Public Record Office of Northern Ireland (PRONI), Belfast Corporation, Town Minute Books, 1884–7, f. 627; 1887–90, f. 246.

passed without the case for promoting Belfast being decided. It was only in May 1888 that the lord lieutenant, the 10th Marquess of Londonderry, wrote to the Home Office to say that he had received the memorial. His letter was endorsed by a civil servant: 'from inquiries made at the Privy Council and in the General Department it appears that there are no precedents for doing what is proposed'. Blackstone, the constitutional lawyer, had taken the view that a city was an incorporated town which either was, or had been, the seat of a bishop. The conclusion, in the words of a further endorsement, was obvious:

> Inform Irish Government that there is no record in H[ome] O[ffice] of any precedent for conferring the title of City on a town and that the officials at the Privy Council Department are also without any such record and do not believe that it has ever been granted. Add that Sec[retary] of S[tate] will if the Irish government desire it take the opinion of the law officers as to the power of Her Majesty to make such a grant and the manner of proceeding if she has....

This was a desperate response given the background work already undertaken in Belfast, and the lord lieutenant simply responded that he had 'already taken the opinion of the Law Officers of the Crown in Ireland on the subject who have advised that it is legally competent for the Crown to confer by Charter the title of City upon Belfast'. Unmoved, the Home Office took its own legal advice, only to discover, somewhat unsurprisingly, that no impediment existed at law to making such a grant.[3]

The Home Office procrastinated as long as it could, but its cover was blown when Thomas Sexton, MP for Belfast West, put himself down to ask a question in the House of Commons on 9 July 1888 about progress on the issue. A civil servant summed up the position in a briefing minute prepared for the Home Secretary, Henry Matthews, written on 3 July:

> The Law Officers are of opinion that the Crown has power to confer by Charter the title of 'City' on a town not the seat of a bishopric. If the government accept this opinion it rests with them to decide on the expediency of creating a precedent for the exercise of a power which, I believe, is unprecedented, and may be quoted for Great Britain as well as for Ireland.[4]

The politicians proved less inflexible than their civil servants. The prime minister, the Marquess of Salisbury, consulted the Queen, who gave her approval. Mr Sexton was told on 9 July that the government 'finding there are no legal difficulties, will take the necessary steps for the grant of a City Charter'.[5] The following morning the *Belfast News-Letter* suggested that 'the announcement will give great satisfaction', and it stressed once again the significance of commercial considerations: 'Belfast has an honourable and a distinguished history, and, now

---

3   PRO HO 45/9774/B1512.
4   Ibid.
5   *Hansard*, 3rd ser., 328, July 1888, col 739.

that it is to be created a city, we trust a new era of prosperity will open before it; while we are certain it will fully justify the action of Ministers in giving an honour that must be acknowledged to be exceedingly well merited'.[6] To establish some decorum, the Home Office insisted that the Law Committee of Belfast Corporation should submit a petition to the Queen,[7] and this was duly put together and submitted to the Home Office through the lord lieutenant on 1 August 1888. In turn, the Home Secretary sought and obtained the Queen's approval on 7 August.

The official announcement of city status was made on Saturday 13 October when the lord lieutenant visited Belfast to open the Free Library, an apt occasion in itself as the library represented a major civic achievement. At a lunch in the council chamber following the ceremony, Lord Londonderry used his speech in reply to the mayor to announce 'that Her Majesty has been graciously pleased to confer on your town the dignity, the honour, and the title of city. And that honour is enhanced by the fact that on no other occasion has this title been conferred except the town was the seat of a bishopric.' As the *Northern Whig* put it, 'it will be seen, therefore, that Belfast is to be regarded as especially and doubly honoured, since it has been created a city without a bishop'. On the other hand, the newspaper wanted to know 'where is the charter?', since it was not mentioned the previous Saturday. The following day (16th) it reported that the mayor had told a meeting of the town council on 15 October that it would arrive by another route, although he had not said which one.[8] What actually happened to the charter is not clear. We know that the relevant legal documents were drawn up on 9 October and sent to Belfast on 12 October, but presumably they did not arrive in time for the free library ceremony, probably to the embarrassment of the lord lieutenant.[9]

Inevitably, Belfast was a precedent. On 4 October 1888 Charles Thomson Ritchie, President of the Local Government Board in Lord Salisbury's government 1886–92, and a native of Dundee with family links in the jute-spinning business, visited his home town to be made an honorary freeman. The provost of Dundee 'thought there could be no harm in indicating our wishes [in regard to city status] to him. We found him most anxious to obtain this honour for his native town.' Ritchie, presumably aware of events in Belfast, and with inside knowledge of the workings of Whitehall, took it upon himself to promote Dundee's case. He wrote from the Local Government Board to the provost of Dundee on 30 November 1888: 'I have much pleasure in informing you that the Queen's consent has been given to the elevation of the Town of Dundee into a City. I offer you and my fellow townsmen my warmest

---

6   *Belfast News-Letter*, 10 July 1888.

7   PRONI, Belfast Corporation, Town Minute Books, 1887–90, f. 246.

8   *Belfast News-Letter*, 15 Oct. 1888; *Northern Whig*, 15, 16 Oct. 1888.

9   A copy of the letters patent was printed in the *Belfast and Ulster Directory for 1890* (Belfast, 1890), 2, which also noted that it was enrolled in the High Court of Justice on 7 Nov. 1888.

congratulations upon an event which I am sure will give the liveliest pleasure in Dundee.'

The town clerk communicated this information to the council at its meeting on 6 December 1888, and on 26 January 1889 Dundee officially became a city.[10] The council was convened on 4 February 1889 'for the purpose of formally receiving the Charter conferring the dignity of a City on the Royal Burgh of Dundee'. According to the *Dundee Year Book*, 'the interest felt by the community in the honour conferred by Her Majesty was manifested by the large attendance of the general public, all the available space in the Town Hall being fully occupied by ladies and gentlemen'. The provost wore 'handsome new robes' for the occasion. Ex-Bailie Gentle told the meeting that 'I am certain an impetus will be given to the industries of this city because of the honour that has been conferred by her Majesty the Queen'. According to the Lord Dean of Guild, Dundee was fully entitled to the status as the third town in Scotland in terms of population and importance.[11]

Belfast had set a precedent which Dundee was quick to exploit, partly because it had a sympathetic champion at the heart of government. Both would-be cities had stressed the likely economic spin-offs which they anticipated from the new status. But this was not to be the primary concern of the larger English boroughs which picked up the baton from Belfast. For them Belfast was a precedent, but they already enjoyed considerable prosperity: city status became bound up with the whole issue of civic pride, a public endorsement of municipal achievement. The physical embodiment of civic pride was in the improvement of public health, the demolition of slums, the acquisition of public utilities, the promotion of new civic buildings and the provision of libraries and museums. Birmingham, under the mayoralty of Joseph Chamberlain 1873–6, is sometimes viewed as the leader of this movement, but it was far from alone as municipal corporations became not simply service providers, but moral agencies committed to promoting 'civilization' within their borders. As one newspaper put it in 1895:

> The larger provincial towns are ... laying out parks and playgrounds using in fact municipal funds to increase the pleasure and health of the community ... the future of life in large cities may be contemplated with the assurance that it will be brighter, sweeter and more appreciative of the necessities of modern life and more anxious to adopt improvements that will add to the happiness of the communities they represent.[12]

---

[10]   NAS, C2/268, Register of the Great Seal.

[11]   *Dundee Year Book* (12th edn., Dundee, 1890); *Dundee Advertiser*, 5 Feb. 1889; *Dundee Town Council Minutes*, 6 Dec. 1888, 4 Feb. 1889. Ritchie must have handled the application himself: at least, there is no Home Office file in the PRO, which suggests that it was not responsible for Dundee's elevation.

[12]   Quoted in D. Fraser, *Power and Authority in the Victorian City* (Oxford, 1979), 170. See also R.J. Morris, 'Structure, Culture and Society in British Towns', in M. Daunton, ed., *The Cambridge Urban History of Britain, III 1840–1950* (Cambridge, 2000), 412–15; J. Stobart, 'Identity, Competition and Place Promotion in the Five

The icing on the cake came in the form of civic buildings, particularly new town halls, guildhalls and civic premises, while the cherry on the icing was in the development of appropriate ceremonies and ritual. Ceremonies needed robes, and robes needed occasions. In Dundee, the provost bought new robes to celebrate city status. Titles, in other words, became part of the recognition and celebration process by the late nineteenth century. Just as individual achievement was increasingly recognized through the conferment of honours, municipal achievement deserved to be crowned in a manner which told the world just how well respected a town was in the eyes of the Crown. City status, granted by the Crown, became the means of achieving corporate recognition. It was transferred from a passive reward granted to places which happened to become the sees of English dioceses, to an overt celebration of the success of large towns. Nor was this all. A symbolic language of civic ritual meant that even the status of the participants was an issue. A city demanded a lord mayor rather than simply a mayor, and the ultimate accolade was for the lord mayor to convert the prefix Right Worshipful into Right Honourable.

These civic distinctions became crucially important. With honours seen as registering an approval rating in terms of civic success, and the Home Office desperately attempting to keep the genie in the bottle, each gradation was turned into a symbol of civic achievement. 'I must freely confess', wrote Professor E.A. Freeman shortly after Birmingham was promoted, 'that I do not know what difference, except difference in rank, there is in England between a city and a borough'. Beyond this he found it 'hard to see what Birmingham or any other borough gains by becoming a city'. The difference in law between a city and a borough was negligible. Although the mayor of a city would take precedence over the mayor of a town, it was otherwise unclear in late nineteenth-century England what was to be gained by obtaining the status of a city.[13] Couched in these legal terms it did indeed make little sense, but the petitions presented by aspiring cities show that they saw the title as carrying a sense of status which differentiated them from those around. The search for honours among the larger English boroughs was about civic pride, about recognition of municipal success.

Birmingham was the greatest of the Victorian provincial towns which by 1889 was not a city. Since Chamberlain's mayoralty in the 1870s, it had been a model of municipal progress. A new town hall was built 1874–9, and the powers of the town council were codified and unified by the Birmingham Corporation Consolidation Act of 1883. In 1884 it became an assize town, and in 1887 Queen Victoria laid the foundation stone of the new law courts. Parliamentary reform in 1885 saw Birmingham divided into seven

Towns', *Urban History*, 30 (2003), 163–82; A. Croll, *Civilizing the Urban: Popular Culture and Civic Space in Merthyr, c.1870–1914* (Cardiff, 2000).
13   E.A. Freeman, 'City and Borough', *Macmillan's Magazine*, 60 (1889), 30.

constituencies, and in 1888 it became a county borough.[14] With a population in excess of 400,000 it stood in size terms behind only London, Liverpool and Manchester among English conurbations – and they were all cities. It was almost inevitable that Birmingham would react to news of Belfast's elevation to city status, but while it used to good effect the precedent established across the Irish Sea, it took as its justification for requesting city status municipal progress rather than economic anticipation.

News of Belfast's success reached Birmingham just as the General Purposes Committee was discussing ways of celebrating in 1888 the jubilee of incorporation in 1838. Edward Orford Smith, the town clerk, suggested that city status might be a suitable promotion for Birmingham, confirming its status among the elite of English towns and its successful conduct of municipal affairs. When Smith and Alderman Pollack were in London on 17 October 1888 they enquired at the Privy Council Office as to how Birmingham might obtain city status. They were told to submit a petition to the Home Office. On their return to Birmingham the two men drafted a letter, which Smith sent to Home Secretary Matthews on 19 October. Birmingham, he pointed out, was about to celebrate (on 31 October) fifty years as a municipal corporation, and this seemed a suitable opportunity for it to be elevated to a city: 'It has occurred to me that Her Majesty might be willing on such an occasion to confer the title of City upon the town. I have mentioned the subject to the mayor, who cordially approves of the suggestion, and has requested me to communicate with you upon the subject.'[15]

The town clerk constructed his argument along lines similar to those used by Belfast: commercial and manufacturing greatness as well as size and municipal achievement. 'Birmingham', he reminded the Home Secretary, 'is now the second largest town in England (excluding London), and it is believed that the municipal work done here during the last fifty years can hardly have been surpassed.' His claim as to size was not borne out by the 1891 census – Liverpool and Manchester both had greater populations – but his emphasis on municipal achievement reflected the idea that city status was an honour to be conferred on large and successful provincial towns. He had noted that 'the title of city is popularly supposed to carry with it a certain accession of dignity', and also that it was 'no longer held to be necessarily connected with the See of a Bishop'. Above all:

> I observe that Her Majesty has within the last few days been graciously pleased to confer a similar dignity upon the town of Belfast, and, with this recent precedent before me, I venture very humbly to suggest that a like act of grace may be

---

[14] Asa Briggs, *History of Birmingham* II (Oxford, 1952), 88–9; Simon Gunn, 'Ritual and civic culture in the English industrial city, c.1835–1914', in R.J. Morris and R.H. Trainor, eds., *Urban Governance: Britain and Beyond Since 1750* (Aldershot, 2000), 226.

[15] PRO HO 45/9799/B5306.

extended to Birmingham, in the belief that such a mark of Royal favour will be heartily appreciated by the town.

This last phrase reflected the idea of an honour conferred by the monarch as a reward for municipal success. He concluded: 'I have confidence in appealing to you, in your official capacity, to favourably consider the proposal I have thus ventured to make'. The reference to 'official capacity' reflected the conflict of interests Matthews was bound to feel since he was not only Home Secretary but also MP for East Birmingham.[16]

Although Sir Godfrey Lushington, the permanent secretary at the Home Office, responded to this letter on 23 October in the deadpan style of a senior civil servant, assuring the town clerk that the contents of his letter would be carefully considered, the Home Office was irritated that this approach had come so swiftly after Belfast, and that promotion for the Irish town was seen as the precedent they feared. Smith's letter is annotated:

See the case of Belfast.... As supported in that case, it has proved a precedent on which to found similar claims, and a word that by association had acquired a definite meaning signifying a certain fact, will now become a meaningless title: in the United States every village is a 'City'. It is a break with History but a cheap way of gratifying large manufacturing towns, strongholds of nonconformity. However, it is purely a question for the government to decide.

The civil servant's logic is not entirely clear, but presumably the 'certain fact' was possession of an Anglican see, hence the conclusion that towns which had no desire to promote themselves as Anglican beacons because of their nonconformist leanings, would still be able to obtain city status. Whatever the case, the key point, as another civil servant noted on the file, was that 'If you grant this, you will be prepared to grant others'.[17]

An informal approach of this nature also upset the civil servants' sense of decorum. Nothing could be done, they told Matthews, without 'a formal petition to the Queen ... from the Town Council'. If Matthews was minded to promote the case, he was recommended to suggest privately to the mayor of Birmingham that a petition should be prepared. The Home Office would not act simply on a letter from the town clerk, and without 'further instruction ... the papers will be put up in our pigeon hole and forgotten'. Matthews clearly thought little of this procrastination but, presumably because he felt compromised by being both Home Secretary and a local MP, he decided to raise the matter in Cabinet. In the meantime he sent a private note to the town clerk on 23 November suggesting that a petition should be submitted. He also told Alderman Pollack in confidence that the Queen would be asked to accept the case for Birmingham's elevation. With

---

[16]   Ibid. The original letter in the PRO file was printed in *City of Birmingham: City Council Minutes 1888–9*, 64.
[17]   PRO HO 45/9799/B5306.

this assurance, the town clerk prepared a petition which he proposed to bring to the town council on 4 December for endorsement.[18]

An element of farce now came into the proceedings. Unfortunately, there is nothing in the Cabinet papers of this period to indicate whether the Birmingham case was discussed and, if so, what opinions were expressed, but the case for Birmingham being given city status was evidently endorsed. Subsequently, Lord Salisbury took the Queen's pleasure on the matter, and on 3 December he told the Home Secretary that she had given her approval. Matthews passed this information directly to Birmingham. As a result, when the corporation met on 4 December it was placed in the awkward position of discussing and approving a petition for an award it already knew it was going to receive. An editorial in the *Birmingham Daily Post* happily pointed out that the corporation 'need not give itself the trouble to discuss the question whether it will or will not petition that Birmingham shall be made a city, for the thing is already done. Her Majesty has approved the issue of the requisite grant, and we are a city from this time forward.'[19]

The corporation went ahead with the planned debate, which at least allows us to see some of the objections which surrounded the proposed promotion. The *Birmingham Weekly Mercury* noted that 'a little amusement was created by Mr Whateley's earnest enquiry whether a bishop and a cathedral would be necessary'. Here was the nonconformist Labour conscience worrying both that the promotion would be seen in Anglican terms and that it might be costly. He was assured that it would not. Alderman Downing was another doubter, but he seems to have received little support for his complaint that promotion would mean the council would need to have a mace and other baubles, and to wear gowns.[20] For many councillors this was probably a boon. The petition mentioned the 1838 municipal charter which had granted the town independence in matters of local government, it stressed population (450,000 by October 1888), size – 'the second town in England in point of population and the largest borough that has not received the title of City' – industrial standing, and municipal achievement. It was accepted on a motion moved by Alderman Pollack, and sent immediately to the Home Secretary.[21]

In the Home Office the civil servants were thrown into a further panic by this turn of events. For the Queen to give her approval before the petition reached Whitehall was a breach of protocol. In the words of one civil servant, this made it look as if 'they were asked to petition apparently after the Queen's pleasure had been taken'. In his view this made the petition an embarrassment: 'If it came it could not be dealt with; the Queen's Pleasure could not be taken again. What has been done is altogether irregular.' The Home Secretary had failed to follow the

---

[18]   Ibid.
[19]   *Birmingham Daily Post*, 5 Dec. 1888.
[20]   *Birmingham Weekly Mercury*, 8 Dec. 1888; *Birmingham Daily Post*, 5 Dec. 1888.
[21]   *City of Birmingham Minutes*, 66–7; PRO HO 45/9799/B5306.

'proper course' of action, which 'would have been for the corporation to have petitioned, and for the Secretary of State to have taken the Pleasure of Her Majesty. As it is the Queen's Pleasure was taken by Lord Salisbury before any petition had been made.' He added that although this was 'irregular', the Queen's permission had to be taken as read: 'Inform the law officers that the Queen has approved without any petition having been presented, and consult them as to the form of warrant which should be prepared by the Crown Office, 5 December 1888'.[22]

To save face, the civil servants now decided that a little sleight of hand was in order: 'Acknowledge & (without saying, in the usual formula, that the Petition has been laid before HM) acquaint the Town Clerk that the Queen has been graciously pleased to signify Her approval of the Borough being raised to the rank of a City'.[23] Lushington wrote to the town clerk on 10 December in a carefully drafted letter which noted that the Home Office had received the petition, 'and I am to acquaint you, for the information of the Mayor and Corporation, that Her Majesty has been graciously pleased to signify Her approval'.[24] If that overcame the awkwardness caused by the politicians' hastiness, it opened up an additional problem of how the award should be made. The government's law officers were asked to find the means of raising Birmingham to a city, because there was 'no Record existing of the issue of a Royal Warrant directing Letters Patent to be passed under the Great Seal for such a purpose, as regards any English Borough except in the case of newly constituted Episcopal Sees'.[25]

Evidently, despite this last ditch attempt to stall, a way was found because the letters patent were prepared on 14 January 1889 and sent to Birmingham the following day. The official announcement appeared in the *London Gazette* on 18 January, and in *The Times* on 19 January 1889. The fees payable were 100 guineas (£105). Birmingham City Council formally acknowledged the promotion at its meeting on 5 February 1889 and sent a motion of thanks to the Queen. The General Purposes Committee consulted the Heralds' Office about the city's future armorial bearings.[26] The celebrations seem to have been strictly in-house although, turning the old order on its head, the newly-created city proposed that it should now have a cathedral. It did not succeed until 1905.[27]

Belfast was in Ireland, and Dundee was in Scotland. The grants of city status could just about be seen as exceptional, but Birmingham was quite clearly a precedent. Professor Freeman, writing soon after the Birmingham

22   PRO HO 45/9799/B5306.
23   Ibid.
24   *Birmingham Daily Post*, 12 Dec. 1888; *City of Birmingham Minutes*, 79, 8 Jan. 1889.
25   PRO LCO2/2013, Home Office to Treasury Solicitor, 5 Dec. 1888.
26   *City of Birmingham Minutes*, 97, 5 Feb. 1889; PRO HO 45/9799/B5306.
27   It became the see of an Anglican diocese in 1905. P.S. Morrish, 'County and Urban Dioceses', *Journal of Ecclesiastical History*, XXVI (1975), 279–300; P.S. Morrish, 'The struggle to create an Anglican diocese of Birmingham', *Journal of Ecclesiastical History*, XXXI (1980), 59–88; Briggs, *Birmingham*, II, 89.

case, noted that 'the creation of cities, once begun, will perhaps not stop. Modern greatness may plead Leeds and Bradford; ancient memories may say something for Shrewsbury and Nottingham.'[28] Freeman rightly predicted that there would now be a queue at the door of the Home Office. 'City' might carry no formal privileges, but it evidently acknowledged size, rank and importance, as well as representing a reward for municipal achievement. In such circumstances, and with no specific qualifications laid down, the demand for city status was unlikely to end with Birmingham's successful application.

Freeman was right, but he might well have been surprised to find that the first major town to put forward a case for city status was Leicester, which submitted a petition in June 1889.[29] Once again, the civil servants were appalled. Belfast 'had special and peculiar claims to consideration which do not apply to ordinary English towns', and Birmingham could be justified because of 'its great superiority in wealth and population' which gave it 'a primacy of its own for exceptional consideration'. Leicester was an also-ran because there were 'nine towns in England superior to Leicester in population and rateable value which at present are not cities'. It had 'no better claims to the distinction than Beverley and Nottingham', both of which also had (or, in the case of Nottingham had had) suffragan bishops, and certainly no better claims than large commercial towns such as Bradford, Hull, Leeds, Portsmouth, Salford and Sheffield. So where should the line be drawn? As one civil servant noted, 'if it is thought that having granted Birmingham there is no occasion to draw a line at the smaller towns', then the Home Secretary should recommend the Queen to grant the petition.[30]

In assessing the Leicester petition, the civil servants were groping towards a new definition of the city. If the status was no longer to be linked directly with ecclesiastical considerations, applicants needed to be able to demonstrate their urban importance. Leicester may have seen it as a form of civic promotion, an opportunity to distinguish itself among a range of medium-sized corporate boroughs, but the clearest and simplest indicator of relative rank was population. Birmingham's case could almost be justified on these grounds alone. To extend the honour to a place of 123,000 people, with limited ecclesiastical claims, while ignoring many other large towns, seemed somehow offensive. A pecking order was emerging together with an unofficial list of qualifications, whether the Home Office perceived it as such or not. Home Secretary Matthews was evidently persuaded by this logic. He agreed to meet with the Mayor of Leicester, Alderman Edward Wood, to discuss the petition, and he 'intimated to him the difficulties under which the Government might feel themselves in dealing with the memorial'.[31] Matthews, having dropped as broad a hint as he could, endorsed

28   Freeman, 'City and Borough', 34.
29   *Leicester Mercury*, 29 May 1889; Leicestershire RO CM1/23, 28 May 1889, 22DE57/97, fos 345, 346.
30   PRO HO 45/13276/1.
31   *Leicester Mercury*, 18 July 1889.

the file on 21 June 'I think this should be declined'. Sir Godfrey Lushington wrote to Mayor Wood on 25 June to say that the Home Secretary had laid the petition before the Queen but was not able to advise her to grant Leicester's wish.[32]

The Leicester case had established that population and municipal importance were key qualifications for a town to be considered for city status, and when Sheffield and Leeds chose in 1892 to follow the lead given by Birmingham the Home Office had no real grounds on which to deny them city status. In the 1891 census the two West Yorkshire industrial towns stood fifth and sixth in the rank order of urban population, behind London, Liverpool, Manchester and Birmingham. Both believed they had an excellent track record in municipal achievement, and Sheffield saw Birmingham as a direct precedent which it might follow. Alderman Batty Langley, Sheffield's mayor, travelled to Birmingham in the autumn of 1892 to discover the procedure for seeking city status. Armed with appropriate information, he proposed to Sheffield town council at its meeting on 9 November that by way of celebrating the golden jubilee of incorporation (due to fall on 24 August 1893) Sheffield should follow Birmingham and seek city status. The corporation agreed, and commissioned him to carry the proposal forward.[33] As in Birmingham, city status was viewed as a potential reward for municipal achievement.

When news of this development reached Leeds, a rival campaign was immediately started. Leeds was an ancient borough, but there was much disquiet at the thought of a relatively new incorporation (and a smaller town in the same county) becoming a city, while it remained a town. On 4 January 1893 the corporation approved a petition to the Queen drawn up by the town clerk on its behalf. The petition followed similar principles to those of Belfast and Birmingham. Stress was placed on the antiquity of Leeds, its various charters, its size (21,572 acres), its population (367,506 in the 1891 census but now considered to be 'approaching 400,000'), the fact that it was the largest municipality in the kingdom not to be a city, and its commercial importance in the woollen trade. The petition was strongly supported by both the *Leeds Mercury* and the *Yorkshire Post*. The *Mercury* provided the context:

> Leeds is at least as worthy of being dubbed a city as either Liverpool, Manchester or Birmingham, to say nothing of Bristol or Newcastle upon Tyne. These cities, with the exception of Birmingham, are the seats of a Bishopric, and an effort is being made to create a bishop of Birmingham. Ripon is the cathedral city in this diocese, but Leeds is its real centre, and even on these grounds could present as strong a claim for recognition as any of the cities we have mentioned.... If it was intended to recognize the work done by the municipal body in Birmingham, the same body in Leeds can point with confidence to the work they have accomplished as entitling Leeds to a like distinction. If the title of city were meant to be conferred as a recognition of good work done for the health and general well being of the

---

[32]   Leicestershire RO CM1/23; PRO HO 45/13276/1.
[33]   *Sheffield Daily Telegraph*, 2 Feb. 1893.

population of the great towns, the fact that Leeds has just been able to show the lowest death rate ever recorded in its history is one that may be pleases as entitling it to the honour.[34]

The newspaper was not certain of the grounds, other than ecclesiastical, required to qualify as a city, but it was sure Leeds had as good a claim as any, and the main emphasis was on its municipal achievements.

In the Birmingham case, Home Secretary Matthews had been content with a petition, but H.H. Asquith, who had succeeded him by 1893, was rather more demanding – perhaps because he was a native of Morley in West Yorkshire, although he had lived in the area only briefly as a small boy. He requested that delegations from Sheffield and Leeds should visit the Home Office to stake their respective claims. For Sheffield, Alderman Langley arranged a delegation consisting of himself, the town clerk (J.W. Pye-Smith), and several of the local MPs. At the Home Office they were introduced by A.J. Mundella, MP for Sheffield Brightside and President of the Board of Trade. The Home Secretary, in the mayor's words, 'listened very patiently' to their presentation. He also asked their view of the pending Leeds application, and on hearing that the two Yorkshire towns were not vying with one another – a suggestion that the delegation was only too happy to deny – he dismissed them with an assurance that he would put their case to the Queen.[35]

All this Langley reported to the first meeting of the Jubilee Committee on 20 January. 'Steps', he told the newly formed committee, 'had [been] taken with a view to obtaining the grant of the title and dignity of "City" to the Borough of Sheffield, and that he and the Town Clerk accompanied by several Members of Parliament for the Borough had had an interview with the Home Secretary on the subject and laid before him the claims of Sheffield to that dignity.' He added that the committee's view was that 'it is desirable that application be made at the proper time to her Majesty in Council to confer the title and dignity of a City on the Borough of Sheffield'.[36]

The Leeds delegation arrived at the Home Office on 27 January. It consisted of the mayor, the former mayor, an alderman, four councillors, and two of the town's MPs: W.L. Jackson, Conservative MP since 1880 and Secretary to the Treasury in Salisbury's government of 1886–92, and Gerald Balfour. Jackson had previously raised the matter of city status in 1890,[37] and he now took the lead, making a speech in which he restated many of the points in the petition. Asquith listened attentively to the Leeds case, and then posed a series of questions to the delegates. 'How does Leeds compare with Sheffield in population?' he asked,

---

[34]   *Leeds Mercury*, 5 Jan. 1893; Arthur Elton, 'Becoming a City: Leeds, 1893', *Publications of the Thoresby Society*, 2nd ser., III (1993), 71.

[35]   *Sheffield Daily Telegraph*, 2 Feb. 1893. No account of this meeting has survived in the PRO file, and even the date is uncertain.

[36]   Sheffield Archives, CA 530(22), 20 Jan. 1893; *Sheffield Daily Telegraph*, 21 Jan. 1893.

[37]   Elton, 'Becoming a City', 70–1; PRO HO 45/9864/B13782.

once again searching for evidence of rivalry between the two towns. It was, replied Jackson, 'about 50,000 more' – the actual total in 1891 was 43,263 – and he added that in case Asquith should have spotted the chronological coincidence between the two applications 'we are not here to say one single word in depreciation of Sheffield'. He went on to suggest additional qualifications for Leeds, but avoided any mention of Sheffield by basing these at least partly on a favourable comparison with Birmingham: Leeds received a charter of incorporation in 1626, Birmingham only in 1838; and Leeds had been an assize town since 1864, Birmingham only since 1884. However, there was more to it than this. Leeds was 'the only University Town in the Kingdom I believe that is not a city', and it had five MPs (only Sheffield of the non-cities had so many). In his response, Asquith acknowledged that the older connection between 'the title of a City and the residence of a Bishop' no longer applied: 'it is impossible that it can now be used in opposition to the claim put forward by any great centre of population'. Jackson commented by way of conclusion that when a new see was created at Wakefield there had been considerable dissatisfaction in Leeds.[38]

Once it became known in Sheffield that the Leeds petition had been presented to the Home Office, the mayor called a special meeting of the town council to approve their own submission. The council met on 1 February 1893, and the town clerk read out the proposed petition, which emphasized the history, size (324,243 population) and industrial importance of Sheffield. Mayor Langley proposed that the corporation adopt the petition, and send it directly to the Home Office. Langley's enthusiasm was not entirely shared by his fellow councillors. Although the resolution was eventually carried unanimously, several speakers were at best lukewarm on the subject. Alderman William Smith admitted that the mayor had asked him to second the resolution, and that he had refused to do so because 'he did not feel himself sufficiently interested in the matter ... he felt there was not much in it'. Alderman Brittain, who did agree to second the resolution, told the council that 'he thought it was desirable to aspire to the dignity of a city', but he agreed with Smith that 'there was not very much in it'. Alderman Bramley 'was not aware that there was a widespread feeling in the town in favour of this proposal ... he saw no necessity for adopting this method for commemorating the jubilee of the corporation'.[39] As in Birmingham, there were those who thought the title unnecessary.

Immediately after this meeting, the Sheffield town clerk sent the petition to the Home Office, and on 3 February 1893 Asquith forwarded to the Queen the petitions from both Leeds and Sheffield with the recommendation that both be raised to the status of cities:

Mr Asquith respectfully points out that Leeds and Sheffield are the only two towns in the United Kingdom with a population exceeding 300,000 to which the title of City, enjoyed by many smaller and less important places, has not been granted; and

---

38   PRO HO 45/9863/B13633. For Wakefield see Chapter 2.
39   *Sheffield Daily Telegraph*, 2 Feb. 1893.

that both appear to be well fitted by their loyalty, public spirit, and industrial progress, for this mark of your Majesty's favour.

Four days later, on 7 February, Sir Godfrey Lushington wrote to the mayors of both Leeds and Sheffield informing them that the Queen had accepted the recommendation and that both would be raised to the dignity of cities.[40] The letters patent for both new cities were sealed on 13 February, and reported in the *London Gazette* on 20 February. Leeds City Council exhibited the document at its next council meeting on 1 March 1893.[41]

Reaction in the two new cities varied. Flags were immediately hoisted in Leeds, and people meeting in the streets shook hands and addressed each other as citizen. Sheffield seems to have been less inclined to celebrate. The town, now city, council held its regular monthly meeting on 8 February at which it simply recorded the receipt of Lushington's letter and agreed to pay the £105 required expenses, before passing quickly to other business.[42] The Jubilee Committee continued its discussions and only the language changed. At its meeting on 14 February no mention was made of the new status, although the draft minutes record the proposal to build a new central library 'in the centre of the Town', with 'town' then crossed through and 'city' inserted. Subsequently, this was referred to as the City Free Library, and a city ball was proposed for August in celebration of the jubilee. City status was simply a boost to the rather more important jubilee celebrations.[43]

If Leeds and Sheffield represented local rivalry, Leeds and Bradford was an even more intense contest. Leeds town hall was built at least partly as a response to Bradford's St George's hall of 1852–3. Bradford, in turn, was cool towards Leeds when it was raised to a city, and this seems likely to have encouraged its own application.[44] In the 1840s there was a long struggle in Bradford to achieve incorporation. The charter was finally granted on 14 October 1847,[45] so that the golden jubilee was fast approaching when on 8 January 1897 the Finance and General Purposes Committee adopted a motion proposed by the mayor to petition for city status. In doing so, it was following precedents set by Birmingham and Sheffield in relation to incorporation, but it also had a strong case based purely on population: in the 1891 census Bradford (216,361) was the largest town in England which was not a city. Also in its favour Bradford could argue that it was

---

40   PRO HO 45/9863/B13633 for Leeds and HO 45/9864/B13782 for Sheffield. Mayor Langley was informed in advance by Mundella that the request was being granted, but the news warranted only half a column inch on p. 5 of the *Sheffield Daily Telegraph*, 7 Feb. 1893. The Sheffield charter is in Sheffield Archives, CA 666/5.
41   Elton, 'Becoming a City', 75; M.W. Beresford, 'A Tale of Two Centenaries: Leeds City Charter and City Square, 1893', *University of Leeds Review*, 36 (1993/4), 331–46; Sheffield Archives, CA666/5.
42   *Sheffield Daily Telegraph*, 9 Feb. 1893.
43   Sheffield Archives CA530(22).
44   Elton, 'Becoming a City', 68–9, 79.
45   Bradford City Archives, 78D80/1–2.

the principal seat of the worsted trade, a county borough spread across 10,776 acres, and with a good record of spending on public works and improvements as well as in pioneering municipal enterprise.[46]

The petition requesting city status for Bradford was discussed in full council on 12 January 1897. Councillor Walter Armitage asked whether, if Bradford was made a city, a bishopric would be founded. Armitage clearly thought the honour hardly worth pursuing. He was reprimanded by the mayor, whose view was that if Leeds and Sheffield thought it was worthwhile being cities, Bradford ought to do so as well. The recommendation to pursue city status was accepted, and copies of the petition were sent to the town's three MPs.[47] *The Times* noted how Bradford's growth as a populous and commercial town 'has been in correspondence with that of Leeds and other West Riding centres'. Yet the old link with Anglican diocesan status still lingered, at least in the eyes of the *Times* writer: 'No mention has as yet been made of Bradford in connexion with the movement for the formation of two new dioceses, but the distance of Bradford from Ripon, in which diocese it is situated, has long been a matter of some inconvenience in the way of episcopal work'.[48] Subsequently, considerable lobbying took place, and a meeting was planned between a delegation from Bradford and Lord Salisbury, the prime minister. In the event this was cancelled due to pressure of other business.[49]

While the Bradford application was still being considered in the Home Office, a petition arrived from Hull in March 1897 which deflected civil service minds in another direction. The petition, which was submitted to the Home Secretary through Sir Seymour King, MP for Hull Central, with the support of Hull's other MPs, Charles Wilson and J.T. Firbank, requested that the town be created a city. The claims to city status were set out along lines familiar from earlier cases: Hull was a county borough of 225,000 people (the mid-1897 estimate), a major port with trading interests around the globe, and 'one of the great and ancient municipalities of the kingdom'. In 1534 it had briefly had a suffragan bishop within the diocese of York. Subsequently, King saw the Home Secretary, Sir Matthew White Ridley, who in turn consulted the prime minister.[50] What made this petition different was that Hull had no municipal celebration looming, and nor did it have the strongest claim on the grounds of population since according to the mid-1897 estimates both Bradford (231,260) and Nottingham (232,934) were larger non-cities. Hull did, however, return to an idea first discussed a decade earlier in Belfast: it proposed that the occasion for a grant of city status was the forthcoming Diamond Jubilee celebrations of Queen Victoria.

We do not know what discussions took place between the Home Secretary and the prime minister, but the upshot was that on 18 June 1897 Lord Salisbury

---

[46]   Bradford City Archives, BBC/1/1/27, f. 203.
[47]   *Bradford Observer*, 13 Jan. 1897; Bradford City Archives, BB/1/14, f. 294; PRO HO 45/10163/B24512.
[48]   *The Times*, 11 Jan. 1897, 5f.
[49]   *Bradford Observer*, 22 June 1897.
[50]   PRO HO 45/9922/B23839.

wrote to the mayors of Bradford, Hull and Nottingham to announce that their towns had been raised to city status as jubilee honours. Hull was the first to hear the news. Salisbury's letters arrived only on 21 June, but Sir Seymour King was told of Hull's elevation on the Sunday (20th) and immediately sent a telegram to the mayor, Henry Morrill. Although it arrived after a civic service commemorating the Diamond Jubilee had taken place, the bells of Holy Trinity were rung in celebration of the news. The local paper declared that 'Hull has obtained a recognition of her historical and other claims', and suggested that doubters who questioned the worth of the title 'are insensible to those influences which make for public dignity and contribute to the elevation and ennoblement of communities'.[51]

The news of city status reached Bradford with the delivery of Salisbury's letter on the Monday morning (21 June), and it was made public just after 1 p.m. This was not, of course, the occasion when Bradford anticipated city status, but in the euphoria of the moment no one seems to have complained. Church bells were rung and arrangements were made to add 'a gas device' depicting 'The City of Bradford' to the town hall illuminations prepared for the jubilee celebrations. Letters of congratulation arrived from the town's three MPs who had been involved in the negotiations, and the following morning a leader column in the *Bradford Daily Telegraph* claimed that:

> This is a great day for Bradford, and, were it not that the attention of the whole country is just now centred upon the unique national celebration of the Record Reign of Queen Victoria, our newly constituted city and the circumstances which have led to its receiving this conferment of honour would have a good deal of interest for others besides those who are its citizens. Even the people of Bradford in the midst of the distractions of their part in the national celebration are perhaps less inclined to be as jubilant about the raising of the town to the rank of a city as they would have been under ordinary conditions; and ... in the public mind the larger event has overshadowed the local one.... Our city has today abundant cause for celebration.

But even in the midst of celebration the question arose of what city status meant:

> The question was asked times without number in the crowd last night What are the precise advantages conferred on the new city? Will it give us a Lord Mayor? No. Will it give Bradford a Court of Assize? No. Will it make the Parish Church a Cathedral? No. It is a mere titular dignity to which all the great modern towns have aspired just in the same way as a successful man has striven to become 'My Lord' or 'Sir Thomas'. Bradford, Nottingham and Hull have been elevated to the baronetage, so to speak, of the municipalities; the peerage is when you get a Lord Mayoralty.[52]

---

[51]   *The Daily Mail Hull Packet and East Yorkshire and Lincolnshire Courier*, 21 June 1897.

[52]   *Bradford Daily Telegraph*, 22 June 1897.

This final sentence was prescient. City status was being seen as a corporate honour, to be dispensed by the Crown on occasions of royal significance as a reward for municipal achievement.

In both Hull and Bradford, the announcement of city status was overshadowed by jubilee day celebrations. Eight thousand Hull children were entertained to tea in Pearson Park, and later in the day bonfires were lit throughout the East Riding and fireworks let off in parks around the town.[53] Bradford's celebrations included a tea for poor children, a trades demonstration and procession, numerous bands playing in the local parks, and the decoration of civic buildings. However, there were no fireworks; the Jubilee Committee considered these to be too great an extravagance.[54]

When, finally, the dust had settled, the mayor of Hull reported on city status to a meeting of the new city council on 1 July 1897. Lord Salisbury's letter was read, and the mayor's response of 21 June when he noted that 'your communication has been received with the most grateful satisfaction'. A copy of the petition was also entered in the council minutes. For his part, the mayor told the meeting 'he was sure there was not an inhabitant of Hull who did not feel in some way gratified by that great mark of Royal favour ... and he trusted the future of this rising young City might be even more glorious than the past, and that it might progress with even greater strides'.[55]

Both Bradford and Hull had applied for city status in 1897: Nottingham, the third town to be honoured, had not done so. We do not know how the decision was reached to treat Bradford, Hull and Nottingham together, but we can speculate that it was based primarily on population figures. The Local Government Act of 1888 had created a new statutory authority, the county borough, and the initial intention was that this status should be awarded to ten towns with a population in excess of 150,000. This figure was later altered, but the original list of ten comprised Liverpool, Manchester, Birmingham, Leeds, Sheffield, Bristol and Newcastle, all of which had city status by 1897, Bradford, Hull and Nottingham. In the 1891 census these three boroughs stood ninth, tenth and eleventh respectively in terms of population among English towns. Above them in the list were London, West Ham – a special case because it was within the London conurbation – and six provincial cities. The mid-1897 population estimates for towns of 200,000 or more placed Nottingham eighth, Bradford tenth and Hull eleventh in rank order. The population figure for Hull was 225,000, the figure quoted by the mayor in the petition. Someone in the Home Office clearly decided that the three cases stood or fell together, and that the jubilee was a suitable point at which to grant the honour. This was a subtle but important shift from civic celebration to royal honour.

---

53   *The Daily Mail...*, 23 June 1897.
54   Bradford City Archives, BBC 1/56/2, Bradford Corporation, Special Committees Minute Book, 2, fos. 479, 484, 497–8 passim.
55   *Hull City Council Minutes*, 1897, 149–52; *The Daily Mail...*, 1 July 1897.

What is perhaps more surprising is that no one in the Home Office apparently tipped the wink to Nottingham to apply. No petition was submitted, and no delegation waited upon the Home Secretary. The mayor, Alderman Edward Fraser, was as surprised as anyone at the news,[56] and there was some confusion at the Home Office when it became clear that a petition had not been received.[57] The Clerk to the Crown noted in the Nottingham case that 'it is an ancient prerogative of the Crown to grant Charters', and therefore (in the absence of a petition) 'I don't think a petition is indispensable'.[58] Since Queen Victoria had always accepted the recommendations of her Home Secretaries, there was no reason to expect anything different on this occasion.

Letters patent for Hull were issued by the Home Office on 6 July,[59] for Bradford on 10 July, and for Nottingham on 7 August. Bradford City Council formally noted the arrival of the letters patent when it met on 10 August.[60] The delay in respect of Nottingham was simply pragmatic: it allowed the town's Improvement Bill currently before Parliament to pass into law and thereby avoid the expense of changing all the terminology.[61]

Inverness also applied for city status in 1897. Dundee's elevation, which had not passed through the Home Office, had raised awkward questions as to which other Scottish burghs were entitled to city status. Professor Freeman, reviewing the case, named Aberdeen, Edinburgh, and Glasgow, although he also thought St Andrews and Perth might have claims to city status, and he recalled that 'I saw some years back a long argument, by which it was said that Mr Gladstone had been convinced, to prove that Dunfermline was a city'.[62] The issue again came up for discussion when in March 1897 an approach was made to Lord Balfour, as Secretary for Scotland, to have Inverness raised to city status 'in connection with the distribution of honours this year'.[63] The idea of city status as a jubilee honour was already under discussion.

---

[56]   Nottinghamshire AO CA.TC 10/57/74/116; P.S. Clay and J.H. Richards, *City of Nottingham: Official Record of the Celebration of the Diamond Jubilee of Her Majesty Queen Victoria* (Nottingham, 1898), 83; John Beckett, 'City Status in the Nineteenth Century: Southwell and Nottingham, 1884–97', *Transactions of the Thoroton Society*, 103 (1999), 149–58.

[57]   There is a minute on the relevant Home Office file which reads: 'In the absence of a petition Mr Digby has written to the Clerk of the Crown. Await his reply': PRO HO 45/9925/B24470.

[58]   PRO HO 45/9925/B24470.

[59]   The wording of the letters patent was also added to the Council's Minutes: *Hull City Council Minutes* (1897), 167–8.

[60]   Bradford City Archives, BB/1/14, f. 483; 78D80/4; *Bradford Daily Telegraph*, 11 Aug. 1897.

[61]   NAO CA.TC 10/57/74/131; *Nottingham Evening Post*, 11 Aug. 1897.

[62]   Freeman, 'City and Borough', 34.

[63]   The Inverness case in 1897 can be pieced together from letters and papers in NAS HH 1/1347.

The confusion caused by Inverness's application is apparent from the annotations on the file made by the civil servants who considered the case. One thought that 'there would be great difficulty in giving Inverness a City Charter while Aberdeen and Perth are without one'. Another compared Inverness with the position specifically of Aberdeen:

> On consideration I see no grave objection if it is thought desirable, that the Burgh of Inverness should be declared a City by charter, as in the case of Dundee. I am certainly of opinion that Aberdeen, as the site of an ancient University and an ancient Bishopric should take precedence rank before Dundee. Aberdeen has, amongst other things, immemorial usage and custom for being called a City, and its Provost a Lord Provost. On the other hand Dundee has received a Charter making it a City and Her Majesty has conferred upon its Chief Magistrate the style and title of Lord Provost. Up to the present time the nice points of practice has fortunately not arisen, and curiously enough Aberdeen (probably resting on its own ancient prestige) raised no objection to Dundee receiving a Royal Charter. As Aberdeen apparently did not raise any objection to the honour awarded to Dundee, I think she would not raise any objection to Inverness receiving a similar honour, because whilst Dundee is a formidable rival to Aberdeen, Inverness can hardly be placed in that category.

Another civil servant considered the population question: 'I have been looking in Whitaker to see if there are any cities in England smaller than Inverness, and find Durham and St Albans, perhaps others. The population of Inverness is 19,000 and that of Perth 24,000.' In the end, after discussion, they took the appropriate avoiding action: 'I do not see that we need raise any objection to Inverness getting the rank of a City, but we must not definitely assume responsibility for it'.

The means of avoiding responsibility was to pass the proverbial buck to the prime minister. Lord Balfour, according to the civil servant who wrote to Reginald Lucas in answer to the original application on behalf of Inverness, lodged on 29 March:

> desires me to reply that although of course it is a very small burgh for such a dignity (the population being less than 20,000) and although he would not himself have thought of conferring such an honour on it, [especially as both my predecessor and I have had a good deal of trouble with the Town Council, who have assumed a most improper attitude towards their Sheriff] still if the Prime Minister sees fit to recommend it to the Queen he is not prepared to raise any objection.

This of course was the draft written in the Scottish Office, from which the words given here in square brackets were eventually erased. The indication is that the recommendation actually made to the prime minister was, at best, lukewarm, and Inverness was not promoted.

In theory, by linking city status to royal events, the Home Office could see a means of presenting the honour as being in the gift of the monarch, and at the same time protecting itself from further claims. The practice was rather different. The demand for city status was now apparently insatiable, especially when the borough of Westminster's claim to city status was confirmed in 1900.[64] In November the same year the mayoress of Leicester wrote to the Home Office enclosing a petition to Queen Victoria asking for the title of city 'on behalf of the women of Leicester'. The Home Office thought Leicester still unworthy of the title and presented the petition to the Queen without a recommendation, so it failed.[65] Portsmouth put in a request in 1901. 'The portsmothians', wrote a local MP, want their borough 'made a city'. The Home Office was not convinced and the petition was rejected. A proposal that Cambridge might be made a city was gently rebuffed by the Home Secretary on the grounds that it lacked a cathedral and had insufficient population.[66]

Cardiff applied in 1902, asking for city status as an honour in conjunction with the coronation of King Edward VII. In doing so it was picking up the scent laid down in 1897 when the Home Office accepted a link between city status and royal events. An MP wrote to the Home Office:

> I venture to ask your kind consideration to submit to His Majesty the proposition of raising the town and parish of Cardiff to the rank of a City with a Lord Mayor.... the population has grown to over 163,000 and the registered export tonnage is the largest of any port in the Kingdom exceeding even London and Liverpool.[67]

Only Leicester seems to have followed Cardiff in spotting the possibility of claiming city status in conjunction with the coronation, and both towns were unsuccessful.[68]

Cardiff failed in 1902 but it succeeded when it applied again in 1905.[69] For Cardiff this was a campaign about the town's claim to be the Welsh capital. The desire to cut a distinction in Wales lay behind the creation of a civic centre at Cathays Park. In 1892 it was proposed to move the town hall to Cathays Park, and after much debate in 1898 the corporation bought the park for £159,323. Approach roads were completed 1893–4, and the town, subsequently city, hall built 1901–6. It was the first major building on the site.[70] In 1902 Cardiff failed to convince the Home Office of its aspirations to capital status, but the desire remained among leading politicians. When in June 1905 the Prince of Wales

---

[64]   PRO LCO2/2013. Technically, Westminster's status was confirmed, on the grounds that it had been, briefly, an Anglican diocese in the 1540s, and had been allowed to retain the status subsequently.

[65]   PRO HO 45/13276/9.

[66]   PRO HO 45/12904/4a; HO 45/1021/B34608.

[67]   PRO HO 45/11090/7.

[68]   PRO HO 45/13276/10.

[69]   PRO HO 45/11090/10. Ironically, the file covering the grant of city status is one of the thinnest in the Cardiff collection and gives little useful information.

[70]   Cunningham describes it as 'the town hall with everything': C. Cunningham, *Victorian and Edwardian Town Halls* (1981), 156.

visited the town to lay the foundation stone of the new University College buildings, the corporation deliberately set out to make an impression. The town was decorated for the occasion, distinguished visitors were invited to dine with the Prince, local people gave him an 'enthusiastic welcome', and before he departed he was made a freeman of the borough. As a result, 'it was then felt that the great satisfaction which His Royal Highness expressed might very well be taken advantage of for the purpose of again renewing the proposal to create Cardiff the Metropolis of Wales'.

A petition was submitted to the Home Office in July 1905, and in October the Marquess of Bute reported that he had learned that the town had been promoted to city and the mayor to lord mayor. On the day of the official announcement, 23 October, the bells of St John's rang 'a merry peel, and the centre of the town rapidly became gay with bunting. Flags floated from the town hall and the principal places of business.' Head teachers summoned school assemblies, told their charges of the significance of the new honours, and gave them the rest of the day off. The mayor declared a public holiday, and at midday he and the corporation appeared outside the town hall, dressed in their official robes, to the enthusiastic applause of a crowd of 6,000. Three cheers were raised, and the Welsh Regiment Depot Band played the national anthem. The *South Wales Echo* had no doubt about the significance of this moment: 'Cardiff is a City, with a Lord Mayor – the question, vexed and vexing, of the Metropolis is thereby settled'. It added that 'the new Town Hall will mark the beginning of the history of Cardiff as a City', thereby nicely juxtaposing city status with civic pride.[71]

Cardiff was the last new city to be created before the First World War, but this was largely because from 1907 the Home Office applied a minimum population qualification of 300,000, which no towns were able to meet. Unofficial approaches from Portsmouth in 1909 and as a coronation honour when King George V came to the throne in 1911 were 'fended off', to use the Home Office's rather inelegant description.[72] Portsmouth had a population of only 218,000 in 1911, and while its claim to be a great naval port with a mayor who 'has at times to entertain the officers of foreign navies' was admitted as relevant to the case, the likelihood of other towns regarding its promotion as a precedent was too much for the Home Office. On 2 June the Home Secretary, Winston Churchill, forwarded the Portsmouth petition to the King with a note recommending rejection. The King agreed. Subsequently, questions were asked in the House of Commons as to why Portsmouth had been refused promotion when it was larger than Cardiff. Churchill responded that Cardiff had been an

---

[71]   *South Wales Echo*, 23 Oct. 1905. There was an unfortunate sequel to the Cardiff case when claims by the mayor – the first lord mayor – that he had been largely responsible for obtaining the grant as a result of his work on behalf of the Conservative party, were firmly rebuffed in the Home Office: PRO HO 45/11090/7–10; *The Times*, 1 Nov. 1905. See also N. Evans, 'Region, Nation and Globe: Roles, Representations and Urban Space in Cardiff, 1839–1928', in A. Fahrmeir and E. Rembold, eds., *Representation of British Cities* (Berlin, 2003), 108–29.

[72]   PRO HO 45/12904/4a, 8.

exceptional case, and Portsmouth did not meet the population criterion – which he carefully failed to define.[73]

Swansea sought city status again in 1911, in conjunction with the coronation and the investiture as Prince of Wales of the future King Edward VIII. The petition was carefully prepared and presented, but it was brushed aside by the civil servants on the grounds that Swansea 'is much smaller than Cardiff [and] far outside the rule laid down by the late king'.[74] No one in Swansea knew the rule, but the new King accepted Churchill's recommendation that the claim should be rejected because Swansea's population was only 111,000 and '300,000 should be the minimum limit'.[75]

Leicester was also caught by the new rule, but the Home Office's dealing with the Midlands town in these years reflected the extent to which even the civil servants had come to see city status as a seal of approval on municipal progress. Leicester's claim to city status was based not on its record of success in civic affairs, but on the grounds that it was seeking the restoration of a lost status. It claimed to have been a diocesan see in the seventh and eighth centuries, that it had been *civitas* in Domesday Book, and that as late as 1220 it appeared as a city in a return made to the Bishop of Lincoln. This long lost history cut no ice at the Home Office, and Leicester's claims to city status were turned down in 1889, 1892, 1900, 1902, 1905, 1907 and 1915.[76] Prior to 1907, the Home Office claimed it could not promote Leicester because Salford, which was marginally larger, could hardly be denied the status should it apply.

Since this was not something they admitted publicly, the civil servants turned down Leicester's application on other grounds, notably what they perceived to be its failings in municipal government: 'the town clerk speaks of the efficient conduct of local business. He can hardly refer to proceedings under the Vaccination Act. We should ask Local Government Board how they are doing before we grant any special favour to them.' This was a reference to the so-called 'Leicester Method' of handling smallpox by isolation rather than vaccination. Although by 1905 it was less of an oddity than it had been in the 1890s, with a number of deaths from smallpox 1902–4 the issue of vaccination had been widely discussed. The Home Office had implicitly accepted that an unblemished record in civic government was a critical qualification as far as city status as concerned, and this was sufficient for Leicester's claims in 1905 to be dismissed.[77] From

[73]   PRO HO 45/12904/11; *Hansard*, 5th ser., XXIX (1911), 1572–3; *Portsmouth Town Council Minutes* (1911), 342, 555–6. I am grateful to Mrs Diana Gregg for drawing these details to my attention. Portsmouth Record Office has no papers relating to any other application from the town for city status.

[74]   PRO HO 45/18697/1.

[75]   PRO HO 45/18697/2. For a detailed account of the Swansea quest see: John Beckett, 'City Status for Swansea, 1911–69', *Welsh History Review*, 21/3 (June 2003), 129–47.

[76]   PRO HO 45/13276/10.

[77]   PRO HO 45/13276/11; S.M.F. Fraser, 'Leicester and Smallpox: the Leicester Method', *Medical History*, 24 (1980), 315–32.

1907 the Home Office could hide behind the population minimum. Leicester argued that its population of 232,000 made it the largest non-city in the country, but the Home Office was unmoved, preferring to recall that 'at [the] HO we chiefly know Leicester as the Mecca of Anti-Vaccinationists'.[78] Local government failings, as perceived in Whitehall, were now a reason for rejection.

Cardiff's celebrations of city status in 1905 were indicative of the sense of achievement generated by what in a simple legal sense was an apparently minor change of status. The public appearance of a robed mayor and corporation reflected the ceremony and dignity which was associated with this new sense of civic self worth. It had other spin-offs. T.H.S. Escott noted in 1897 the growing habit of inviting titled aristocrats to assume the position of mayor. Town councils, David Cannadine has argued, were:

> dominated by professionals and businessmen who believed in private property, and they were much concerned to proclaim the greatness and the unity of their communities by appealing to history, to pageantry, and to glamour. They built elaborate town halls rich in civic iconography; they were greatly concerned with municipal etiquette and ceremonial; and they acquired aldermanic robes, coats of arms, maces, and regalia. After the royal family, these city fathers were the greatest inventors of tradition between the 1880s and the 1930s.

Men of ancient lineage and high social standing embodied municipal pride, and their prestige was used 'for the furthering of civic dignity'.[79] Not all cities sought such mayors – Sheffield did, but Birmingham, Leeds, Manchester and Nottingham did not. Yet the new cities recognized the importance of the position of mayor, and civic pride also raised the question of how he should be addressed.

Until the 1890s the title of mayor had no prefix in English towns, except for London and York. 'Lord' had been added to mayor in London in 1354 and to York in 1389. Dublin obtained the appellation from 1665. The situation was slightly different in Scotland, where the position of provost was the nearest equivalent to mayor. The title lord provost was used by the leading municipal figure in Aberdeen, Edinburgh, Glasgow and Perth. Professor Freeman noted that when Birmingham was raised to a city no one appeared to consider it strange that the title of the mayor did not change, but that when Dundee was made a city in 1889 its chief magistrate acquired the right to be called lord provost. Freeman took the view that this was by way of precedent rather than law: 'his Lordship is inferred from the grant of the rank of city to the burgh'.[80] Technically this was correct because at the town council meeting on 4 February 'the Magistrates and Council unanimously Resolve[d] and declare[d] that the Chief Magistrate of

[78]   PRO HO 45/13276/12.

[79]   D. Cannadine, *The Decline and Fall of the British Aristocracy* (Yale, 1990), 564–5; T.H.S. Escott, *Social Transformation of the Victorian Age* (1897).

[80]   Freeman, 'City and Borough', 29, 34.

the City shall hereafter resume and assume the style and title of Lord Provost', a move said to be to restore a title used 'antecedent to the present century'.[81]

Many people, even today, mistakenly believe that outside of Scotland a city automatically has a lord mayor rather than simply a mayor. This has never been the case, and many cities do not have lord mayors. The two 'promotions' have only ever been granted simultaneously in the case of Cardiff in 1905. Until the 1890s there was no specific link between the title of city and the claim to a lord mayoralty, but precedents established in the final years of Victoria's reign suggested that while a town could never be granted a lord mayoralty, a city had a prima facie claim to a lord mayoralty, although it was granted only on a separate application.

The principle that a town could not have a lord mayor was laid down by the Home Office in 1887 when Cardiff applied for the title in conjunction with Queen Victoria's Golden Jubilee. The initial Home Office response was to favour the request: 'the national feeling exists in Wales and little favours such as this are more likely to allay rather than to intensify it', but discussions among senior ministers suggested they opposed the idea of treating England and Wales separately, 'and if it is treated as the same country then obviously Manchester, Liverpool and Birmingham would have claims superior to Cardiff'. That was it as far as Cardiff was concerned, although spoiling tactics from Swansea – which made a similar application when it heard of Cardiff's move – would probably have ensured it was not successful.[82]

It was only a matter of time before the Dundee anomaly noted by Freeman was picked up elsewhere, and once again the initiative came from Belfast. On 22 February 1892 William Johnston, MP for Belfast South, asked the Home Secretary in the Commons if Belfast might be granted the title of lord mayor, 'now that Dundee, recently granted a City Charter, and with a population considerably less, has just had its chief magistrate raised to the position of Lord Provost'. Home Secretary Matthews replied that the government was ready to consider the case for Belfast 'having due regard to what has been done in other parts of the United Kingdom'.[83] This being, in political terms, a green light, Belfast subsequently renewed its claim through the lord lieutenant. He approached the Home Secretary who, in turn, acquired the approval of the Queen in April 1892.[84] As far as the Home Office was concerned, the justification was simple: Belfast was a city of a quarter of a million people, and the 'capital of the province of Ulster, in population and importance the first town in Ireland. Enormous and growing increase in population and revenue, centre of the linen manufactory and ship building industry in Ireland, four MPs.'[85] As with city status, so now with lord mayor, Belfast was considered to be an exception.

81   *Dundee Town Council Minutes*, 4 Feb. 1889.
82   PRO HO 45/11090/1–2.
83   *Hansard*, 4th ser., 1, Feb.-March 1892, col 875.
84   PRO HO 45/9774/B1512.
85   PRO HO 45/11090/8.

Unfortunately for the Home Office, even in Ireland this was interpreted as a green light, and Cork, Waterford and Limerick all applied for lord mayoralties. The Home Office turned them down on the grounds that they were not supported by the lord lieutenant.[86] Cardiff, which also enquired, was turned down as well.[87]

The Home Office was already moving towards a position it would formalize in 1907, by which the title of lord mayor was given only to cities, and to cities which had held the status for some considerable time. In June 1893, the Queen approved requests for the mayors of Liverpool and Manchester to be raised to lord mayors.[88] Birmingham followed in May 1896,[89] and Leeds and Sheffield had their chief magistrate raised to the position of lord mayor as part of the Diamond Jubilee honours in June 1897.[90] Bristol, an ancient city, received the honour in 1899.[91]

All of these cities had populations in excess of 300,000, but outside of England the rules were applied differently. The mayor of Cork was raised to lord mayor as one of the honours granted by Queen Victoria following her visit to Ireland in April 1900, although this award from the Crown did not please nationalist sentiment in the town. Cork had a population of 76,000.[92] Further afield, Sydney and Melbourne were granted lord mayoralties in 1902,[93] but in England the case for Bradford, which hoped to receive the honour 'during the year of His Majesty's coronation' was sent to the prime minister and not acted upon.[94] Cardiff received a lord mayoralty in 1905,[95] and Newcastle in 1906, but here a new precedent was set. The Home Office had 'some doubt' about Newcastle, fearing a rush of requests from other provincial towns, but the balance was tipped because King Edward VII was visiting the city on 11 July 1906 to open Armstrong College and the Royal Victoria Infirmary. The Home Office took the view that Newcastle was 'the chief town and seaport in the North of England', and the King told the council in response to their loyal address that 'I am of opinion that the chief magistrate should bear the honourable title of Lord Mayor and I will have much pleasure in giving the necessary instructions to grant it'. On 1 August the grant of a lord mayoralty was confirmed.[96]

[86]   PRO HO 45/21712.
[87]   PRO HO 45/11090/3.
[88]   PRO HO 45/9872/B14680; HO 45/10129/B14679/1–3.
[89]   PRO HO 45/9799/B5306A.
[90]   PRO HO 45/9925/B24509, B24510.
[91]   PRO HO 45/21712.
[92]   PRO HO 45/11090/7–10; HO 45/10467/B32037; *Cork Weekly News*, 5 May 1900; *Cork Evening Echo*, 27 April 1900.
[93]   PRO HO 45/22625/1.
[94]   PRO HO 45/21712.
[95]   PRO HO 45/11090/5, LCO2/2013; *South Wales Echo*, 23 Oct. 1905.
[96]   *Newcastle City Minutes 1905–6*, 553. For Home Office doubts, PRO HO 45/16147/10; HO 45/12904/11; HO 45/10345/141982; *Newcastle Daily Journal*, 12 July 1906.

Bradford renewed its claims to a lord mayoralty after Cardiff was promoted in 1905, pointing out that it was considerably larger than the Welsh capital. Once again it was turned down, but in April 1907 a delegation from the city secured an audience with the Home Secretary, Herbert Gladstone, in order to put their case in person. It was as a result of the discussions surrounding Bradford's application that the Home Office subsequently worked to a rule-of-thumb population figure of 300,000,[97] although that did not prevent them from immediately allowing Bradford to have the title of lord mayor despite failing to meet the minimum qualification. Its claims were accepted on the grounds that its population 'is over 290,000 at the present time and in a very few years it will have reached 300,000'. King Edward VII accepted this rather speculative logic, and the grant was made in September 1907.[98] However, Exeter, despite being a cathedral city, was turned down in 1908 on the grounds of inadequate population.[99]

The population minimum was always subject to royal intervention, both for grants of city status and lord mayoralties. The Newcastle lord mayoralty had shown how such grants could be used as marks of royal favour, and the same principles were applied in other cases. In 1910, the King agreed to break the rule for Norwich, a city by ancient prescriptive right, by virtue of being the seat of a bishop. Norwich had a population of only 124,000, but was given a lord mayoralty by the King's 'express wish ... as the capital of East Anglia', and 'in view of City's close association with HM', but with the proviso that this was not to constitute a precedent.[100] An even clearer example of royal favour was Hull. When it applied in 1911 for a lord mayoralty the Home Office accepted that it had a good claim to the title as the largest city which did not have a lord mayor, but it was still turned down because its population of 278,000 was below the prescribed minimum. However, three years later King George V set the guideline aside so that he could make an announcement of the lord mayoralty when he visited Hull to open a new dock.[101] Royal visits were not an automatic route to promotion. Nottingham (despite the grants to Bradford and Hull, with whom it had been joined for city status in 1897), was turned down on population grounds when it applied for a lord mayoralty as a coronation honour in 1911, and in conjunction with royal visits in 1914 and 1919.[102]

These various grants raised yet another problem: how should a lord mayor be addressed? In the wake of the mayoral promotions in Manchester and Liverpool in 1893 the Heralds' Office proposed that lord mayors should be addressed as 'right honourable'. The Home Office questioned this view. It accepted that the lord mayors of London and York had the right to this prefix, but left the question open otherwise. Not surprisingly, the prefix was then adopted, notably in

---

97 This is fully discussed in Chapter 4.
98 The memorandum and correspondence is in PRO HO 45/10163/B24512.
99 PRO HO 45/16067.
100 PRO HO 45/11090; HO 45/12904/11; HO 45/16147/10.
101 PRO HO 45/12904/11; HO 45/16147/10.
102 PRO HO 45/12938/1–5.

Birmingham and Bristol, but that in turn annoyed the civil servants. In February 1902, they decided that the prefix applied only to Dublin, London and York, as well as to the lord provost of Edinburgh.[103] But then in 1903, 'by analogy from the usage in respect to London and Edinburgh', the King granted the prefix to the lord mayors of Sydney and Melbourne,[104] and in 1912 Glasgow was permitted to use the title lord provost. The Chairman of the London County Council was also permitted the title. Yet another precedent was slowly evolving: a large and important town might be a city; an important city (as opposed to one of the old cathedral towns) might have a lord mayor; and a really important city with a lord mayor might be granted the right to use the title right honourable.

Civic pride was a driving force in British towns from the 1860s, and by the 1890s many sought to add marks of distinction including city status and lord mayoralties. This restless search for status sprang largely from a desire to distinguish the new cities from their lesser neighbours, but at the same time both city status and lord mayoralties represented a town hall honour. Civic dignitaries sought it, although many councillors, especially nonconformists, were often lukewarm on the subject. Few townspeople, or citizens as they became, quite understood what the fuss was all about. The Nottingham Diamond Jubilee chroniclers recalled 'a flutter of excitement through the town' when city status was announced, which 'gave evident satisfaction to all classes'.[105] This was hardly public rejoicing, but it seems to have been fairly typical although, of course, when the announcements were made in conjunction with other celebrations including the Diamond Jubilee they were never distinctive moments in their own right.

So what did the new cities expect to gain from their raised status? The petitions they sent to the Home Office indicated how they saw the title as bringing a status which would differentiate them from other towns. In his list of reasons for seeking city status for Belfast, F.D. Ward referred to the commercial success which he believed gave the town the right to rank alongside Liverpool and Manchester. City status, he believed, would make a statement about Belfast's international trading importance. The town clerk of Birmingham stressed the size of the town, and both size and commercial success were claimed in the cases of Sheffield, Leeds and Hull. The mayor of Leeds thought that the title 'has some influence abroad', and the *Yorkshire Weekly Post* commented in respect to Sheffield and Leeds that 'men of business whose affairs take them beyond the marketplace know to what extent the world is influenced by sentiment, and by what simple methods the importance of a place may be gauged in distant countries'.[106] Hull claimed in its petition that city status would mean it was recognized as 'one of the great and ancient municipalities of the kingdom'. The *Nottingham Daily Express*

103   PRO HO 45/10129/B14679.
104   PRO HO 45/22625/5–6.
105   Clay and Richards, *City of Nottingham*, 50.
106   Elton, 'Becoming a City', 79–80.

commented that city status was 'indirectly advantageous', because Nottingham would be 'elevated in the eyes of all with whom it has commercial relations'. Perhaps because this seemed rather vague, it added that: 'it must be for the future to decide what benefit will accrue from the change'.[107] The South Wales press assumed when Cardiff was promoted that it would be an 'advantage socially' within the United Kingdom, and that it would 'have a stimulating influence' on its industrial and commercial interests.[108]

These comments collectively suggest a sense of achievement, but the lack of real substance was perhaps most accurately reflected in the local response to city status. In 1897 the *Nottingham Daily Guardian* reported that city status had 'occasioned locally the most lively satisfaction', while according to the *Nottingham Daily Express* the news was received with 'evident satisfaction by all classes'. The *Guardian* added that 'the new dignity has not been conferred without adequate reason', but it made no attempt to suggest what that reason might be.[109] According to the *Express* the honour was 'tangible evidence of appreciation of the progress Nottingham has made during [Victoria's] reign', which was similarly vague.[110] The newspapers were struggling for adequate words to convey any sense of the significance of the promotion. Other new cities, such as Sheffield, made little attempt to celebrate the award.

Promotion was certainly used to bolster civic pride. Sheffield was in the process of building a new town hall (subsequently opened in 1897 by Queen Victoria) when it applied for promotion in 1893.[111] Belfast compared itself with Liverpool and Manchester in commercial terms, and then used its promotion as a reason for funding new civic buildings: in 1897 the corporation began building City Hall, a magnificent palace in an architectural style based on Wren's St Paul's cathedral, and 'one of the splendours of Edwardian Baroque architecture'.[112] Leeds took the opportunity of naming a major area of urban redevelopment about to be started in 1893 'City Square' – thereby putting to an end a prolonged correspondence in the local press concerning a possible name. Alderman T.W. Harding donated several statues, including a depiction of the Black Prince, a figure with heroic overtones who carried images of city decoration and civic patronage.[113] Bradford considered a town hall extension to include an art gallery, but did not subsequently go ahead,[114] and a newspaper correspondent in Sheffield suggested renaming the new town hall as the city hall.[115]

[107]   *Nottingham Daily Express*, 22 June 1897.
[108]   William Rees, *Cardiff: A History of the City* (Cardiff, 1962),
[109]   *Nottingham Daily Guardian*, 22 June 1897.
[110]   *Nottingham Daily Express*, 22 June 1897.
[111]   PRO HO 45/9799/B5306.
[112]   A. Service, *Edwardian Architecture* (1977), 143; Cunningham, *Victorian*, 157.
[113]   Beresford, 'Tale of Two Centenaries', 343–5; E.P. Hennock, *Fit and Proper Persons* (1973), 282.
[114]   Bradford City Archives, BBC 1/1/27, fos. 226, 238, 355.
[115]   *Sheffield Daily Telegraph*, 8 Feb. 1893.

Nottingham, perhaps because of the unusual way in which it became a city, did not aspire so high. When the new city council met on 19 July 1897 to discuss the honour, the mayor presented a report recommending 'that a Memorial bronze be placed in the Guildhall to commemorate the event, and also that a proper Badge should be obtained (similar to those worn by the Mayors of many large towns) for future Mayors to wear on special occasions'. The *Nottingham Daily Guardian* argued that an opportunity was being passed over to promote the new civic buildings which had been under discussion since the 1850s, and 'of which so much has been said in the past …a city certainly wants a city hall to round off its dignity'. Maybe, but that involved an expense the corporation was not willing to entertain.[116]

The new cities also used their status as jumping-off points for further developments. Asa Briggs has written of Birmingham that the post-1889 city council made decisions which turned it into 'the best governed city in the world'.[117] Much the same seems to have been true of Leeds where the effect of city status was to galvanize the new city council which 'sought to repair the neglect of the previous century ... to improve the deficient water supply', to acquire the utilities, and generally to set about improving the new city.[118] Perhaps Leeds was aware that it lacked the municipal track record which other would-be cities had stressed in their applications.

City status has to be seen as part of a wider movement which was all about civic pride. Lord mayoralties, civic buildings, the so-called civic gospel itself, all suggested a desire to improve and decorate the commercial and industrial towns of industrial Britain. It was not just a matter of being a city rather than a town: a whole culture of representation was being developed which can loosely be described as civic improvement.[119] Becoming a city was one part of this process, and even in Whitehall it was recognized that size now mattered. The old Anglican qualification was swept away as the idea of a 'city' took on an entirely new meaning: the civil servant who feared an American-style proliferation of cities misunderstood the fundamental shift of thinking which was taking place. A city was now a great place. It was distinguished primarily by population size, but in itself population reflected commercial and industrial success, and in turn this was expressed in civic pride as municipal authorities sought to cleanse their streets, to build bigger and better buildings, to lay out parks and gardens, and to create a concept of the 'city' which was quite distinct from the norm in past decades.

---

[116]   *Borough of Nottingham: Reports to Council, 1896–7*, 227; *Nottingham Daily Express*, 20 July 1897; *Nottingham Daily Guardian*, 20 July 1897; NAO CA 3656, 184.
[117]   Briggs, *Birmingham*, II, 116.
[118]   A.J. Taylor, 'Victorian Leeds', in D. Fraser, ed., *A History of Modern Leeds* (Manchester, 1980), 396; Hennock, *Fit and Proper*, 227, 231–91.
[119]   Briggs, *Victorian Cities*, 205; W. Hamish Fraser and Irene Maver, eds., *Glasgow, Volume II: 1830–1912* (Manchester, 1996), 420–1; Hamish Fraser, 'Municipal socialism and social policy', in R.J. Morris and Richard Rodger, *The Victorian City* (1993), 258–80.

CHAPTER FOUR

Civic Status and Civic Promotion: the Inter-War Years

In 1932 Sunderland was in the grip of the inter-war depression. The male unemployment rate stood at 36.6 per cent, largely due to the collapse of shipbuilding. It would get worse before it improved, but the corporation responded by looking for ways of promoting the image of the town, and one of these ways was to petition the Home Office requesting city status:

> Sunderland has been passing through a period of severe trade depression and it is felt that the raising of the town to the dignity and status of a city would assist considerably in the efforts which are being made to secure a revival of trade and the establishment of new industries in our midst. I may mention that when travelling abroad I have been struck with the attitude of the foreigner when considering the importance of towns in England and have definitely formed the conclusion that he looks upon a town upon which the dignity of a City has been conferred as being of the highest importance whilst generally regarding the other towns as of secondary degree.[1]

Sunderland was dissuaded from sending a delegation to the Home Office, and although the petition was accepted the claim to city status was rejected, but the wording of the claim was significant. In one sense Sunderland was looking backwards to the claims made by Belfast and Dundee in the 1880s, but in another sense it was chiming with the mood of the times. In the inter-war years, British industrial promotion was largely concerned with regeneration, the search for replacement industries in areas of depression.[2] This clearly was what Sunderland had in mind when it thought in terms of securing a revival of trade and setting up new industries, and it saw this process in terms of the contrasting images conveyed abroad between a town and a city. While city status for Birmingham and many of the other provincial towns had been about approval, an honour conferred on the municipality as a mark of royal favour for services completed, in the inter-war years it came increasingly to be sought as a way of encouraging civic promotion. As the Sunderland application hinted, 'city' was a title which it was hoped would raise it in the international pecking order.

---

[1]   Tyne and Wear Archives, 209/271, fos, 395–412. There is no file in the Public Record Office on this application. For the economic background, G.L. Dodds, *A History of Sunderland* (Sunderland, 2001), 120.
[2]   Stephen V. Ward, *Selling Places: The Marketing and Promotion of Towns and Cities 1850–2000* (1998), 151.

This shift from city status as a confirmation of civic importance to a tool of civic promotion was relatively slow to take off. In part this was because the whole idea of promotion was still in its infancy, but it was also for other reasons. These included the lingering but still potent belief that city status went hand in hand with Anglican diocesan status; an ongoing and significant link with royal events which could be allowed to over-ride other considerations if the monarch so wished; and, above all, a context laid down by the Home Office. Potential applicants were vetted in Whitehall no longer according to the intrinsic worth of their case, but according to rules and regulations which proved unenforceable, except insofar as they could be used to turn applications down rather than filter – as was intended – the chaff from the wheat. What Sunderland's unsuccessful application of 1932 reflected more than anything else of the inter-war years was the conflicting priorities of a Home Office trying to limit promotion to the really worthy (in its eyes), and a rising tide of applicants who came to view city status as a means of promoting their towns in a national and increasingly international context.

The Home Office guidelines which operated through these years have to be understood to appreciate how the civil servants set about assessing city status claims. When in 1907 Bradford applied to have its mayor raised to lord mayor the Home Secretary, Herbert Gladstone, asked his civil servants to draw up some ground rules for future grants.[3] The Home Office had clearly been moving in this direction since the link with diocesan status was uncoupled in 1888, but this was the first time civil servants had actually drawn up guidelines which they could refer to in assessing any claims. Summarized, they included three main qualifications. The first, and most critical, qualification for consideration as a city was to be population. Applications for city status were in the future to be considered only from boroughs with populations of 300,000 or more. This was a straightforward demographic qualification, based on the precedent of Victorian urban growth, but soon to become a millstone around the neck of the Home Office.

Clearing the population hurdle represented a prima facie case to be considered for city status, but a second qualification was introduced to avoid a mechanistic situation whereby any town reaching the magic figure of 300,000 would expect automatic promotion to city: 'even where the population reaches 300,000 consideration to be given to the position of the city as regards its local metropolitan character, its credit in respect of education, refinement, efficiency and splendour of its public works, and so forth'. The logic here was that a town 'which had a certain Metropolitan position from its history or geographical position or its education and refined society would, in most people's eyes, be more worthy of the title than a mere collection of mills and factories and working people without any of these advantages, but with a large population'.[4] Thus, to quote a phrase deployed on many subsequent occasions by the Home Office to explain its actions, in order to qualify for the title a town should not be 'a mere

---

[3]   The memorandum and correspondence is in PRO HO 45/10163/B24512.
[4]   Ibid.

formless collection of inhabitants but a place of outstanding importance, with a character and identity of its own, and preferably having the position of a capital in a substantial and well-defined district'.[5] These high-sounding words were fine, but unlike population figures established from the census they left a good deal to interpretation and prejudice. The third guideline set out in 1907 was that lord mayoralties should be granted only to cities.

The guidelines were accepted by the Home Secretary and approved by King Edward VII. His private secretary told Gladstone: 'The King thinks that the general principle advanced by Mr Gladstone in regard to the granting of the title of "City", and also for the grant to the Chief Magistrate of a City of the title of "Lord Mayor" is right, but he desires me to say that practically he greatly deprecates the number of "Lord Mayors" being increased'.[6] King George V confirmed his acceptance of the guidelines on coming to the throne in 1910, although he then found reasons for making additional grants, often in defiance of Home Office policy and sometimes even in contradiction of earlier statements of his own.

These guidelines were to influence Home Office thinking through and even beyond the inter-war period, but they proved far easier to set down on paper than to enforce in practice. In fact, the population guideline was unworkable from the start. The 300,000 figure had been set in the confident expectation that urban growth on the scale achieved in the nineteenth century would be sustained in the twentieth century. The Home Office could not have predicted that it would peak in 1911. As it transpired, no town reached the magic figure of 300,000, at least without the benefit of a boundary extension, and these were usually granted on only a relatively small scale in these years.[7] In the circumstances, enforcement of the population rule would have meant no promotions to city and possibly only one or two lord mayoralties as existing cities achieved the magic figure. In practice, the queue for honours was so long and so pressing that the Home Office found itself using the rule selectively. Leicester, Stoke, Portsmouth, Salford, Plymouth and Lancaster all achieved city status between the wars, but none of them met the Home Office's primary population qualification. Many other towns, including Sunderland, were turned down as the Home Office enforced the qualification when it wanted to reject an application. Over time, in any case, it had little option but to lower the qualifying figure, initially to 250,000, and eventually to 200,000. The most that can be said for the implementation of the 1907 guidelines between the wars is that relatively few towns achieved promotion and, within the British Isles, none outside of England.

The queue for honours might have been shorter if the guidelines had been published. In practice, their very existence was scarcely acknowledged. In June 1910, in response to a question from an MP, the Home Secretary told Parliament that 'to maintain the value of the distinction' a rule had been laid down 'as to the

---

5   PRO HO 45/18697/19.
6   PRO HO 45/10163/B24512/10.
7   V.D. Lipman, *Local Government Areas, 1834–1945* (Oxford, 1949).

minimum population which should ordinarily be regarded as qualifying a borough for the higher status'. He was careful to avoid spelling out the minimum figure.[8] Enquiries to the Home Office invariably produced a bland response. When in September 1915 James Jackson, chairman of the Liverpool district of the Lancashire Congregational Union, wrote to the Home Secretary asking for information on how a town could be promoted to city, he was told simply that it occurred when letters patent were issued. Undaunted by this deliberate attempt to miss the point, Jackson wrote again with specific questions about population, municipal enterprise, and so on, to which Arthur Locke of the Home Office responded that the Home Secretary 'cannot give the detailed particulars for which you apply.... A minimum limit of population has been laid down, but the Secretary of State regrets that he cannot make any general statement of the grounds which he would regard as justifying a recommendation to His Majesty to grant the title in question.'[9]

A.L. Dixon, giving evidence in 1923 to the Royal Commission on Local Government, refused to acknowledge the rule. In reply to the chairman's question as to whether city status 'has anything to do with the size of the population?' he replied 'There is no population limit or anything of that kind'.[10] Even the Earl of Onslow, enquiring on behalf of Guildford in 1927, could elicit nothing more than a generality: 'the title is only recommended in the case of towns of the first rank in population, size, and importance, and having a distinctive character and identity of their own'.[11] Over time, a number of people became aware of the 300,000 rule, and the Home Office was less guarded in its responses. Yet because applications which failed the population test, and of which the Home Office disapproved, were not forwarded to Buckingham Palace, a number of towns fell at the first hurdle without ever knowing why. For the Home Office it was always possible to hide behind the convenient excuse that as a constitutional matter city status issues were confidential, and no feedback was offered. The same situation continues today.

With the population rule relatively easily enforced in the demographic conditions of these years, the Home Office could quite easily have closed the door on promotion to city status. With urban population growth slowing, and boundary extensions only reluctantly conceded in Whitehall, the possibility of any towns satisfying the first rule, in order even to be considered under the second, was beginning to look remote. This, of course, was to reckon without the willingness of politicians or the monarch to waive the rules when it suited them.

Leicester was to be the first beneficiary of this flexible approach to the 1907 guidelines when in 1919 it hosted an official visit by King George V and Queen Mary. The town had been seeking city status since 1889, and from 1907 the Home Office was able to enforce the population rule. When in 1915 the town

---

[8]   *Hansard*, 5th ser., XXVII (1911), 150.

[9]   PRO HO 45/24601/2.

[10]   Royal Commission on Local Government, Cmnd 3213, Minutes of Evidence, part IX, question 29,560. Dixon's evidence is given in PRO HO 286/40.

[11]   PRO HO 45/24601/5.

clerk sought an interview at the Home Office to put the case for Leicester, he was refused: 'even allowing for change of circumstances since 1907 the case of Leicester falls so far outside the rules laid down by Edward VII, and approved by the present King that it would not be proper for me to make a recommendation to His Majesty'. With a population believed in Whitehall to be 227,000 it was well below the threshold, which was all the evidence the Home Office required because of its distaste for public health policies in the town.[12]

The royal visit of 1919 changed the situation. It was viewed as an opportunity for the people of Leicester to celebrate military victory in Europe, but the corporation saw it as an opportunity to renew the request for city status.[13] The King made it clear in advance that he was 'anxious if possible to meet the wishes of Leicester', and although no public announcement was made while he was in the town on 10 June, he evidently assured the mayor privately that the title of city would be forthcoming. He signed the necessary documents on 13 June.[14] The following day, the Home Secretary, Edward Shortt, wrote to the mayor, Alderman Walter Lovell, congratulating him on the arrangements made for the royal visit, and adding: 'I am very glad also to be able to inform you that His Majesty has been graciously pleased to approve the restoration of your Ancient Town to its former status of a city'. The formal announcement was made a few days later.[15] Leicester 'should never have been divested' of the title, the *Leicester Mercury* informed its readers in a leader column accompanying the announcement.[16] Leicester's promotion was billed as a restoration of city status. Home Secretary Shortt emphasized that it was receiving 'exceptional treatment' with 'the restoration to your ancient town of its former status of a city'. A civil servant added to the file:

> As you know, the standard prescribed is a population of 300,000. Leicester in 1911 had a population of about 230,000, but at the present time it is probably over 250,000. The ground on which Mr Shortt thinks the case calls for exceptional treatment is that Leicester is of very ancient origin and appears in early days to have enjoyed the status of a City. The proposed charter would therefore restore to Leicester its ancient privilege....[17]

The wording may have been careful but it was never likely to fool other aspirant cities. Leicester's historic claims were hardly unique, but just as

---

[12]   PRO HO 45/13276/13.
[13]   Leicestershire RO, 22D57/219, Pritchard to the Earl of Cromer, 29 May 1919, to the Secretary of the Association of Municipal Corporations, 27 May 1919, and to the Home Secretary, 31 May 1919.
[14]   PRO HO 45/13276/14.
[15]   Leicestershire RO, DE 1973/20/194; PRO HO 45/13276/14; *The Times*, 17 June 1919. Similar announcements on the same date in *Daily Telegraph, Morning Post, Daily Chronicle*.
[16]   *Leicester Mercury*, 15 June 1919.
[17]   PRO HO 45/13276/13.

importantly the Home Office (and the King) had bent the guidelines in the cause of expediency, in this case a royal visit. It was hardly surprising to find other towns jumping on the 'royal' bandwagon. In July 1920 the mayor of Swansea renewed the Welsh town's application in relation to a visit by the King and Queen to open the new University College buildings. On this occasion the Home Office was unmoved,[18] but it anticipated further applications, and the naval towns of Portsmouth and Plymouth were both expected to apply, emphasizing their royal links: 'no doubt there will be renewed applications from them which will have to be considered when they are made'.[19]

Plymouth had, in fact, applied a month before the Leicester grant, in May 1919, and been turned down, but its claims were urged again in 1920.[20] The case for Plymouth was coloured by its royal connections. The town itself had grown rapidly in size as a result of legislation in 1914 which joined it to Devonport and the urban district of East Stonehouse to create a new and enlarged borough. It enjoyed royal patronage because the King had been – and the Prince of Wales currently was – its Lord High Steward. Finally, it could claim – as could Portsmouth – a particularly important wartime role as a naval port. Its cause was taken up by Lord Astor, Unionist MP for Plymouth 1910–19, and *de facto* owner of the Sunday newspaper the *Observer*. Astor succeeded his father in the peerage in 1919 and his wife Nancy was elected in his place as an MP for Plymouth, to become the first woman to sit in Parliament. Astor was parliamentary secretary to the Ministry of Health 1919–21, and influential in government circles. He took great interest in Plymouth, subsequently helping to plan its reconstruction after the Second World War, and serving as lord mayor 1939–44. In February 1920 he wrote to the Home Secretary urging that both Plymouth and Portsmouth should be granted city status on the grounds that 'the two chief Naval Ports should have this honour conferred upon them in commemoration of the splendid services rendered by the Navy during the War'. The Prince of Wales had been canvassed, and had raised the matter with the King. Astor, who knew of the 300,000 rule, claimed it had been honoured rather more in the breach than the letter. Home Secretary Shortt passed Astor's letter to Lord Stamfordham, the King's private secretary, with the comment that 'so far as we are concerned there appears to be no reason why the decision of May [1919] should now be reversed'. The King agreed: 'His Majesty sees no reason for not adhering to the decision come to on this subject last year'.[21]

The King's support for the Home Office in the case of Plymouth enabled the civil servants to maintain the fiction that Leicester was an exception because it

---

[18]   PRO HO 45/18697/9.
[19]   PRO HO 45/13276/14.
[20]   The Plymouth case is difficult to reconstruct. There is no Home Office file on the town's promotion to city in the Public Record Office, and the town clerk's papers held in the West Devon Record Office are patchy for the period prior to 1939, largely because of destruction during bombing raids in 1941.
[21]   Royal Archives, Windsor Castle, RA PS/GV/PS22361; PRO HO 45/12904/19.

was a restoration – however remote – and not a new creation. Yet the rule, which had been so conveniently overlooked in 1919, was again breached in 1925 in similar circumstances. In January 1925 John Ward, MP for Stoke-on-Trent, led a delegation to the Home Office with two specific requests: first, to ask for 'what most towns of a similar size have attained, namely the dignity of a City'; and second, to request that the king should visit Stoke to lay the foundation stone to the extension of the North Staffordshire Infirmary. The county borough of Stoke-on-Trent was a relatively new conurbation, the result of an amalgamation in 1910 of the six Potteries towns of Burslem, Fenton, Hanley, Longton, Stoke and Tunstall. The borough had a population in 1911 of 234,553, rising to 240,428 in 1921 prior to a boundary extension in 1922. Mr Ward's deputation claimed that by 1924 the total was 294,000, although where this figure came from is uncertain given that the 1931 census figure was 276,639.[22] More importantly, according to the deputation, Stoke was the 'centre of the pottery industry which provided employment for 50,000 persons and was unique in being the only pottery town in the world'. Stoke wanted promotion not because of its current size or even its civic track record, but because of the recognition it expected would follow: 'The Mayor said that it was desired to make the place better known and it was thought that this would be done if it were made into a city. Mr Clows (MP) mentioned that last year the exports of pottery had been increased by £1,000,000.' The view in Stoke was that if it was to promote the new borough internationally it needed the boost of national recognition in the form of city status.

The initial response of the Home Office was simply to reject this line of argument on the usual grounds:

> There does not seem to be sufficient ground for making an exception to the general rule, particularly as any exception (unless some very special and obvious grounds exist) is certain to make difficulties with other towns. It is suggested therefore that the request should be refused, in which case no submission to HM is necessary as there is no formal petition to HM. If it is thought desirable to soften the refusal it might perhaps be accompanied by a hint that their request should be renewed when they can show a population of 300,000.

The mayor was informed on 4 February that Stoke could not be considered until its population reached 300,000.[23] Unfortunately for the Home Office, the position was less clear cut than it seemed because Mr Ward's delegation of January 1925 had also asked the King to pay a visit to Stoke. The King accepted the invitation, and as with Leicester in 1919 he wanted to make a gesture. The most obvious way to do this was via grant of city status. Given that Stoke was the largest town to propose itself for promotion since the 300,000 rule had been introduced, and that it was very close to the winning post, the Home Office had little option but to

22   VCH, *Staffordshire*, VIII (1963), 252-71, especially 263.
23   PRO HO 45/12950/244729/2.

relent. It was agreed that Stoke should be promoted, and that the King should make the announcement during his visit.

The royal visit to Stoke took place on 4 June 1925, and in his reply to the corporation's loyal address the King announced that:

> the development and importance of your town and industry enable me gladly to consent to the request that the title and status of a City shall be conferred upon your County Borough. I pray that the Divine Blessing may rest upon your labours, and that the City of Stoke-on-Trent may enter upon and enjoy a future of even greater usefulness and prosperity.

It took a few moments for the news conveyed in this announcement to sink in, and then 'the demonstration of cheering was like a thunderclap. His Majesty's speech was interrupted for a moment or two until the rounds of cheers had subsided.'[24] So secretly had the negotiations been conducted that the announcement was said to have come 'as a complete and pleasurable surprise'. The King paid 'high tribute' to the pottery industry during his visit.[25]

The Stoke case highlighted the conflicting interests at play in these years. The initial response of the Home Office to the request for city status was negative, an insistence on enforcing its own rules which showed little or no appreciation of the importance towns were beginning to attach to city status. It gave way reluctantly: as one civil servant pointed out: 'I fear it will cause HM trouble and embarrassment if the idea gets about that the visit of HM to a town is an occasion for asking special favours'. Yet the King's words at Stoke reflected the new reality: city status was granted in the hope of ensuring 'a future of even greater usefulness and prosperity'. Did it succeed? Maybe it contributed to the success of the corporation in attracting the French Michelin Company to the city in 1927.[26]

Leicester and Stoke sowed doubts in the King's mind about the fairness of the 300,000 rule. Lord Stamfordham told the Home Secretary in May 1925 that 'His Majesty would be prepared to reduce the qualifying figure from 300,000 to say 250,000'.[27] 'It is', he added, 'almost inevitable that bestowal of this favour will result in applications from Portsmouth and Plymouth for similar consideration, which the King feels could hardly be refused.'[28] Portsmouth was particularly dismayed by events in Stoke. It had applied for city status in 1901 and 1911, and had been mentioned in passing by Lord Astor when he brought forward the case for Plymouth in 1920, but it had been turned down again early in 1925 on the population rule: the Home Secretary told the mayor, 'I think it right to say to you at once that there is an old standing rule here that the limit of

---

[24]   *Staffordshire Sentinel*, 5 June 1925.
[25]   *The Times*, 6, 8 June 1925. Stoke-on-Trent Archive Service was unable to find any additional information relating to the grant of city status, beyond the letters patent. I am grateful to Mrs M. Beard for help on this point.
[26]   PRO HO 45/12950/244729/3; Ward, *Selling Places*, 154.
[27]   PRO HO 45/12950/244729/3.
[28]   PRO HO 45/12950/244729/4.

population must be 300,000 before this takes place and I have only last week refused another town whose population is 294,000'.[29] The other town was, of course, Stoke, but once this decision was reversed and Stoke was granted city status in June 1925, Portsmouth had good reason to be aggrieved; indeed, foreseeing its likely annoyance, the Home Secretary proposed reopening the case even though the town 'is, of course, below the minimum of 300,000 which was fixed by one of my predecessors, and if we make it a City there will probably be a demand from one or two other places'. He accepted that royal links were significant:

> I gather that the Prince of Wales is coming back to Portsmouth. I do not know whether His Majesty will personally meet him there. If so, there is sure to be a tomasha of sorts and the King might like to make a gesture (to use that loathsome expression) such as was made when His Majesty went to Stoke-on-Trent.

Far from making a gesture, the King objected to the case being revived because Portsmouth's population was only 257,000, and Sir William Joynson-Hicks, the Home Secretary, took this as sufficient grounds for refusing to meet a delegation from the town.[30]

At this point, the Home Secretary was steering fast towards some very jagged rocks. On 3 July 1925, just a month after Stoke was raised to city status, Salford submitted an application. It claimed to have a population in excess of 300,000, although the civil servant handling the case disputed this figure: his statistics suggested a total of 234,045, and 'this alone seems to be fatal to any prospect of conferring the title of city'. What really caused alarm in the Home Office, however, was Salford's position on the second qualification laid down in 1907: the local metropolitan character of a potential city. To London-based civil servants this was not the image they had of Salford:

> It has always been held that in addition to mere population a city ought to be a place of outstanding importance having a character and identity of its own. Stoke-on-Trent of course fulfilled this condition in virtue of its reputation as the centre of pottery manufacture. Salford, I understand, does not.... [it] is merely a scratch collection of 240,000 people cut off from Manchester by the river. On all grounds it seems that any application from Salford for the title of city had better be discouraged.[31]

What concerned the civil servants was that Joynson-Hicks, who had begun his political career as MP for North-West Manchester (1908–10), was evidently sympathetic to the Salford cause. On 25 August 1925 he received a delegation including the mayor, Alderman G. Billington, the MP for West Salford, F.W. Astbury, and the town clerk, I.C. Evans. Billington pointed to Salford's high

29   PRO HO 45/12904/18.
30   PRO HO 45/12904/19.
31   PRO HO 45/16147/2.

rateable value, its population, 'the fact that it was the third largest town in Lancashire, and that other towns, notably Stoke, which were not so large as Salford, had already been made cities'. Joynson-Hicks proved 'only too willing to lend a sympathetic ear to Salford's claims',[32] although he initially rejected the case.[33]

Simply by seeing the Salford delegation Joynson-Hicks enraged the mayor of Portsmouth. On 31 August 1925, acting on the King's advice that the Portsmouth case should not be reopened, Joynson-Hicks wrote to Mayor Privett refusing to meet a delegation because Portsmouth was not yet large enough for consideration for city status. Privett received the Home Secretary's letter in the same post as his copy of *The Municipal Journal*, in which he read with disbelief that a deputation from Salford had recently been received at the Home Office. Since Privett believed Salford to have a smaller population than Portsmouth, this looked like straightforward discrimination. Privett demanded to see Joynson-Hicks: 'the general feeling in Portsmouth is very strong that the first Naval Port of the kingdom receives no recognition, moreover there are some points that are at present inexplicable to me, which doubtless could be made clear by an interview'. Privett also persuaded a number of influential local people to write to the Home Office, only to find that he was forced to kick his heels while Joynson-Hicks was away on a shooting holiday.

When he returned, the Home Secretary duly received a delegation from Portsmouth on 9 October 1925.[34] They discussed population, Portsmouth's role in naval affairs, and the anticipated arrival of the Prince of Wales on 16 October. The delegation 'pointed out that Portsmouth was the gateway of the Empire, and held the sea history of England, [and] that as the chief Naval port of the Empire the town had sent many fleets to victory'. They also noted that it had 'welcomed home warriors who had led our fleets and armies to victory', but they left the Home Office empty handed and for several months there was silence.[35] Early in February 1926 Mayor Privett complained that it was four months since he had visited the Home Office, and nothing had been heard of the matter since. Joynson-Hicks told him a decision could not be taken speedily, but he did refer the case back to Lord Stamfordham. The King, Stamfordham responded, had reconsidered his position on the matter since 'the fixing of a certain population as an additional qualification for becoming a City, is really an unofficial, and indeed private understanding between His Majesty and the Home Secretary'. He was ready to approve Portsmouth's promotion 'on the understanding that the granting of this privilege is not made a precedent for other cases, such as Plymouth, Salford etc. The fact that Portsmouth is regarded as the first Naval Port and Dockyard in the world should be regarded as a justifiable reason for making an exception.'[36]

32   *Salford City Reporter and Salford Chronicle*, 3 April 1926.
33   PRO HO 45/16147/2.
34   PRO HO 45/12904/19.
35   *Portsmouth Times*, 16 April 1926.
36   PRO HO 45/12904/21.

For Joynson-Hicks this was welcome relief, but he was reluctant to overlook the claims of Salford. He counter-proposed to the King that both towns should be promoted, and he would then 'erect a formidable barricade against all the others for some time to come and keep them at bay'. After some sparring between Whitehall and Buckingham Palace, the King backed down and agreed that both towns should become cities. Joynson-Hicks's campaign for Salford was probably crucial, since the Home Office would subsequently argue that the grant to Salford had been given 'with considerable hesitation', and that it was 'a doubtful case'.[37]

In Portsmouth the official announcement was made by Mayor Privett at a public meeting in the Town Hall Banqueting Room on 25 March 1926. Subsequently, Privett made a formal announcement to the council on 13 April at which it was decided to invite the Prince of Wales to become the first freeman of the new city: 'Councillor J.W. Perkins congratulated the Mayor and Town Clerk on their efforts, and said the distinction was one of which they might feel proud'.[38] Letters patent for both Portsmouth and Salford were issued on 22 April 1926.[39]

Salford was much more appreciative. News of city status reached the town on Tuesday, 30 March, when the mayor immediately issued instructions for flags to be flown on the municipal buildings. The Police Band played celebratory music in Bexley Square during the afternoon, and at the request of the mayor schoolchildren were granted a holiday to mark the occasion. Tram cars were decorated, bunting put up in Chapel Street, and the tramway poles at the entrance to the new city were 'decorated with flags and shields bearing the words "City of Salford"'. When the council met on 21 April it looked at ways of celebrating the new status, but preliminary plans for a gala and children's entertainment were put on hold and then abandoned as the city was crippled by the general strike and the subsequent coal shortage.[40] The Salford press believed that the new city would now be able to escape from the shadow of Manchester:

> There is no gainsaying that in the past Salford has been overshadowed by her near neighbour, with the result that her possibilities and her resources alike have not received the attention they merited. This situation has acted as a check on her commercial and industrial development, but the elevation to the status of a city will do more to remove that obstacle than any other step, provided it is wisely and persistently supported.[41]

---

37   PRO HO 45/16147/10; HO 45/18697/19.

38   *Portsmouth Times*, 26 March, 16 April.

39   PRO HO 45/12904/21; HO 45/16147/4–5; *The Times*, 26, 30 March 1926.

40   *The Reporter for the Borough of Salford and Salford Chronicle*, which renamed itself *Salford City Reporter and Salford Chronicle*, 3, 16, 23 April, 8 May 1926.

41   Ibid., 3 April 1926. No papers survive for the Salford town clerk. I am grateful for clarification of this point to Mr A.N. Cross, retired Salford City Archivist.

Here, as in Stoke, the emphasis was placed on city status providing a welcome boost to Salford's economic standing, and being a city would help to promote its economic importance.

Joynson-Hicks had promised to erect formidable barricades because he knew how disturbed the King was over the whole honours question in the 1920s,[42] but he could not stop further applications. Both Plymouth and Southampton submitted petitions in the wake of the Portsmouth grant. Plymouth's claims could hardly be denied once Portsmouth had been promoted, and in June 1928 the King made it clear that he would not object to city status if the case was to be brought forward again by Lord Astor. On 12 October, the King signified his agreement to Plymouth's promotion, and Joynson-Hicks conveyed the good news to Lord Astor.[43] The Home Office wrote to the mayor of Plymouth on 16 October. The local press hailed the new status as 'a justification for the amalgamation of Plymouth and Devonport ... marking the inception of a new era in their joint history when post-amalgamation feuds should be forgotten and a new spirit of unity and co-operation engendered'. Various local people expressed the hope that city status would have 'a decidedly beneficial effect upon the business life of the port and on its claims as a holiday centre'.[44] Here again, the stress was on the promotional benefits of city status. The formal announcement in the press was made with the issue of letters patent on 18 October 1928.[45]

With Plymouth's elevation, King George V made it plain he hoped 'that we have now come to an end of city making'.[46] It was a decision welcomed in the Home Office; indeed, nearly forty years later a civil servant noted that in 1928 'His Majesty expressed the opinion that the list of towns qualified to become cities was exhausted'.[47] This King kept to his word, which was bad news for several aspirant cities. Southampton applied unsuccessfully in 1929. The Home Secretary told the mayor:

> I fully realize the great and increasing importance of Southampton as a Port but, rapid as its development has been, I am afraid that it cannot be said to have reached a point at which I should feel justified consistently with the practice which has prevailed for many years, in recommending The King to grant it the title of City.... the time for putting forward your request is not yet.[48]

Southampton had still to reach a population of 200,000, but with Plymouth and Portsmouth having become cities it considered itself slighted. Sunderland, as we have seen, missed out in 1932, and Swansea unsuccessfully renewed its case in

---

[42]   H. Nicolson, *King George V: His Life and Reign* (1952), 513.

[43]   PRO LCO6/1391; *The Times* 18 Oct. 1928; Royal Archives, Windsor Castle, PS/GV/PS 22361.

[44]   *The Western Morning News and Mercury*, 18 Oct. 1928.

[45]   C.E. Welch, *Plymouth City Charters, 1439–1935* (Plymouth, 1962), 35, 43.

[46]   PRO HO 45/18697/17; Royal Archives, Windsor Castle, PS/GV/PS 22361.

[47]   PRO HO 286/66, endorsement of 7 Jan. 1966.

[48]   PRO HO 45/13487.

1935 by asking for city status as a Silver Jubilee honour. It was turned down because it failed to meet the population minimum, and when it put out yet further feelers early in 1936 the Home Office officials were so annoyed that the letter was left unanswered.[49]

The only other town to achieve city status during the inter-war years was Lancaster, which was a coronation honour at the accession of King George VI. As such, Lancaster was the first and, indeed, remains the only town to be made a city in conjunction with such an event. Technically, the 1907 guidelines were still in place, although the 300,000 rule had gradually been relaxed. Lancaster, however, drove a coach and horses through the rule since its population was only 51,650. In this case the emphasis was laid firmly on royal links: 'His Majesty carries the title Duke of Lancaster'. Alderman Edward Parr, chairman of the Finance Committee, and the driving force behind the application, admitted that 'if I had any misgivings it was on the score of population', but he refused to be swayed by the pessimists on the council. He approached the town's MP, Herwald Ramsbotham, who not only expressed his support but immediately canvassed Sir John Davison, the Chancellor of the Duchy of Lancaster. Ramsbotham sorted out procedural matters and advised Middleton how best to prepare a memorial to the King,[50] since a grant to Lancaster was to be regarded as an honour bestowed by the monarch and no petition was required.[51] The King gave his assent: in the words of his private secretary, Sir Alexander Hardinge:

> although according to the usual criterion of numbers, the application is not one that could be favourably considered, His Majesty feels that the long association of Lancaster with the Crown would justify a departure from the rule that exists ... this privilege has only been granted to Lancaster in virtue of this town being the County Town of the Duchy of Lancaster, and in fact the Castle is The King's personal property.[52]

The case for Lancaster was subsequently defended as 'long association with the Crown, the county town of the King's Duchy of Lancaster', a specific exception to the rules as a result of its special association with the Crown.[53]

By 1939 the Home Office had effectively backed itself into a position where it could reasonably enforce the 1907 rules only by making exceptions, usually on the basis of royal connection. Its main success in holding the line was in rejecting the claims of new diocesan towns. The Anglican church went on promoting new dioceses, and where the cathedral was in a town which did not already have city

---

[49]   PRO HO 45/18697/17, 18.

[50]   Lancaster City Museum, LM73.50/1, 'How Lancaster Became a City'.

[51]   *Lancaster Observer and Morecambe Chronicle*, 14, 28 May 1937; *Municipal Review*, June 1937, 225.

[52]   Royal Archives, Windsor Castle, PS/GVI/PS 1909.

[53]   PRO HO 45/18697/19; HO 286/66, 67.

status, applications for promotion continued to flow into the Home Office.[54] The diocese of Southwark was created in 1905. Southwark applied for city status in 1907 and was turned down: 'the wide-spread and popular impression that the seat of a bishopric is necessarily a city' was 'a mistake', and the title arose 'only by prescriptive right or by direct Royal Grant'.[55]

The message had not been very well broadcast, and when the new bishopric of Chelmsford was announced on 23 January 1914 the town clerk found to his surprise that before the borough could use the title of city it needed to obtain letters patent by petition to the King. Having no idea of the procedure, he wrote to the Patent Office, which passed on his request to the Home Office. The town clerk, who seems to have thought it was only a matter of form to ask for the requisite documentation, must have been even more nonplussed when he received a distinctly dusty response from the Home Office: 'the creation of the Bishopric of Chelmsford does not give the Borough any claim to the title of City and ... the Secretary of State cannot hold out any hopes that he will be able to recommend compliance with the prayer of the Petition'.[56] Bury St Edmunds had also applied for city status with the foundation of the bishopric of St Edmundsbury and Ipswich in 1914,[57] which at least forced the Home Office to recognize that its message to Southwark in 1907 had still to be heard elsewhere:

These applications from Chelmsford and Bury St Edmunds are the result of the wide-spread popular impression that the seat of a bishopric is necessarily a city. This is a mistake ... though for many centuries the actual correspondence between the cities and the bishoprics was so close as to give some excuse for the idea that there was a causal connection. The title comes only by prescriptive right or by direct Royal Grant. For a long while the Home Office acted on the principle that any town which became the seat of a new bishopric was entitled on application to be created a city. This rule was broken through in the case of Southwark, when the title was explicitly refused.... it is perfectly clear that no encouragement should be given to the idea that the possession of a new bishopric in itself gives a town any claim to be granted the title of city, and that minor towns like Bury St Edmunds (16,785), Chelmsford (18,008), and even Ipswich (73,932) – which is sure to apply if the authorities know that Bury St Edmunds has applied – should certainly not be made cities.

The position could not have been clearer, but once again the information was contained in an internal memorandum prepared for the eyes of Home Office officials.[58] Consequently, when Blackburn learned early in 1924 that it was likely to become the seat of a bishop, preparations were made to apply for city status. The Home Office offered no encouragement: 'this would not give any claim of

<hr/>

[54]   Existing cities which became sees in these years included Birmingham, Sheffield, Leicester and Bradford.
[55]   PRO HO 286/37; HO 45/24657.
[56]   PRO HO 45/24657.
[57]   No file has survived for the Bury St Edmunds application.
[58]   The memo, dated 16 March 1914, is in the Chelmsford file.

right to the title which is now conferred only on the most important boroughs and after full consideration of all facts of the application'. With a population of 122,000 it had no possible chance of success.[59] Undaunted, it made a further informal approach in 1934, and a more formal one in 1935. Despite submitting an impressive account of its industrial history, the Lancashire town was simply too small: 'there can be no question of granting the title here', wrote a civil servant on the Home Office file, and the case was closed.[60]

Guildford applied in 1927 when it became a diocesan see,[61] and Derby used the same pretext in 1928. On 7 May 1928 G. Trevelyan Lee, the town clerk of Derby, wrote to J.H. Thomas, MP and the Duke of Devonshire to ask if they could propose Derby for city status: 'You are of course aware that it has just become the seat of a new Diocese and in addition to this it has always been the County Town. There is no other town in the country which is not already a city in which all these circumstances apply....'[62] Sir John Anderson, under-secretary of state at the Home Office, brushed off Derby as he had Guildford, but the local MPs asked for a meeting with the Home Secretary. This took place on 15 July. The Home Secretary told the deputation that Derby was too small because of the 300,000 rule, and that even when that had occasionally been broken no town below 250,000 had been honoured. (This was an interesting piece of political deviousness from Home Secretary Joynson-Hicks, who had already more or less promised the King he would oversee Plymouth's promotion, knowing its population to be well below 250,000.)[63]

Derby was persistent. After Plymouth was promoted it restated its case in 1929, and again in 1931 when it sought to use as leverage a forthcoming visit to the town by the Prince of Wales. Each request was turned down, primarily on the grounds that with a population of 176,000 Derby was too small, but with two other significant factors thrown in. Promoting Derby would, potentially, lead to claims from larger towns such as Birkenhead, Bolton, Brighton, Oldham, Southampton, Sunderland and Swansea, as well as others of much the same size – Blackburn (another cathedral town), Gateshead, Middlesbrough, South Shields, Southend, Stockport, Wolverhampton and Preston – which would see Derby as a precedent. Second, the civil servants objected to the difficulties likely to arise by encouraging the theory that a county town as such had a preferential claim to be a city: Reading, Northampton, Ipswich and Cambridge were others in a similar position. Derby, in other words, was nowhere near the top of any potential

[59]   PRO HO 45/21692/1.
[60]   PRO HO 45/21692/2–4.
[61]   PRO HO 45/16995, 286/40; Surrey History Centre, 5337/9/39; *Surrey Times and County Express*, 14 May 1927.
[62]   PRO HO 45/14110, Sir John Anderson to J.H. Thomas, 11 May 1928.
[63]   PRO HO 45/14110, Home Office notes, 18 July 1928; Home Secretary to Sir Richard Luce, 27 July 1928.

pecking order.[64] Even so, Derby's persistence may be seen as part of its policy of industrial promotion, in which it was particularly active during these years.[65]

What then of the third guideline set out in 1907, that lord mayoralties should be granted only to cities, and among existing cities (which included cathedral cities by ancient prescriptive right) only those with a population of 300,000 or more? Part of the thinking represented Home Office prejudice. As one civil servant wrote:

> There is a further consideration of some ?small importance viz: the capacity and refinement of the persons who enter into municipal life in the various boroughs and may expect to obtain the position of Lord Mayor. I suggest that even Cities of enormous population and wealth often fail to find creditable Chief Magistrates and if the tangible standards of wealth and population are lowered below 300,000 there would be still greater risk of the title Lord Mayor becoming contemptible.[66]

Whatever the truth of this assertion, in the years between 1907 and the Second World War no city without a lord mayor passed the 300,000 barrier, so that the rule would have excluded any additions to the lord mayoralty had it been applied rigidly. Like city status, it has in fact been employed with a good deal of expediency. Bradford, which had been the test case in 1907, was still deemed to qualify for a lord mayoralty despite having fewer than 300,000 people, and similar flexibility was applied subsequently.

The first application for a lord mayoralty after the First World War came from Coventry in 1918, citing its service in the wartime munitions industry. A civil servant noted that 'it is to be remembered that the manufacture of munitions, though unquestionably praiseworthy, is also very profitable; and that it would be a very delicate and invidious task to distinguish the degrees of merit of different towns in the production of munitions.... Coventry falls far short in every way of the qualifications ordinarily required.'[67] Adelaide applied successfully in 1919,[68] but Londonderry was turned down in 1923 because it was too small and 'must accept British standards in such matters'.[69]

Newly-created cities in these years were usually surprised that they did not receive a lord mayoralty automatically. The mayor of Leicester wrote to the Home Secretary on 24 June 1919, having had time to study the letters patent raising the borough to a city, to complain that there did not seem to be any provision for a lord mayoralty. He was rebuffed with the comment that as the government was restoring city status to Leicester, there was no question of a lord

---

[64]   PRO HO 45/14110, Mayor of Derby to the Home Secretary, 19 Aug. 1929; Home Secretary to the Mayor, 29 Aug. 1929; Home Secretary to the Duke of Devonshire, 17 June 1931.
[65]   Ward, *Selling Places*, 153, 156, 164, 169.
[66]   PRO HO 45/10163/B24512.
[67]   PRO HO 45/24696/2.
[68]   PRO HO 45/22625/7.
[69]   PRO HO 45/16147/10.

mayoralty, which would have been a new grant.[70] Stoke discovered the same omission in June 1925 and immediately applied to the Home Office asking for the title, only to be refused.[71] When the Portsmouth delegation visited the Home Office in October 1925 seeking city status, the Home Secretary pointed out to Mayor Privett that he would not automatically be promoted to lord mayor: 'this appeared a great disappointment to the Mayor, who evidently thought that the status "City" and title "Lord Mayor" went together'. The refusal of the title when city status was granted in 1926 annoyed Privett. Announcing the grant of city status he told his audience that 'unfortunately the honour now conferred did not carry with it the full dignity which it was felt by his colleagues that the new City deserved, but they were not without hope that with the assistance of their friends the full dignity would be conferred'. An application was turned down in 1927.[72] Nottingham was again refused a lord mayoralty the same year because 'though large and important [it] is hardly of such outstanding importance as to justify exceptional treatment', and perhaps also because the petition included 'unsuitable matter, e.g. a glowing account of the town's success in combating venereal disease', as a civil servant recalled thirty-five years later.[73]

The Home Office decided it should try to sort out the apparent inconsistency in government policy on grants of lord mayoralties when Portsmouth applied for a third time in 1928. A civil servant drew up a list of potential candidates:

There are four cities (of a size comparable to Portsmouth) which have not at present Lord Mayors, viz Nottingham (268,000), Leicester (244,000), Stoke-on-Trent (276,000) and Salford (247,000). Nottingham has the strongest case of the four in view of its antiquity, importance and general standing. It was made a city in 1897 on the occasion of the Diamond Jubilee. The city has made several applications for a Lord Mayor, and it would be very difficult to continue to refuse, if the grant were made to Portsmouth.[74]

It was also noted that both Stoke and Portsmouth were 'inclined to be dissatisfied because they were not also given Lord Mayors', and that Leicester 'has always been extremely jealous of Nottingham' so that applications could be expected from Leicester, Stoke and Nottingham in the event of Portsmouth being successful. In these circumstances, the Home Office recommended – and King George V accepted – that lord mayoralties should be bestowed on Nottingham, Leicester, Portsmouth and Stoke, but not on Salford, which had also renewed its application.[75] The King agreed to make the announcement apropos of Nottingham during his speech at the opening of the new University College building on the

70   PRO HO 45/13276/14, 19.
71   PRO HO 45/12950/244729/7.
72   *Portsmouth Times*, 16 April 1926; PRO HO 45/12904/19, 21, 24.
73   PRO HO 45/12938/6; HO 286/70, file annotation 14 Sept. 1962.
74   PRO HO 45/12904/26.
75   PRO HO 45/12938/4, 6.

Highfields campus on 10 July.[76] Arrangements were made for simultaneous announcements to be made in the other three cities,[77] but the letters sent out by the Home Office arrived only on 11 July, much to the chagrin of Leicester's mayor, Alderman James Thomas, who was an invited guest at the University College celebrations in Nottingham on 10 July. He heard of his own promotion via a phone call to his home from the chief clerk in the town hall at 8 a.m. the next day.[78]

The King intimated to the Home Office in 1928 that with the accession of Plymouth he had done with city making, and that with the four lord mayoralties he had finished with lord mayoralties 'unless there was some marked change in the position'. The two obvious losers, Salford and Plymouth, were not amused. Salford complained within a week about its omission, unaware that its case had been considered and specifically rejected within the Home Office.[79] When the King and Queen paid a visit to the city in 1934 an application submitted for a lord mayoralty was summarily turned down, and an informal approach was rejected early in 1935.[80] Plymouth was promoted to city in 1928 on the understanding that it would not receive a lord mayoralty.[81] It was ill-disposed to take this apparent snub without protest, and both towns were considered for lord mayoralties at the time of King George V's Silver Jubilee celebrations in 1935.

In the event, Plymouth succeeded, and Salford did not. Plymouth, it was decided in the Home Office, was worthy of a lord mayor because it was 'the largest municipality in Devon and Cornwall', and also because 'there is no doubt that in the West it does occupy a quasi metropolitan position and has a character and identity of its own'. This made it suitable for a lord mayoralty. By contrast, Salford lacked the proper sense of identity, 'because it is really an appendage of Manchester; it is part of a larger unit – Greater Manchester – and falls to be treated on the same lines as Croydon and West Ham which, although not metropolitan boroughs, are mainly dormitories of London and are not at all likely to be the recipients of the dignity of City'. The Home Office, now under Sir John Gilmour, was still shuddering at the way in which it had fallen for Joynson-Hicks's Salford recommendation in 1926. Letters patent for Plymouth were dated 6 May 1935.[82]

Salford took this further snub badly. Lord Derby wrote to Gilmour on 13 May 1935 to ask, unofficially, 'whether you could tell me whether there is any chance of their being able to get it or if there is any reason which would prevent their application ever being considered'. The answer to the latter question was probably Home Office prejudice – one file is annotated

76   PRO HO 45/12938/8–9.
77   PRO HO 45/12904/26.
78   Leicestershire RO, 22D57/310.
79   PRO HO 45/16147/5, 8, 10.
80   PRO HO 45/16147/10–12.
81   Royal Archives, Windsor Castle, PS/GV/PS 22361.
82   PRO HO 45/16147/13, HO 286/65; Plymouth City Charters, 35.

'practically indivisible from Manchester' – but clearly this was not the answer Gilmour was likely to offer. His diplomatic reply of 14 May squashed Salford's chances: 'In connection with the Jubilee celebrations I went into the question whether there was any justification for the creation of any further Lord Mayors. In the course of this review I specifically considered the position of Salford, but I had to come to the conclusion that their case was not strong enough.'[83]

The Home Office had fewer quibbles with Australian towns, and Perth (1919), Brisbane (1930), and Hobart (1934) all had their mayors promoted in these years. The population of Hobart was just 57,000.[84] In England, however, Wakefield was turned down for a lord mayoralty as a coronation honour in 1937,[85] and Lancaster was told when receiving city status that there was no possibility of a lord mayoralty.[86]

The question of which lord mayors were entitled to use 'right honourable' periodically came up for discussion during these years. Australian cities, because they were state capitals, were invariably awarded the prefix when the lord mayoralty was awarded.[87] Occasionally, British cities adopted the title without permission. In 1927 the Home Secretary issued instructions to the lord mayors of Liverpool, Bristol and several other cities to the effect that they were not to use the prefix right honourable, which could be conferred only by the sovereign. 'My duty', the Home Secretary told the House of Commons, 'is to see that the prerogative is not infringed by the assumption of titular distinctions of this kind without the permission of the Sovereign'. Although one MP pointed out that 'the great mass of the people of England remain entirely unmoved by the controversy', it was brought back to the Commons only two days later after newspaper reports that the lord mayor of Cardiff also had the right to use right honourable. On this occasion one MP suggested that 'in a civilized community it is about time we were stopping the use of these nicknames altogether'.[88]

Between the wars, six towns were raised to cities, and after a suitable period of reflection four of them (Salford and Lancaster being the exceptions) were given lord mayoralties. City status was usually linked with royal matters: Leicester and Stoke were promoted on the occasion of visits by King George V, Portsmouth and Plymouth because of their naval connections with the royal family, and Lancaster as a specific grant in connection with the coronation of King George VI. Salford was essentially a political promotion. The numbers might have been greater if the Home Office had not conveniently hidden

83   PRO HO 45/16147/14; HO 45/21712.
84   PRO HO 45/21712.
85   PRO HO 45/16841/B4371/3.
86   Royal Archives, Windsor Castle, PS/GVI/PS/1909; *Lancaster Observer and Morecambe Chronicle*, 14 May 1937.
87   PRO HO 45/22625.
88   *Hansard*, 5th ser., 209 (1927), 853 (25 July 1927), 1243 (27 July 1927); PRO HO 286/41.

behind guidelines prepared in 1907, and perhaps had it been more aware of or even convinced of the benefits of city status. It continued to perceive of these honours as it perceived of honours to individuals – to be used sparingly for fear of debasing the coinage. And with the possible exception of Salford it maintained the idea that city status was not a political honour, and nor was it a mark of religious favour.

The result of these views was that relatively few towns were promoted, but more importantly the growing assumption that city status was a means of promoting a town in a national and international context was lost on the civil servants. Mostly towns promoted in these years saw their new status in terms of a step up into a higher league which would be recognized in the wider community and would help to maintain and enhance their prosperity. Sunderland argued the case in 1932, and was still saying much the same sixty years later when it was finally promoted. As such, it was of a piece with the attitude of civic authorities towards grand civic gestures: most of the applications (and successes) date from the 1920s, a decade of relative prosperity marked by the building of some flamboyant town halls such as Leeds' civic hall and Nottingham's council house. By contrast, in the depression and its aftermath in the 1930s there seem to have been fewer applications for city status, just as new civic buildings such as in Derby were reduced in size and architectural complexity, even if this was partly a result of changing styles on a European level.[89] Yet city status had clearly passed from being a reward for civic achievement to being regarded as a means of civic promotion, and this would become increasingly important in the post-war world.

---

[89]   Ian Murie, 'Inter-war Town Hall Design' (B.Arch. thesis, University of Nottingham, 1980), 31, 33.

CHAPTER FIVE

Politicians and City Status, 1945–69

In the autumn of 1941, with Britain struggling for survival in the heat of the Second World War, there took place in Whitehall what in retrospect appears to have been an extraordinary internal disagreement in the corridors of power as to whether or not Coventry should be granted a lord mayoralty. Coventry had city status by virtue of ancient prescriptive right as the seat of a bishopric. It tried on a number of occasions to acquire the title of lord mayor, notably in 1918 and 1929, and again in 1940. The last of these bids was put together hastily in time for a visit from the King on 16 November in the wake of a heavy German air raid. The bid was not successful, but Coventry clearly believed that the title was in its grasp in view of its wartime experiences, and it applied again in 1941. This time the request reached the prime minister, Winston Churchill. Given the weight of enemy action suffered by Coventry, Southampton and Swansea, Churchill – who visited Coventry in September – was all in favour of giving lord mayoralties to each of them, but despite the extraordinary circumstances of the time the Home Office had no intention of bowing to what it clearly believed were the unreasonable demands of the prime minister.

In 1940, the Home Office had prepared a memorandum outlining reasons for Coventry's case to be rejected: 'to give a Lord Mayoralty to Coventry because of what it had suffered would be inequitable in itself and would cause great difficulties'. This memo was forward to Churchill on 10 October 1941. The prime minister was furious, and wrote a personal minute on 29 October:

> I have now read the note which the Home Office prepared last November on the subject of a Lord Mayor for Coventry. This note achieves its negative purpose by breaking down successively every separate argument in favour of the honour. Antiquity is no guide. Population cannot be trusted. Air raid damage is novel and invidious. One might agree that each of these in itself could form no foundation. The case for Coventry is that all three come together in a peculiarly high degree. Coventry has been a city, as the Home Office note says, 'from time immemorial'. It has a population of 237,000, which places it well in the list of population claims. Finally it has suffered the most spectacular bombing and has been selected as the special victim of German malice. It is the conjunction of these three claims which gives Coventry its unique position at the present time. No other city can show the same combination and there should be no difficulty in resisting other claims, if it were desired to do so. I hope therefore that the matter may have your further consideration.

In response to this tirade Austin Strutt, the career civil servant who ran the Home Office's Constitutional Unit, prepared a memorandum on 31 October to the effect that Churchill had overlooked the need for a city wanting a lord mayoralty to be not just large but to have a special importance and dignity of its own, something approaching the character of a metropolis in its region. But precedent was the real problem:

> The real point is the practical difficulty in which the Secretary of State will be involved if he once gives way on the question of granting civic honours as a recognition of air raid sufferings. If Coventry is given a Lord Mayor it will be interpreted universally as a reward for being bombed, and no argument would carry the least weight, for if air raid sufferings are allowed to turn the scale and the other grounds are insufficient the award is, for practical purposes, an award for air raid damage. There is intense competition for civic honours in this country and any grant to Coventry would inevitably, despite what the Prime Minister says, bring in claims from other bombed towns which would be extremely difficult to deal with. Coventry's position is really only unique in the sense that it is the only one of the large towns which has been bombed which is a City and has not a Lord Mayor.... I suggest that it is a complete mistake to think that the case of Coventry can be isolated from that of the other bombed cities, and that any grant to Coventry will upset the whole practice with regard to civic honours which has developed under the instructions of successive Sovereigns for the past fifty years.

This dispassionate narrative, which seemed almost to ignore the war going on around the Home Office, was, in so many words, the response passed to Churchill on 11 November, and there the matter seems to have rested. Coventry continued to pursue its case, in 1944, 1945 and 1948,[1] until it was successful in 1953.[2]

Apart from the image of Churchill becoming almost apoplectic with rage over what must have appeared a minor issue in the context of the war, there is a more pertinent point in this exchange which was soon to become increasingly apparent, and this was the growing intervention of politicians in what had been in the past essentially a constitutional matter. Although the war years were hardly conducive to campaigns for city status, the increasing concern which towns developed with promoting themselves,[3] together with the apparent collapse of the old rules when Lancaster was promoted in 1937, led almost inevitably to an increase in demand. With it came politicization of the whole process. In the memo he prepared for Churchill, Austin Strutt set out the unwritten principles employed in the Home Office: 'The grant of these civic honours proceeds on a scale. First, a place is made a City, then it receives a

---

[1]   PRO HO 286/69.

[2]   PRO HO 45/24696.

[3]   On the use of the planning procedure in post-war Britain to 'boost' civic images, see P.J. Larkham and K.D. Lilley, 'Plans, Planners and City Images: Place Promotion and Civic Boosterism in British Reconstruction Planning', *Urban History*, 30 (2003), 183–205.

Lord Mayor and very rarely the Chief Magistrate is granted the style of Right Honourable. These grades have to be considered together.'[4] No one really questioned this ladder of preferment, although in the post-1945 era the key measure of success came increasingly to be city status. What changed was the recognition by politicians that city status was worth seeking for political, not simply commercial reasons. After Cambridge had been allowed to follow Lancaster in breaking the rules, only Southampton and Swansea were promoted in the twenty-five years after 1945, and in both cases politicians played an important part in securing the status, for overtly political reasons.

The rhetoric of royal connections which surrounded Lancaster's promotion in 1937 cut no ice with those towns coveting city status. If Lancaster, a town of only just over 50,000 people, could achieve city status, it seemed the old rules no longer amounted to much at all. Even relatively small towns now came to believe that they might be eligible. In the summer of 1944 the Estates and General Purposes Committee of the Lincolnshire port of Boston held informal discussions about applying to have their town raised to the status of a city in conjunction with the forthcoming 400th anniversary of incorporation, due in May 1945.[5] Their role model was Lancaster. C.L. Hoffrock Griffiths, the town clerk, was privately pessimistic about the chances of success, but he approached R.H. Middleton, his opposite number in Lancaster, for advice. Armed with useful information on 3 August he asked the lord lieutenant of Lincolnshire, Lord Brownlow, to lead a campaign for city status. Stress was laid on the antiquity of the borough, its medieval importance as a port, its continued significance within the Holland district of Lincolnshire, its strong links with Boston, Massachusetts, and its cathedral-like church of St Botolph. Brownlow approached Winston Churchill, the prime minister, through Brendan Bracken, the Minister of Information.[6] He in turn passed the request to the Home Office.

Brownlow's letter, together with the town clerk's statement of the case for Boston, dropped onto the desk of a Miss Usher, who was not, it has to be said, very flattering. Boston, she wrote, 'is a large, rich, but unimposing (bordering on sordid) market town, with very little architectural beauty apart from the church, and with a population in 1931 of only 22,190. Lancaster is in quite a different category.... There are no grounds on which a case could be built for raising Boston to city status.' Miss Usher then drafted a response for the Home Secretary, who wrote to Bracken on 5 September 1944 to say that there was no case to be made in Boston's favour: 'While I appreciate the history and

---

4   Ibid.

5   Constitutional issues like this have always been regarded as highly confidential and so nothing was minuted. Consequently there is no reference to this episode in the minutes of Boston Corporation or of its Estates and General Purposes Committee: Lincolnshire AO, BB, 2/A/30. Confidentiality also explains why nothing was known of the application beyond a small circle of Boston politicians. No relevant papers of Lord Brownlow are known to have survived. I am grateful to Adrian Wilkinson for help on this point.

6   Lincolnshire AO BB, Boston Letter Books, 25, 1943–4, fos. 757, 771, 773, 777.

interesting features of Boston's position in the fen country, and also recognize American interest in the development of the town, I am afraid that, having regard to the general principles governing policy in this matter, I could not make a favourable recommendation to the King'.[7] Bracken passed the news to Brownlow, who conveyed the gloomy tidings to Hoffrock Griffiths. In his response, the town clerk noted that the members of his Estates and General Purposes Committee were 'naturally somewhat disappointed at the reply which you have received from Mr Brendan Bracken' but, he added, 'they quite appreciate, as I do myself, the necessity for complying with precedents in such matters as this'.[8] Not everyone was to prove so accommodating, particularly as the next successful applicant, Cambridge, also broke all the rules.

At a meeting of the Association of Municipal Corporations early in 1950, Alderman W.L. Raynes of Cambridge sounded out Alderman Parr of Lancaster about city status. After all, if Lancaster, with its historic connections, was large enough to be a city, surely Cambridge ought to qualify, even with a population below 100,000? Parr advised him on procedure and the need for secrecy.[9] Raynes confided in Alan Swift, the town clerk, Alderman Sir Montagu Butler, senior member of the university group on the council, and Councillor G.F. Hickson, chairman of the council's Local Government Reform Committee and also secretary of the university's Board of Extra-Mural Studies. The four men became what Swift described as 'the self-appointed sub-committee', and by the autumn of 1950 they were preparing the Cambridge case for city status. On 1 November Hickson saw Austin Strutt, who helpfully provided him with guidelines on how Cambridge should proceed:

> The Petition, which comes up to the Home Secretary for submission to The King, should start with a short historical statement dealing with the town and the University and should give particulars of local government activities, e.g. what the Corporation had done in the matter of education, housing, town and country planning, and should emphasize directions in which the Corporation have been pioneers in any of these fields. The petition should emphasize the quasi-capital position which Cambridge holds as a seat of the regional headquarters of many Government Departments and of the Regional Commissioner in time of war. If the point can be made emphasis should be placed upon the way in which Cambridge functions as the natural centre for the county and, say, the Isle of Ely, in the matter of agriculture and commerce while it would also be as well to say something about the administrative arrangements and the excellent relations which exist between the town and the county as well as between the town and the University. Something should also be said about the financial position of the borough.

Strutt, an Oxford graduate, offered to look at the petition off the record, before it was submitted to the Home Office. Hickson and the town clerk set to work

7   PRO HO 45/23202.
8   Lincolnshire AO BB, Boston Letter Books, 25, 1943–4, f. 908.
9   Cambridgeshire RO, R101/47, Raynes to Hamilton Kerr, 3 April 1950; Kerr to Fitzroy Maclean, 4 April 1950 and Maclean's replies, 24, 27 April 1950.

drafting 'this all-embracing memo',[10] which was approved by the sub-committee and forwarded to Strutt in mid-December.[11]

Swift met Strutt at the Home Office on 3 January 1951. As a result of their discussions, several revisions were made to the draft petition, particularly over the relationship between the university and the city. These alterations were circulated to the sub-committee early in February, and subsequently Swift wrote again to Strutt, a letter he marked 'Secret', enclosing 'four copies of the memorandum for your use.... The matter has been kept entirely secret in Cambridge and is known only to the persona mentioned above, to my secretary and myself. I must thank you most sincerely for your kindness in seeing me and for the helpful suggestions which you made.' Only eight people knew of the plans being drawn up.[12] Strutt acknowledged the town clerk's letter, but then there was silence for a month, until on 10 March he wrote 'in continuation of my letter of the 13th February, I write to say that if the Corporation decide to adopt the petition in the form of the document of which you sent me copies on the 12th February it will receive the favourable consideration of the Secretary of State'.[13]

Assured now of success, the sub-committee convened a meeting of the town council on 17 March 1951. Alderman Raynes moved a motion proposing that they should petition the Crown seeking city status. He argued that the standing of Cambridge in world affairs was such that 'we might well petition the King to grant us the title of City.... We are proud of the fact that His Majesty, as was his grandfather, is a member of Cambridge University, and the bestowal by His Majesty upon Cambridge of the title of City would be a welcome culmination of the favours bestowed by his Royal ancestors.' The motion was seconded by Alderman W.L. Briggs: 'The City of Cambridge denotes standing: the Borough of Cambridge is simply a geographical area'. It took all of twelve minutes for the resolution to be passed unanimously. Cambridge, it was noted, was the only one of the six ancient seats of learning in England and Scotland not to enjoy the status of either a city or a royal borough:

> Cambridge is proud to be the seat of a University famous throughout the world. To all in Cambridge it is a source of gratification and pride that His Majesty is, as was his grandfather, King Edward VII, a member of the University. The bestowal by His Majesty upon Cambridge of the title of "City" would be a welcome culmination of the favours conferred by his Royal ancestors.[14]

---

[10]   Ibid., Strutt to Hickson, 2 Nov. 1950; Hickson to Swift, 3 Nov. 1950.
[11]   Ibid., Swift to Butler and Hickson, 4, 13 Dec. 1950; and to Strutt, 27 Dec. 1950.
[12]   Ibid., Hickson to Swift, 26 Jan. 1951; Swift to the sub-committee 3 Feb. 1951; Swift to Strutt, 12. Feb 1951.
[13]   Ibid., Strutt to Swift, 13 Feb., 10 March 1951.
[14]   Ibid., copy of memorandum and petition.

Professor G.M. Trevelyan, master of Trinity College, and one of a number of prominent local people specially invited to attend the meeting,[15] added his backing to the petition: 'Why should Oxford be a city if Cambridge is not?'.[16]

Immediately after the meeting on 17 March, the petition was despatched to the Home Office, and on 22 March Strutt wrote to confirm that the King 'has been graciously pleased to raise the Borough of Cambridge to the title and dignity of City'.[17] Alan Swift was not quite sure if all the effort had been worthwhile:

> apart from the fact that a large amount of re-painting and over-printing will be necessary, the alteration does not make much difference to us, except, of course, that the Chief Executive and Administrative Officer of the Corporation has to remain content with the mean and unworthy sobriquet of Town Clerk, whilst the other Chief Offices are given the grandiose and high sounding title of City Treasurer and City Surveyor etc.[18]

Considerable discussion took place with the Heralds' Office, the Home Office, and the university, as to the correct wording that should now appear on the city's seal. The vicar of Holy Trinity had to be reminded that when the mayor and corporation attended a civic service in his church on 20 May he needed to make necessary alterations to the prayers to acknowledge that Cambridge was now a city. The mayor hosted a civic dinner on 27 April, at which the guests of honour were the Home Secretary, James Chuter Ede, who proposed the toast, Austin Strutt, the Bishop of Ely, the chairman of the county council and the vice chancellor of the university. Subsequently, this was described as 'quite a small affair', attended mainly by councillors and representatives of the university. And when on 14 July Alderman Raynes was made a freeman of the city, he presented a silver-gilt cup which the council agreed to call The City Cup and to use at mayor-making and on other civic occasions. However, the suggestion of a firework display was not taken up.[19] What Cambridge really wanted was for the King to present the letters patent in person.[20] This was not to be, although Queen Elizabeth formally presented them at a ceremony in the Guildhall in 1955.[21]

---

[15]   Ibid., Swift to Charles Phythian, to the Lord Lieutenant and to the High Steward of the University (G.M. Trevelyan), 13 March 1951.

[16]   *City of Cambridge, Council Minutes, 1951*, p. 625; *Cambridge Independent Press and Chronicle*, 23 March 1951; Cambridgeshire RO, R101/47, Alan Swift to the Under Secretary of State at the Home Office, 17 March 1951.

[17]   Cambridgeshire RO, R101/47, H.A. Strutt to the Mayor of Cambridge, 22 March 1951, and the mayor's response, 24 March 1951; *The Times*, 19, 24 March 1951; PRO LCO 6/2325.

[18]   Cambridgeshire RO, R101/47, Swift to Phythian, 28 March 1951.

[19]   Ibid. The file includes numerous letters on these subjects. Also *Minutes*, 626, 109, 112; *Cambridge Independent Press and Chronicle*, 4 May 1951.

[20]   Cambridgeshire RO, R101/47, Major Edward Ford, Assistant Private Secretary to the King, to the Mayor of Cambridge, 22 March 1951, and the mayor's reply on 24 March; Swift to Under Secretary of State for the Home Office, 20 April 1951; *Cambridge Independent Press and Chronicle*, 27 April 1951; Sir Michael Adeane, Buckingham

As with Lancaster, the Home Office was careful to emphasize what it referred to vaguely as the 'quite special reasons' which explained the Cambridge grant.[22] Since it had a population of only 81,000, it was held to have succeeded on 'ancient historical grounds'.[23] Not everyone was so easily convinced. Maidstone MP, Alfred Bossom, approached the Home Secretary in May 1951 asking for promotion for Maidstone as part of the Festival of Britain celebrations. Bossom received a typical civil service reply: 'I fully appreciate the historical and other features of Maidstone and its position as the County Town of Kent, but I am afraid that the title of City would not, as a general rule, be granted to a town of this size'. Unwilling to be sidelined quite so easily, Bossom asked 'could you let me know what the general principles are, which you refer to as governing this kind of thing?'. The Home Office was irritated by this attempt to break confidentiality. The file is endorsed:

> Mr Bossom in effect is asking the Secretary of State to indicate the principles on which he acts in deciding what advice he shall tender to the King in the exercise of the prerogative as fountain of honour. It is the Secretary of State's long standing practice to decline on constitutional grounds to give reasons for or explanations of his policy in these matters.

Bossom was told as much but he would not be deflected. He arranged to see the Home Secretary on 20 July 1951, when Chuter Ede explained to him that:

> among the considerations which he had in mind in making recommendations in these cases were the town's population, the standard of its local government administration, and the extent to which it provided a centre for a substantial region. He doubted whether Maidstone qualified on the first count or the last, but provided it was understood that the chances of a favourable recommendation were very slender indeed he would be prepared to authorize Mr Strutt to talk to the Town Clerk and explain the kind of information which a petition would have to contain.

Subsequently, Maidstone's town clerk made a further approach to the Home Office which – in effect – took up references about the town with the Ministries of Education, Transport, Health, and Housing and Local Government. As a result of the replies received, the Home Office concluded that 'no case has been made out for a favourable recommendation', and that it was time to tell the tiresome Mr Bossom as much.[24]

Palace, to Swift, 8 Jan. 1952; Swift to Adeane, 13 May 1952; Adeane to Swift, 14 May 1952; Swift to S. Tapper-Jones, 16 April 1951.
[21]   Ibid., Town Clerk of Cambridge to Norman Schofield, 27 Feb. 1964.
[22]   PRO HO 286/67.
[23]   PRO HO 286/38, Memorandum dated 5 Aug. 1953. There is no HO file relating to this grant in the Public Record Office. The file (HON/152/3/1) seems never to have been deposited.
[24]   PRO HO 286/64. The file includes the comment written on 19 March 1952 of Bossom: 'he is quite persistent and seems to be ill-disposed to take no for an answer'.

Croydon also noted events in Cambridge. It submitted a draft petition to the Home Office on 15 September 1951. References were taken up from the Departments of Education, Transport, Health, and Housing and Local Government, but the results were not encouraging. According to the Ministry of Education 'we do not feel that Croydon has any greater title to "Metropolitan" status than one would expect in the case of any County Borough of reasonable size'. The Ministry of Housing and Local Government also refused to back the application: 'It has always been held that boroughs which are parts of the metropolitan aggregate are not suitable for the honour; in the view of the Ministry Croydon is still largely a dormitory town and is likely to remain so for some years'. A civil servant annotated the file: Croydon's 'only claim is on the score of population, the other necessary attributes of a City does not succeed'. The town clerk was told that a petition was unlikely to be successful, but on request a delegation from Croydon was received at the Home Office on 12 December 1951. It was unable to change any minds, and the Home Secretary told the mayor in February 1952 that he could not recommend the submission of a formal application.[25]

Other would-be cities sought advice from Alan Swift, town clerk of Cambridge. In January 1952 his opposite numbers in Blackpool and Middlesbrough asked him how to go about making an application for city status. Swift sent them a copy of the Cambridge petition and supporting memorandum and stressed the secrecy surrounding the whole business:

> As you will be aware, the matter is one of very great delicacy, and therefore I shall be glad if you will return the copy Petition and memorandum, and refrain from telling anyone that I have lent it to you.... As you will appreciate, it is not advisable for the matter to receive any local publicity whatever unless you are pretty sure that the Petition is going to be granted.[26]

It was all to no avail.

The Home Office also expected to play a role in the creation of cities in the Dominions and other parts of the Empire. A number of colonial capitals raised themselves to city status by acts passed in their own legislatures, including Port-of-Spain (Trinidad) in 1914 and Belize (British Honduras) in 1942. Others asked for Whitehall support. In 1949, Nairobi specifically requested that city status should be granted by letters patent, and they were presented to the mayor by the Duke of Gloucester at a ceremony on 30 March 1950.[27] Gibraltar, with a population of 732,000, followed in July 1951,[28] but the Colonial Office objected to Suva, the capital of Fiji, declaring itself to be a city

25   PRO HO 286/65.
26   Cambridgeshire RO, R101/47, Trevor Jones, town clerk of Blackpool, to Alan Swift, 24 Jan. 1952 and Swift's reply 28 Jan.; E.C. Carr, town clerk of Middlesbrough, to Swift, 28 Jan. 1952.
27   PRO CO 1032/31/R.1909; PRO HO 45/24313.
28   PRO HO 45/24601/7.

under the older dispensation in 1952, and introduced guidelines for colonial governors to follow. The intention was that London should control future city status grants to ensure that potential cities were 'in the first rank in terms of size, dignity and importance'. The municipal authority was to 'enjoy a reputation for efficiency in the performance of its functions' and 'have a high degree of autonomy'. These terms were used throughout the 1950s and 1960s to assess grants of city status to growing colonial centres – just as they were to towns in the British Isles.[29]

Lancaster's success as a coronation honour in 1937 encouraged would-be cities to view the anticipated coronation of Queen Elizabeth II in 1953 through hopeful eyes. Alan Swift of Cambridge was approached by Blackburn in July 1952, and by Southampton, both asking for advice as to how they might frame applications, with the coronation in mind.[30]

The Southampton case was the longest running of any in these years. When C.F. Carr, editor of the *Southern Daily Echo* found himself seated next to Ernest Bevin at a Savoy lunch in May 1948, he took the opportunity of sounding him out about Southampton's promotion chances. Quite what influence he thought the Foreign Secretary had in such matters is unclear, but Carr wrote immediately to the mayor of Southampton to say that Bevin had 'left me with the impression that not only was he interested but that he was going to look into the matter'. The mayor approached the lord lieutenant of Hampshire, Lord Portal, for advice 'as to whether now is the appropriate time to press for what we feel is our justifiable claim'.[31] Nothing more was heard of this initiative, but in November 1949 the next mayor, Alderman P.W. Blanchard, visited the Home Office and broached the subject of city status, only to be told the time was not right.[32]

This did not satisfy Southampton, which was still smarting from being overlooked when Portsmouth and Plymouth were promoted in the 1920s. Mayor G.H. Barendt proposed that the town should apply formally for city status in 1951, the centenary of the University College and of the Chamber of Commerce, 'the oldest and most active in the country'. The town clerk approached local MPs and the Duke of Wellington, lord lieutenant of Hampshire, who wrote

---

[29]   PRO CO 1032/31, document dated 15 Jan. 1954; CO 554/2469, 2633; CO 822/2062–3, 3222; CO 1023/229; CO 1030/393, 809; CO 1036/1648.
[30]   Cambridgeshire RO, R101/47. Charles Robinson, town clerk of Blackburn, to Swift, 2 July 1951, Swift's response on 7 July, and Robinson's further letter on 11 July; Gordon Sewell to Alan Swift, 10 July 1952; A. Norman Schofield to Swift, 6 Feb. 1953. As long after the events of 1951 as 1968 the town clerk of Cambridge was approached by agents working on behalf of Kuala Lumpur asking for advice about city status: letter of 16 May 1968.
[31]   SCA, SC/TC, box 220/1, C.F. Carr to the mayor of Southampton, Councillor Frank Dibben, 26 May 1948; Dibben to Lord Portal, 31 May 1948.
[32]   SCA, SC/TC, box 220/1, Memorandum, 10 Nov. 1949.

immediately to the Home Office 'warmly supporting your petition'.[33] The Home Office decided to take soundings as to Southampton's suitability. The Ministry of Health noted that with a population of 180,000, and no evidence that it was considering applying for a boundary extension, Southampton was well below the minimum of 200,000 set by the Home Office, although from the local government viewpoint 'Southampton's record is very good', even if it was not 'so outstanding as to cause us to dissent if you took the view that the population criterion must be maintained'. This was the first occasion on which the minimum population figure had been lowered to 200,000 from the 250,000 approved by King George V in 1926. These investigations took months. The Home Office had backed itself into a corner, because it could hardly reject Southampton's claims on the population figures while simultaneously recommending to King George VI that Cambridge should be promoted. Despite a letter to the mayor on 24 April 1951 saying that the case remained under consideration, the matter was effectively dropped.[34]

Southampton regarded the forthcoming coronation of Queen Elizabeth II as a further opportunity to stake its claim. The mayor secured an interview with the Home Secretary in January 1953, and the following month his town clerk, A. Norman Schofield, saw Austin Strutt at the Home Office. Schofield established that Southampton's application for city status was receiving serious consideration, and Strutt made it clear where his sympathies lay:

> Eventually towards the end of our discussion Mr Strutt said that he proposed making two recommendations to the Home Secretary, one that the mayor of another city should receive the title of Lord Mayor and the other that Southampton should be granted by letters patent the title of 'city'. He said that if all goes well he will indicate personally by letter to me 'everything going according to plan', but if there is any doubt he will write 'when next in London please call and see me'. He impressed upon me the following points which are conditional to any further consideration of the application (1) the absolute secrecy of my visit and a report to no-one but yourself [the mayor], (2) no further correspondence or calls and no petition as the grant of this honour is to have the appearance of the spontaneous wish of her Majesty. The grant is to form part of the Coronation Honours List and will appear in the *London Gazette* about that time.[35]

---

[33]   SCA, G.H. Barendt to R.R.H. Negesson, 4 Dec. 1950, Negesson's reply of 5 Dec. 1950, and copies to MPs and the Duke of Wellington; Wellington's response of 7 Dec. 1950.

[34]   PRO HLG 43/1195. The Home Office case can be followed through the letters it exchanged with the Ministry of Health, which are in this file. The file itself was opened only in 1995: SCA, Home Office to mayor, 16 Feb., 24 April 1951.

[35]   SCA, Memorandum, written by A. Norman Schofield. There is no date on the memorandum but from other papers in the file we know that Schofield approached Strutt on 9 Feb. 1953 proposing that they meet in London 'in order to continue the discussion which the Mayor of Southampton had with you recently'. We may confidently date the memo to February 1953.

Sadly from Southampton's point of view all did not go according to plan, even though its case was acknowledged to be stronger than Preston, turned down 'by reason of its size' (119,243) and Wolverhampton (162,669), which was 'thought not to possess ... individual character'. Promoting Southampton before it reached 200,000 was creating an unacceptable precedent, and no new cities were made at the coronation.[36]

Several towns, including Coventry, Salford, Lancaster, Cambridge, Exeter, Wakefield and Canterbury, expressed an interest in receiving a lord mayoralty as a coronation honour, and on this occasion Coventry was successful.[37]

The fact that no town succeeded in achieving city status at the coronation made no difference to the flow of applications reaching the Home Office. Each was carefully assessed in terms both of population and local government performance. Croydon applied in December 1953, and the Home Office duly conducted a round of enquiries to education, health, transport, and housing and local government. The replies were far from encouraging, but Croydon refused to take no for an answer. It sent a delegation to the Home Office in November 1954, and submitted another application in 1955. This was also turned down. Croydon tried again without success in 1958, when a civil servant noted that the real problem was its lack of 'a Metropolitan character'. The application was rejected. And so it went on, with further applications in 1962 and 1965. Soundings were taken on each occasion, but, as R.J. Guppy, Assistant Under Secretary of State at the Home Office, wrote of the 1965 application, 'the real case against Croydon is that, whatever its past history, it is now just part of the London conurbation and almost indistinguishable from many of the other Greater London boroughs. But the local people will not readily accept this.'[38]

Derby entertained hopes of promotion in 1954, when the town clerk sought advice from Alan Swift in Cambridge, who warned him about the need for secrecy: 'This business of trying to get City status is one of the most ticklish that one has to handle. The Crown does not like any preliminary publicity and if it is humanly possible any sort of publicity in minutes and agenda and in the press should be avoided at all costs.'[39] Derby went ahead and submitted a draft petition in 1955, but was turned down.[40] Southwark also applied in 1955. After the usual enquiries had been made, its claim was rejected on the grounds that the Home Office had long resisted applications from metropolitan boroughs (which, if successful, would have put themselves on the same level as London and Westminster) and the evidence from other departments did not suggest a

[36]   PRO HO 286/62, 111.
[37]   PRO HO 45/24696; HO 286/62, 69; *Coventry Evening Telegraph*, 1, 2 June 1953.
[38]   PRO HO 286/65.
[39]   Cambridgeshire RO, R101/47, Alan Swift to G.H. Emlyn Jones, town clerk of Derby, 26 Nov. 1954.
[40]   PRO HO 286/67; HLG 43/1195.

pressing case. The town clerk was told not to pursue the matter further.[41] Swansea was unsuccessful again in 1956,[42] and Sunderland in 1957.[43]

Despite Sunderland's latest disappointment, it was clear to the Home Office by the late 1950s that it was one of only two serious candidates for city status among English towns. The other was Southampton. Strutt, now Sir Austin Strutt, must have been embarrassed by the turn of events in 1953. He told town clerk Schofield at some point in 1954 that 'the time is now opportune', and acting on this hint a draft petition was submitted to the Home Office early in 1955. Southampton's population, however, was still below 200,000 and its only hope was that 'all the County Boroughs larger than Southampton have been made Cities so that Southampton might be regarded as the next on the list'.[44] Strutt told Schofield privately on 20 December, in a letter endorsed 'this is for your own eye and is to be destroyed, as I am not putting a copy on the file', that Southampton's case was well thought of in the departments of state, but that 'as you know, we attach importance to maintaining a minimum population limit of 200,000'. The registrar-general's mid-1955 estimate was only 194,000.[45]

Southampton was tantalizingly close, and Norman Schofield's hopes were raised again when the registrar-general's mid-year population estimate for 1957 was 197,300. In June 1958 he wrote to Strutt to ask 'whether you feel that the time has now arrived when Southampton could profitably present a petition for this advanced civic status'.[46] He evidently received an amber light which turned green over the following months, because he prepared a petition which was submitted to the Home Secretary on 13 September.[47]

Strutt made clear within Whitehall his support for the Southampton petition. Writing to Philip Allen at the Ministry of Housing and Local Government on 22 September as part of a round of letters seeking further information about Southampton, he suggested that 'we feel that to all intents and purposes Southampton is on the 200,000 mark, and that a grant now would not really breach the rule'. Unfortunately, Dame Evelyn Sharp, the formidable Permanent Secretary at the Ministry of Housing and Local Government between 1955 and 1966, was less supportive. She was in no doubt that all applications for grants of city status should be put on hold until the local government commission had

---

[41]   PRO HO 286/37.
[42]   PRO HO 286/66.
[43]   PRO HO 286/67.
[44]   PRO HLG 43/1195, M.M. Dobbie to Strutt, 12 Nov. 1955.
[45]   This paragraph is based on correspondence in the SCA bundle, but we know that the 200,000 rule was enforced from information in a Home Office file relating to Sunderland: PRO HO 286/67; HLG 43/1195.
[46]   SCA, Schofield to Strutt, 27 March, 2, 6 June 1958. The trail goes dead after a telephone conversation (noted in the file) between Schofield and Strutt on 10 June.
[47]   SCA, Schofield to heads of department, 7 Aug. 1958, and responses to Schofield's request for redrafted sections of the petition are all in the file, together with a copy of his formal letter to the Home Office on 13 September. Two copies of the petition are in the SCA file.

completed its work.[48] The 1958 Local Government Act set up commissions for England and Wales. The commissions asked local authorities to submit their views about future boundaries, and they then began a series of visits to individual areas to discuss with local people and politicians the way forward. This was an extraordinarily long-winded and inefficient way to proceed, but in respect of city status it gave Whitehall all the ammunition it needed to put applications on hold until the commissions had reported. Southampton was to be the first victim of this process. Quite when Norman Schofield heard of this latest obstacle is not clear, although he warned his heads of department on 2 December that in view of the local government commission's review 'the question of city status is likely to be postponed for some time'.[49]

Schofield was evidently disappointed by this turn of events, and on 21 January 1959 he secured an interview with Dame Evelyn 'in the hope that I may convince her that the granting of this honour will in no way interfere with the consideration by the Boundary Commission'.[50] Following the meeting he was more optimistic. He hoped he had persuaded her that 'the change in the dignity of the town would not affect any of its functions or administration, and, therefore, the Boundary Commission could not possibly be prejudiced by such a change'. He also argued that there seemed every chance that when the Boundary Commission reported on Southampton it would extend rather than contract its boundaries.[51] Dame Evelyn told Strutt on 23 January that while 'it would be awkward to confer city status on a county borough at the present time ... it would not really embarrass the commission'.[52] However, after discussing the matter with her minister, Henry Brooke, she told both Strutt and Schofield that the Ministry of Housing and Local Government was not willing to support the case: 'it will not hurt them to wait for a few years yet, and it is better to defer the title of City until the boundaries are settled'.[53]

Dame Evelyn's veto on Southampton's application appeared to put an end to all city status claims until the apparently interminable local government commission had completed its work, but a new impetus arose in 1963. Grants of city status and lord mayoralties had been regarded as constitutional matters, to be assessed in the Home Office and passed to the monarch only when a case was thought strong enough. Above all, the Home Office liked to believe that the process remained above politics, despite the fact that petitions were often spearheaded by MPs. This potential conflict of interest came to a head in 1963. With a general election looming, and the prospects for the Conservatives looking gloomy in Southampton, John Howard, MP for the Test constituency, sought an

[48]   PRO HLG 43/1195, Sharp to Strutt, 27 Oct. 1958.
[49]   SCA, Schofield to heads of department, 2 Dec. 1958. The letter also rescinded an earlier warning about buying too much (non-city) stationery which might soon be redundant!
[50]   SCA, Schofield to Sir Robert Dempster Perkins, 12 Jan. 1959.
[51]   SCA, Schofield to the mayor of Southampton, 21 Jan. 1959.
[52]   PRO HLG 43/1195, Sharp to Strutt, 23 Jan. 1959.
[53]   PRO HLG 43/1195, Memorandum written by Sharp, 27 Jan. 1959.

interview with the Home Secretary to discuss city status. The town was, he noted, 'the only major seaport which does not enjoy City status', but the sting in the tail of his letter was the suggestion that if it could be conferred within the next twelve months it would 'enhance the standing of the Conservative Party in the town enormously'. Howard suggested that as the government had accepted the need for Southampton to be developed as a seaport, the boundaries commission was more than likely to recommend that its borders should be expanded. As this would give Southampton virtually a cast iron case for city status it made little sense to delay the decision when – in Howard's view – much political good would arise from granting city status in advance of the election. The Home Office accepted the non-political aspects of the argument since 'the population of Southampton is now about 205,000', and 'there is little doubt that, but for local government reorganization, the status would by now have been given to Southampton'.

Dame Evelyn Sharp, however, still ruled at the Ministry of Housing and Local Government, and she could see no reason to depart from the 1959 decision. Furthermore, the Home Secretary was none other than Henry Brooke, who as her minister four years earlier had endorsed the decision to deny Southampton promotion. He met Howard on 18 July 1963, when, to the obvious annoyance of the MP, he insisted on following the civil service line. Howard, with his seat under threat, was ill-disposed to accept Whitehall niceties lying down, and on 31 July he wrote to Brooke insisting that city status would:

> do nothing but good for the Conservative Party.... Believe me, we shall need a bit of goodwill in places like Southampton if we are to have any hope of winning the seat in the next General Election and it really seems pointless to refrain from using the power to confer City status and thus enjoy some immediate popularity, purely on account of an overall "standstill" which, presumably, could be revoked at any time.

Brooke demurred.[54]

Through the summer recess little could be done, but in November 1963 Howard returned to the offensive, writing on the 12th both to the chief whip, Martin Redmayne and, once again, to Henry Brooke. To the chief whip Howard pulled no punches:

> My subsequent enquiries locally have caused me to form the opinion that once again we are the victims of obstruction from the Civil Servants in the Ministry of Housing. The award of City Status to Southampton ... would be of great political significance in the town. My prospects of retaining the seat are not very good because of ... the contraction of the population in the Conservative residential wards.... I do hope we shall look at this question in a politically realistic fashion and not be put off by the attitude of the Civil Servants whose cry is that everything is 'premature'.

[54]   PRO HO 286/63; HLG 43/1195.

Howard said much the same to Brooke: 'this question is fast becoming a local issue and it could well be a decisive factor at the next Election in the Test Division of Southampton. Surely, we cannot afford to risk throwing away seats like this simply to meet the susceptibilities of those responsible for planning Local Government boundaries?' He added that with a Conservative mayor and an election in the offing, 'the award of city status in a year's time as has been suggested in certain quarters, is not the slightest use politically'.

Brooke was uncomfortable. He forwarded Howard's letter to Sir Keith Joseph, the Minister for Housing and Local Government, asking for a definitive judgement, and he assured Redmayne that 'the whole matter has been handled at ministerial level throughout'. Joseph asked his civil servants to review the case. They concluded that it would be another 12–18 months before the commission considered Southampton, and since the town had reached the target population figure of 200,000 already, further delay was difficult to justify.[55] While these deliberations were in progress Redmayne found himself hounded by Howard: he told Brooke on 5 December that 'Howard has asked me three times this week whether I can let him have any news'. On 10 December Howard 'buttonholed' Brooke in the lobby of the House of Commons, and the following day he wrote again to Redmayne urging that everything should be done for Southampton, and in such a manner as 'to ensure that the Conservative Party snatch the credit because this is the main purpose of the operation'.[56]

By now, however, the wheels were turning. On 10 December 1963, Joseph wrote to Brooke to suggest on the basis of his briefing, 'I wonder if we couldn't now change our minds about this. Certainly we here don't now believe that to make Southampton a city would be taken as pre-judging issues between the town and Hampshire when it comes to reorganization.' Brooke, evidently relieved to have had the decision taken out of his hands, accepted Joseph's recommendation.[57] But wheels still had to be turned properly. Howard was asked to suggest to Norman Schofield that he should write to the Home Office asking whether, in view of the changed population figures since 1958, the petition for city status might be reconsidered. Both Howard and Schofield were quite capable of taking a hint, and in the latter's words:

I wish to remind you that Southampton's Petition for City Status was lodged with the Home Office on 13th September 1958. I understand that it has been the view up to the present that before a decision could be reached on the petition the views of the Local Government Commission on the future area and status of Southampton

[55]   The Southampton case in 1963–4 can be pieced together from two PRO files: HO 286/63 which provides the Home Office view, and HLG 43/1195 from which the Ministry of Housing and Local Government's perspective can be gleaned. The crucial memo proposing that the Southampton claim be allowed to proceed was written on the HLG file on 28 November by WMF, and subsequently endorsed by two other civil servants. One was probably Dame Evelyn Sharp, although the initials are obscure.

[56]   PRO HO 286/63.

[57]   Ibid.

should be available. It will obviously be some time yet before the Commission's study and report on the Southampton area will be available. It is felt that it is somewhat unfair to Southampton that this delay should hold back the consideration of the petition. I should be obliged if the position could be reviewed and the petition considered at an early date. It is generally felt locally that the merits of Southampton shown in the petition of 1958 are more valid today than in 1958, and that awaiting the views of the Local Government Commission are not really necessary.[58]

On 21 January R.J. Guppy wrote to him from the Home Office to say that 'it would be wrong to defer action any longer'. The Home Secretary, he added, 'proposes to resume consideration of the petition'. The petition, as amended, was approved by the Queen on 26 January 1964.[59]

Meantime Howard, having achieved his first aim, was anxious to ensure that he and his Conservative friends in Southampton were able to derive the maximum political capital from the elevation. He told Brooke on 24 January, 'It would be helpful if credit for this matter could accrue to me and the Conservative Party and it may be that a Parliamentary Question at a strategic moment would establish this point'. Celebrations, he added, ought to be timed to occur within the term of office of the serving mayor (Alderman Ronald Pugh), and it would help if he could crown his year of service with a knighthood. The civil servants, having lost the political battle, at least won the constitutional war. Brooke agreed that despite Howard's pleas the normal practice should be followed with a letter to the mayor announcing the grant and with information given to the press to appear simultaneously with the letter. The date fixed upon was 11 February 1964.[60] The same day Dame Evelyn Sharp wrote to Schofield, 'I am delighted to learn that The Queen has approved that the Town of Southampton shall be raised to the title and dignity of a City'. Schofield responded: 'our new status has already set off a wave of good feeling in the City'.[61] Everyone was delighted, including Howard, because the Conservatives held Southampton Test in 1964.[62]

Nothing can have surprised Home Office civil servants less than the arrival two months after the Southampton announcement in 1964 of a further application from Wearside. In August 1957 Sunderland had submitted a draft petition, hoping that 'the population requirement of 200,000 (minimum) ought not to be the deciding factor in an application for City status (without Lord Mayor)'. The Home Office canvassed the departments of state, but most of the

---

[58]   SCA, Schofield to Under Secretary of State, Home Office, 8 Jan. 1964. This is the copy of the original, which is in PRO HO 286/63.

[59]   PRO HO 286/63.

[60]   Ibid.

[61]   SRA, Sharp to Schofield, 11 Feb. 1964; PRO HLG 43/1195.

[62]   Howard had held the seat since 1959 when he was returned with a majority of 6,766 over the Labour candidate. Perhaps surprisingly in view of his enthusiasm for city status he did not stand in 1964. His successor, Sir J. Fletcher-Cooke, was returned but with a majority of just 348. When a Liberal candidate stood in 1966 he split the vote, and R.C. Mitchell, unsuccessful for Labour in 1964, was returned.

replies were negative: 'on the inland transport side and the shipping side, there are no circumstances which would justify us in supporting the proposed petition', wrote the Ministry of Transport. According to the Ministry of Health, there was 'nothing outstanding about the services provided by the council under the Public Health Acts, the National Health Service and National Assistance Acts.... A fair summary of the position would be to say that they are neither very good nor very bad.' 'Sunderland's performance in the educational field is undistinguished ... we could not seriously support any suggestion that a favourable recommendation would be appropriate', wrote the Ministry of Education. Finally, from within the Home Office came a memo to the effect that 'The Sunderland police force was inspected in February of this year and was found to be efficient but there is no mention in the inspection report of any exceptional features which would strengthen the case for City status'. In November the application was rejected, and when the mayor and town clerk visited the Home Office they were told only that 'in a prerogative matter of this kind no Minister ever gave the reasons for the advice which he would, or would not, tender to the Sovereign'. The mayor was told that he could pursue the case if he had additional information. In February 1958 he submitted a letter containing some new matter on Sunderland as a centre of trade and industry, which he thought should be considered. It was not sufficient: the application was turned down on 4 March 1958.[63]

Sunderland tried again in 1962, noting that its current population of 190,000 was about to rise to around 218,000 once the Boundary Commission's recommendations were implemented. The Home Office recognized that this development might alter its position, but no action followed.[64] Southampton's success in 1964, despite the ongoing boundary review, stirred Sunderland once again. Local government officials asked for a copy of Southampton's petition and any other advice the southern port could offer. Sunderland felt that its claims were now materially stronger than on previous occasions. It cited as evidence in its favour the housing programme, spending on education and the arts, the new Civic Centre to be designed by Sir Basil Spence – itself a sign of the town's desire for self-promotion – shipbuilding and other thriving industries, redevelopment, the civic theatre, and the fact that 'Sunderland is a town of distinctive character and there is no question of it being absorbed into Tyneside or Teesside Conurbations'. Internally, the Home Office accepted that following the Southampton grant Sunderland 'heads the queue', and that 'there would probably be no embarrassing repercussions if the grant were to be made to Sunderland'. In the end, however, it refused the application on the usual grounds that no decisions could be taken until the review of local government in the area had been completed.[65]

63   PRO HO 286/67.
64   Ibid.
65   Ibid.

The review was still in progress when Labour came to power in 1964. Richard Crossman, the new Minister of Housing and Local Government, quickly became concerned that extensions of county borough areas often included the incorporation of 'residential' (Conservative) suburbs, which was likely to endanger the slim Labour majority. Although Dame Evelyn Sharp urged him to leave the commission to its work, in September 1965 – while she was on holiday – he told the Association of Municipal Corporations meeting in Torquay that he was going to appoint a new commission to examine the structure of local government. Dame Evelyn, who retired in 1966 and became a life peeress, was appointed to what became known as the Redcliffe-Maud commission. Meantime the old commission went out of business, having achieved a series of alterations to boundaries across the country which, in terms of city status, altered the rules of engagement because a number of substantial conurbations rose well above the 200,000 mark.[66]

The consequences were soon clear. Croydon renewed its application in 1965 after it was joined with Coulsdon and Purley and had, as a result, a population of 327,000. To the Home Office this was striking evidence that they had been right all along, since the figures 'only confirm the previously held belief that Croydon is a dormitory with few of the essential characteristics necessary to the grant of city status'. Soundings were taken with other Whitehall departments, but the results were not encouraging and early in 1966 the application was rejected.[67] When local government reorganization came into effect in Wolverhampton on 1 April 1966, the borough boundaries were extended with the effect of increasing the population from 150,000 to 267,000. A month later the town clerk wrote informally to the Home Office asking 'in strict confidence, as before [1953], what would be our prospects if we were minded to petition'. The Home Office treated his enquiry as an application and took the usual soundings. Wolverhampton's case for efficiency in local government was not helped when a major overspend on a new inner ring road was reported at length in the *Daily Telegraph* on 23 and 24 May 1966. It was also up against the problem of establishing its 'individual character':

> it can no more be judged as a centre for South Staffordshire than can Croydon as a centre for North East Surrey. Like Croydon it has a certain individuality – more perhaps than Walsall, Warley or West Bromwich, but scarcely more than Dudley, but its claims are not sharply distinguishable. On the Croydon precedent I do not see how an application could be entertained.[68]

Far more damaging to its case was the reaction of Winifrid Fox, who had succeeded Dame Evelyn Sharp at the Ministry of Housing and Local Government. She was unhappy about handling individual cases when the

---

[66]   B. Keith-Lucas, and P.G. Richards, *A History of Local Government in the Twentieth Century* (1978), 209–12.
[67]   PRO HO 286/65.
[68]   PRO HO 286/111.

overall picture remained unclear. Her research showed that Sunderland would have a population of 221,000 after it was extended on 1 April 1967, Derby 217,000 as of 1 April 1968, and the new county borough of Teesside 386,000 as of the same date. Fox was also aware that the Redcliffe-Maud proposals were just around the corner:

> On the whole the feeling here is that it would be preferable for no further grants of city status to be considered until the Royal Commission [Redcliffe-Maud] have reported. With the future structure of local government so much in doubt it might prove a mistake to do anything in this interim period which might intensify resistance to change.[69]

These words sounded suspiciously similar to those of Dame Evelyn in 1959, since they counselled a do-nothing policy while boundary changes were being considered, but the Home Office was happy to take the hint and on 23 November 1966 the town clerk of Wolverhampton was told that 'an application made in the present state of uncertainty about local government would have little chance of success'.[70]

No such easy get-out was available in respect of Sunderland once the extension took effect on 1 April 1967, and this was certainly what the town clerk thought when on 27 June he called at the Home Office to ask whether Sunderland was now entitled to city status. He coupled the argument with a claim that the county borough had a reputation for efficiency and that the town 'was truly the centre of the area in which it stood'. The Home Office continued to stonewall. Winifrid Fox's view had prevailed, and no further grants, he was told, could be made while the Royal Commission was still sitting. Perhaps not surprisingly, the town clerk then asked whether, if there was to be a standstill in the making of cities, Sunderland could be at the front of the queue should decisions by the commission prove consistent with further creations. The Home Office would make no promises, pointing out that population shifts meant that Sunderland was not alone in the field now. The town clerk left, the civil servants recorded, 'with some disappointment'.[71] In retrospect he had every reason to be unhappy: Sunderland would have to wait a further twenty-five years.

The complexity and confusion involved in local government reform in the 1960s was predominantly an English question. The boundary commission established for Wales in 1958 reported as early as May 1961, and provided the background against which Swansea returned to the hunt for city status. In January 1967 Swansea's two MPs, Neil McBride and Alan Williams, approached the Home Secretary, Roy Jenkins:

[69]	PRO HO 286/65.
[70]	PRO HO 286/111.
[71]	PRO HO 286/66, 67.

> Sometime in the near future, HRH Prince Charles will be presented to the people of the Principality as the Prince of Wales and we feel that in according this matter of distinction to Wales, that in addition, Her Majesty may be graciously pleased to mark this auspicious occasion by according a further mark of distinction by the according of City Status to the County Borough of Swansea, and we further believe that this would render formal approval of the widely held view that Swansea is the Second City of Wales.[72]

For the moment this cut no ice with the Home Office, and in July 1967 the White Paper on local government reform in Wales proposed that there should be no changes as far as Swansea was concerned. This appeared to leave the town out in the cold, since its population was only 171,000. The Home Office, as ever, was concerned that to offer promotion to Swansea, when several English towns had greater populations, could not be justified 'without raising a whole host of consequential and embarrassing claims from other places, many of which are likely to be larger'.[73]

McBride and Williams were unwilling to be put off. They returned to the Home Office late in 1968 to re-state the case for Swansea being created a city. It cannot have been to the town's disadvantage that the Home Secretary was now the Cardiff MP James Callaghan.[74] He asked the civil servants to draw up a paper on the subject, but it was clear that Swansea would not meet the population criteria, so a case had to be made on other grounds:

> Population aside, the requirement is that to qualify a place must be of the first rank in dignity and importance, preferably having the position of a metropolis in its own neighbourhood. On this test it has always seemed to me that Swansea's claims are unusually strong. In Wales it is second only to Cardiff (which is already a City) in general size and importance, and it has far more of the character of a metropolis than many larger towns in England. It is, in fact, the indisputable centre for a very large area of south-west Wales. If it were judged in the context of Wales rather than that of England and Wales together, and on the scale of population in Wales, its claims would be very difficult to resist. And with the growth of national sentiment, that is a standard to which, I believe, we must have increasing regard. It may not be easy to continue to justify a situation in which in the whole of Wales there is only a single city.... If there is to be a second city in Wales then Swansea must, I believe, be the choice.... It would, it seems to me, be entirely fitting to confer this honour upon Swansea in association with the forthcoming Investiture of the Prince of Wales. Not only, I suggest would the recognition be particularly

---

[72]   PRO HO 286/66.

[73]   Ibid.

[74]   The Swansea case is referred to in neither Callaghan's memoirs, *Time and Chance* (1987) nor his official biography, Kenneth O. Morgan, *Callaghan: A Life* (Oxford, 1999 edn.), but in private correspondence Callaghan recalled that in his view 'the case was fairly straightforward' and that he was happy to support it: letter to the author 25 Jan. 2000. Callaghan had been approached about a possible move to become member for Swansea East in the early 1960s.

appreciated in that context, but it would help to mark off the occasion in such a way as to minimize the danger of repercussions among places in England.

This was classic Home Office speak: the case for Swansea would have to be put in terms of the exceptional situation arising from the forthcoming Investiture, in order to ensure that it was not regarded as a precedent by larger English towns. As a result, the Home Office now put its weight behind the Swansea request. A further endorsement of the file on 18 March noted:

> I think that Swansea has a good case on the criteria that have been applied in the past and that there is appropriateness in conferring this civic honour at the time of the investiture of the Prince of Wales (though I suppose that the grant of City status to Swansea would not necessarily give pleasure in Cardiff or elsewhere in Wales).[75]

On 15 April 1969 the Home Secretary wrote to George Thomas, Secretary of State for Wales, and Anthony Greenwood, Minister of Housing and Local Government. He was well aware of the growth of nationalist sentiment following Gwynfor Evans's election for Carmarthen in 1966 and strong Plaid Cymru showing in by-elections in the Rhondda (1967) and Caerphilly (1968). Consequently, he was now willing to consider the case for granting Swansea city status in conjunction with the investiture. Thomas supported the proposal, but Greenwood was more circumspect, fearing 'irresistible claims' from larger English towns. The three ministers quickly became entangled in a dispute. For the Home Office, the Swansea proposal was to be seen entirely in the light of the investiture so that the grant 'would thus not affect in any way the claims of English cities, which would still fall to be dealt with under established policy'. Greenwood stood his ground, arguing that Swansea should not be treated as a special case simply because it was in Wales. The Home Office, pressed by George Thomas, wanted to reject Greenwood's viewpoint on the basis that Swansea's standing in Wales:

> is a good deal higher than that of larger cities in England ... it is at least arguable that with the growth of nationalist sentiment the arithmetical criteria applied ought to be adapted to take account of the smaller scale of Welsh affairs ... the investiture plays a part which makes it particularly appropriate to make a gesture of this kind to Wales at the present time.

Callaghan's civil servants advised him to overrule Greenwood, but he was reluctant, arguing that his colleague's objections had some 'force in them. We should face the fact that if Swansea is made a city there will be some discontent among English aspirants.' In the end Callaghan, who was as wary of Welsh nationalist resurgence as was Thomas, accepted their advice, and wrote on 11

---

[75]   PRO HO 286/66.

June to Greenwood to say that the Home Office would proceed with the recommendation:

> In my view the claim of Swansea is justified by the two-fold consideration that Wales has at present only one city compared with six in Scotland and 48 in England – a distribution which does not reflect national populations – and, notwithstanding your comment on timing, the occasion of the Investiture does provide an opportunity to redress this imbalance which will not re-occur. Considered in this light, I think that the grant of 'City' status to Swansea can be regarded as taking into account the special circumstances of Wales – where the different scale of affairs justifies an adjustment of what must always be somewhat arbitrary population criteria – and need not be regarded as involving any implications for other English towns. Moreover, as regards timing, the fact that the Royal Commission report will only just have appeared will make it possible to demonstrate more clearly that the decision is related to the Investiture, and has been taken without regard to the possible future pattern of local government in England and Wales, the details of which are unlikely to be decided for some time.[76]

It was left to the Welsh to decide whether or not to view Swansea's promotion in relation to the nationalist movement, which peaked around 1969.[77]

From this point onwards there could be no going back. On 17 June the Queen's private secretary, Sir Michael Adeane, was asked to obtain Her Majesty's consent, which she gave by letter from Windsor two days later, and on 23 June, the prime minister, Harold Wilson, signalled his assent. Greenwood was still unhappy, and wrote directly to Wilson on 24 June complaining that the proposed grant to Swansea would damage the ongoing work of the Royal Commission examining the future of local government in England and Wales: 'It is for this reason that I thought, and still think, it would be untimely to give Swansea the title of city at this particular juncture. I would much prefer the whole question of city status to be reconsidered in the light of whatever local government changes are ultimately introduced in the three countries.' Wilson chose to take no action.[78]

At this juncture the Home Office became concerned that, as the case for Swansea had been masterminded by the two MPs, the civic authorities had not been consulted. In view of the number of occasions in the past when the town clerk, supported by the corporation, had pressed for Swansea's elevation, this was a remarkable turnaround. To make sure there would be no embarrassment, on 25 June Callaghan spoke in confidence to the mayor of Swansea and was assured 'that the proposed City status will be welcomed by the Council'. Prince Charles was to be invested as Prince of Wales by the Queen at

---

[76]   PRO, PREM 13/3033. In this, and previous quotations, reference is made to there being only one city in Wales (meaning Cardiff). In fact, Bangor held city status by ancient prescriptive right as a cathedral city.

[77]   John Davies, *A History of Wales* (Cardiff, 1993), 662–71.

[78]   PRO, PREM 13/3033.

Caernarfon Castle on 1 July 1969, and then to embark on a tour of Wales. He was due in Swansea on 3 July, and it was arranged that he would make the announcement during his visit to the Guildhall on that occasion.[79] No prior information was given to the press, so the announcement came as a complete surprise to all but a handful of people who had been informed in advance. On the same day, the Home Office wrote to the mayor of Swansea announcing the promotion.[80]

Swansea was still not satisfied. Normal practice was for the formal announcement of the conferment of city status on a town to be followed by the dispatch of letters patent. Swansea, however, wanted to make something more of the grant than simply receiving a communication through the post. The new city wanted nothing less than a return visit from the Prince of Wales, and suggested that there should be a formal ceremony on 31 October. The Prince was less enamoured of the idea than the people of Swansea, and when his equerry suggested that he did not need to attend he happily wrote 'I agree' on the memorandum. As a result, on 13 August the Prince of Wales's office informed Swansea that the proposed date of 31 October was not convenient because Prince Charles would be back at Cambridge University, where he was currently a student, studying for his final examinations. Rather than take no for an answer, the town clerk, Iorwerth Watkins, responded on 3 September offering to change the date to the university vacation. Still without a great deal of enthusiasm, the prince responded that 'I suppose I could do it sometime in week beginning 15th December'. He proposed a short 'flying visit' on Monday, 15 December.[81]

On 15 December Prince Charles flew to Swansea for the official handing over of the letters patent at the Guildhall. In the presence of James Callaghan, the Home Secretary, George Thomas, the Secretary of State for Wales, and Colonel Sir Cennydd Traherne, the lord lieutenant of Glamorgan, he handed the document to the mayor of Swansea, Councillor David Bevan. Perhaps it was a reflection of his reluctance to make the trip in the first place that he was reported the following day as having passed the letters patent to the mayor with the quip 'I entrust this charter to the Mayor and hope that he will look after it as well as possible. All I say is, if he loses it, he is unlikely to get another one.'[82] Subsequently, 700 invited guests joined the Prince for lunch at the University College of Swansea – vast numbers of people applied for tickets[83] – and the

---

[79]   PRO HO 286/131.

[80]   Council Minutes (printed copy in West Glamorgan Archive Service, Swansea).

[81]   Checketts wrote to Sir Cennydd Traherne at Buckingham Palace on 20 October to say that 'The Prince of Wales tells me that he succumbed to a fierce attack about Swansea', and has now said that he is prepared to consider a short 'flying' visit on Monday 15 December: PRO, HO 286/131.

[82]   *Daily Telegraph*, 16 Dec. 1969 (including a picture); *Guardian*, 16 Dec. 1969; *Municipal Review*, 40 (1969), 371.

[83]   West Glamorgan Archive Service, Swansea, TC.54/8700. I am grateful for help with the Swansea case from Professor David Howell, Professor Kenneth Morgan, and Mrs Wilma Thomas.

25,000 schoolchildren given the day off their studies by way of celebration doubtless also enjoyed themselves.[84]

While city status has been sought by numerous towns during the present reign, interest in the lord mayoralty has been less marked since Coventry was successful at the coronation in 1953. Among the handful of successes has been Oxford, where the search for a lord mayoralty began in 1956, but was considered not to be a realistic possibility at that time. It was raised again by the town clerk (Harry Plowman) in a letter to the Queen's assistant private secretary Sir Edward Ford in July 1960, asking that the honour should be granted in conjunction with a forthcoming royal visit:

> It will, of course, be said that this would be contrary to modern precedent as the population of the City is considerably below the current standard for the purpose but the City qualifies on all other counts as being the County Town and the natural centre of a considerable surrounding area, an education centre known the world over, an industrial City of considerable importance to the export trade, and a City whose Council can show a good record of administration.

Ford sent the letter on to the Home Office, which rejected the application: 'on the principles on which the Sovereign has been pleased to create Lord Mayors during the course of the present century there is no case at all for a grant of this dignity to the Mayor of Oxford'. Nothing further was done until 1962 when, with prime minister Harold Macmillan as chancellor of the university, the city council thought a further application might succeed. Macmillan himself was happy to see the claim proceed, and the relevant departments of state all viewed Oxford's situation favourably. The Home Office had to admit defeat: 'it cannot be contested that Oxford has a history and associations which give it a special place among English cities; and it might not be impossible to treat it as a special case and defend ourselves against attacks from cities other than Cambridge'. The Queen gave her approval in September 1962, and the announcement was made in October.[85]

When Westminster applied for a lord mayoralty in November 1965 the main objections within the Home Office concerned the likely knock-on effect elsewhere in London. There was opposition from the City of London, described by a civil servant as 'entirely emotional. The special position of the City and the Lord Mayor of London is in no way affected by the conferment of the title of Lord Mayor on the Mayor of Westminster.' Other concerns related to Croydon, which submitted a claim for city status almost simultaneously, but the Home Office thought it could handle that particular problem:

> Westminster can fairly be distinguished from Croydon and other London boroughs; for one thing it has been a city for over four hundred years. Nevertheless the conferment of Lord Mayor's status on Westminster would

84   *South Wales Echo*, 15 Dec. 1969.
85   PRO HO 286/70.

make the rejection of Croydon's claim for city status more unpalatable and might well have the effect of causing Croydon, and perhaps other London boroughs, to press their claims more strongly.

Even the Queen had concerns. Through her private secretary, Sir Michael Adeane, she told the Home Office that she approved of the Secretary of State's submission, but that 'in doing so there were clearly some doubts lingering in her mind. She said "I suppose it is right to have two Lord Mayors in London?" and she would certainly be sorry if, for example, the elevation of the Mayor of Westminster were to lead to any sort of protest by the Lord Mayor of London.' The Home Office had no doubts, and after consulting the various departments of state the town clerk was told on 10 March 1966 that the petition had been successful.[86]

In other cases the link between a lord mayoralty and city status has proved hardly worth pursuing. Southampton applied in 1967 when the town clerk wrote to the Home Office:

I understand that in the past it has been the custom to wait for a few years after the grant of City status before the grant of 'Lord Mayor'. I feel that Southampton has justified the grant of City status. It has a very good administration, has fallen into line with Government policy ... [it] is being rapidly modernized and developed and has completely recovered from the ravages of the last war.

The reply was an emphatic rejection on the grounds that it had simply not waited long enough:

it would be most unusual for this privilege to be conferred on a city within so short a period of its achieving city status. There are other cities, of older standing, which still do not enjoy this additional recognition. We have considered whether there are circumstances here which would warrant an exceptional step being taken in respect of Southampton, but I am sorry to say that we have been forced to the conclusion that the time has not yet come when the Home Secretary would be justified in recommending this distinction.

No doubt someone pointed out that neighbouring Portsmouth had received a lord mayoralty only two years after being created a city, but the Home Office was keen to emphasize that this was:

considered altogether exceptional and was mainly the result of the Lord Lieutenant of Hampshire's having secured somewhat unconstitutionally the ear of the King's Private Secretary. Plymouth had to wait seven years and then the grant, after years of continued pressing, was made on the special occasion of the Royal Jubilee and because of the personal interest of the Prince of Wales as

[86]   PRO HO 286/108.

High Steward. Birmingham waited eight years and Salford has not, in spite of repeated pressure, yet been granted this additional honour.[87]

The application made no further progress.

At the coronation in 1953 several industrial cities sought to distance themselves from their lesser neighbours by adopting the style 'right honourable' for their lord mayor. Sir Robert Cary, MP, approached the Home Secretary, Sir David Maxwell Fyfe, in April 1953. He wondered:

> whether the privilege might be granted to Liverpool, Manchester and Birmingham as a Coronation Honour on the ground that these three cities are the next three in importance? As a matter of past history I believe it is rather a sore point that Manchester assumed the prefix of 'Right Honourable' many years ago as a result of a ruling from the Garter King of Arms, but a little while before the last war the Home Office intervened in the case of Liverpool and told them that they were not entitled to use this prefix. Liverpool, Manchester and Birmingham have ceased to use it.[88]

After some deliberation, the Home Office decided that this was an honour too far: 'London and York are cities with great and long histories. Birmingham has no real history before the last 150 years ago or so: Manchester and Liverpool are much older but their real importance dates from the days of the Industrial Revolution.' In these circumstances, the Home Secretary told the town clerks of Manchester and Birmingham 'bluntly that there is no likelihood of any such civic honour being conferred on any Lord Mayor and have told them not to submit petitions even in draft. To contemplate three grants at one time is fantastic, the currency would be irretrievably debased.' The Home Secretary also told Cary of the outcome.[89] However, the style was conferred on the lord mayor of Cardiff in 1956 in order to distinguish it as the capital of Wales. When the Home Secretary (Gwilym Lloyd-George) visited on 26 October to be made an honorary freeman he made the announcement at the city hall.[90]

City status went through various changes in the post-war years. Initially, the Home Office held the line as it had always done, resisting claimants with a population lower than 200,000. Southampton, the strongest candidate, succeeded in 1964, but with a political link which was resented in the Home Office. By then the whole process of granting city status had fallen foul of the protracted business of local government reorganization. As a result, the Home Office was faced with enforcing a population rule (200,000) which was likely to be achieved by reorganization rather than natural growth, and in the process

---

[87] Ibid.

[88] Cary is referring here to the exchange of 1927: see Chapter 4.

[89] PRO HO 286/71.

[90] PRO HO 286/41. Canterbury was told in 1988 that the grant of a lord mayoralty did not include the prefix Right Honourable, which is a separate grant given only in exceptional circumstances: Canterbury Cathedral Archives, CC\A\AA65.

to upset the natural order of succession. The possibility of personal opinion swaying a particular case was reduced by the developing practice of responding to city status claims by an audit of local government in the applicant town. In the words of an internal memo written in the Home Office Constitutional Unit in 1959:

> The Home Secretary, as a general rule, only recommends the grant of the dignity of City to towns of the first rank in respect of size, services and general importance. It is not given on account of population alone, although one of the requirements is a population of 200,000. To qualify for the rank of City a town should be not a mere formless collection of people but a place of outstanding importance, having the position of a metropolis in its own neighbourhood; at any rate with a character and identity of its own. The Home Secretary has regard to the record of the authority in the field of local government and for that purpose, he consults Education, Transport and Health, as well as [Housing and Local Government].[91]

In theory this assessment process had two further benefits. First, it enabled the myth to be maintained that the fount of all honours remained the Crown, and this meant that special dispensations could be made for towns with royal credentials such as Cambridge. Second, it suggested that however strongly local politicians might be tempted to press for city status, the checks and balances were such that success could be achieved only if hurdles were successfully cleared. For all the efforts in Whitehall, this distinction gradually started to unravel in the 1960s. Southampton may have had an excellent case for promotion but the final hurdle was undoubtedly cleared as a result of political pressure. In an attempt to prevent a repeat of what it clearly regarded as an unfortunate precedent, the Home Office fought to link honours to royal occasions in the hope of restoring the political neutrality of previous grants. It managed to push Swansea past the winning post in 1969 on the coat tails of the Prince of Wales's investiture, but even so no one could have much doubt that worries about the Welsh Nationalists played a significant role in making up political minds.

---

[91]   PRO HLG 43/1195, Sir Austin Strutt to Dame Evelyn Sharp, 23 Jan. 1959.

CHAPTER SIX

Boosting the Town, Selling the City, 1970–2000

Over the past thirty or so years, the competition for city status has grown out of all proportion to anything that had gone before, and it has done so within the context of new ways of thinking about the roles of cities. Promoting an image takes us back to the inter-war years, but since 1970 town councils the length and breadth of the United Kingdom have come to recognize that 'city' is a title which is worthwhile having despite its lack of tangible benefits. Since the grant of city status to Swansea in 1969, the Home Office has sought to avoid the embarrassment of political intervention by ensuring that promotions take place only in conjunction with royal events. In this process it has been aided by the present Queen's longevity, using the jubilees of 1977, 1992 and 2002 as promotion opportunities and usually refusing claims at other times (except for the millennium year, 2000). It has also introduced an element of competition, both for city status and lord mayoralties. Nine towns sought promotion in 1977, but 23 in 1992, 39 in 2000, and 41 in 2002. Applications for lord mayoralties have risen from five in 1977 to nine in 1992, and to 17 in 2002. So important has the 'city' image become that the Home Office even used the millennium as a non-royal but national event to run a competition, and on that occasion the infighting was of such intensity that final decisions were taken in 10 Downing Street. We shall come to the 2000 and 2002 competitions in Chapters 7 and 8, but the growing need to sell cities in the years since 1970 has brought with it a queue for honours which in its wake has provoked political intervention on a new level. In this chapter we look at how the search for city status moved decisively into the promotional arena in conjunction with convenient royal events, and in the next two chapters we examine the consequent results in terms of modern competitiveness.

Until the 1970s the Home Office was able to implement with reasonable efficiency its checklist of qualifications for city status. It had been bounced into making Southampton a city, but this was hardly a significant precedent, given that it was acknowledged to be the next candidate in the pecking order. Developments in England between 1970 and 1974 altered the position. The 1950s and 1960s had seen long and inconclusive discussions about the future of English local government. In 1969 the Labour government accepted the Redcliffe-Maud reform proposals, but these had yet to be implemented when the 1970 general election saw the return of a Conservative administration. Almost immediately a further enquiry was ordered, and under the terms of the

1972 Local Government Act a new administrative order was introduced on 1 April 1974.

The most significant impact of the 1974 reforms was on county boroughs. In many respects, the Conservatives' scheme was accepted because everyone knew change was needed. The proposals looked rather less radical than the Redcliffe-Maud scheme. County boroughs due to be merged into adjacent counties and lose their responsibilities for major spending areas such as education and social services inevitably complained, but since many were Labour-run the Conservative government was able to ignored their protests.[1] What about city status in this new context? The Home Office could no longer use the excuse of forthcoming local government reform to stall on promotions, but it was also faced with potential claims from 'a greatly enlarged set of urban authorities with populations over 200,000, i.e. the Metropolitan districts ... some of these have been big towns in their own right for many years, even centuries'.[2] At the other end of the scale, because the 1972 Local Government Act abolished many of the prerogative titles previously enjoyed by some local authorities, doubts were raised as to whether all the existing cities retained or even ought to retain their status in the newly reformed world of local government.

Early in 1976 when plans were being drawn up to celebrate the Queen's Silver Jubilee due in 1977, the Home Office approached Buckingham Palace with the suggestion that one of the ways of marking the occasion would be through a grant of city status. When the Queen indicated her assent to this particular proposal, the Home Office began sounding out potential candidates and assessing their qualifications.[3] In total, nine candidates were identified: Blackburn, Brighton, Croydon, Derby, Dudley, Newport, Sandwell, Sunderland and Wolverhampton. Most, but not all, satisfied the Home Office's minimum qualification of a 200,000 population, but they failed the test of being 'the acknowledged cultural and commercial centre of the surrounding area ... with a character and identity of its own'. Blackburn was too small (142,000), and its application was 'based on its being the only cathedral town in the present county of Lancashire', which ensured that it did not have 'a sufficiently strong case ... to put it among the leading contenders'. Brighton 'occupies a central position within the surrounding area', and could be regarded as a cultural centre with a developing international conference trade, 'but it has a population of only 160,000 and ... Brighton's smallness considerably weakens its case.' Croydon's case was considered to be weaker 'since the reorganisation of London government', and it was dismissed as

---

[1]   B. Keith-Lucas, and P.G. Richards, *A History of Local Government in the Twentieth Century* (1978), 224-30.

[2]   PRO HLG 120/1714, C.J. Pearce to R.F.D. Shuffrey, 22 March 1976.

[3]   PRO HO 286/126, R.F.D. Shuffrey to Sir Philip Moore, 3 Aug. 1976, 4 Jan. 1977.

'essentially a part of Greater London'. Dudley lacked 'the individuality and character which would merit its elevation to city status', and it met the population criterion only because of the addition at local government reorganization of two boroughs in the former borough of Dudley, which previously had a population of only 190,000. Newport was disqualified by the recent elevation of Swansea, and the Metropolitan Borough of Sandwell – a late entrant – was simply 'a product of urban amalgamation' which had 'scarcely had time to acquire a distinct character and identity'. That left Derby, Sunderland and Wolverhampton.[4]

Sunderland had, of course, long had its hat in the ring. Derby had been interested in city status periodically since 1908, and Wolverhampton, had been anxious to acquire the status since at least the 1950s.[5] Derby applied formally when it became a diocesan see in 1927, but it had no realistic hope of success while its population remained below 200,000; indeed, having reached 142,403 in the 1931 census, Derby's numbers declined to 132,325 in 1961. Initially, no-one in Derby seems to have noticed the potential significance of the 1968 boundary reorganization for the town's hopes of city status, which increased its population to 218,000. Local pride was roused when the terms of the 1972 Local Government Act proposed that the town should be demoted to the status of a District Council. Gerald Toft Andrews, who was a Conservative councillor 1968-72, had the idea that the reduction in standing might be compensated by the award of city status.[6] Andrews sounded out local councillors to see if there was any enthusiasm for an application, but he quickly came to the conclusion that the political climate in the ruling Labour group was unsuitable. In 1975 he submitted a private application to the Home Office, but he was told he needed the backing of Derby District Council. Ernest Preston, the borough secretary, was not encouraging: 'with regard to the question of city status, all that I can say is that this is not a matter presently under consideration by the Council'.[7] However, the Conservatives returned to power in Derby at the local government elections on 6 May 1976. Gerald Andrews was among their successful candidates, and the first meeting of the new General Purposes Committee on 26 May 1976 agreed to promote an application for city status in conjunction with the Queen's Silver Jubilee in 1977. The petition was sent to the Home Office on 15 July with the

[4]   PRO HO 286/126, Annex, 'Silver Jubilee, City Status'.
[5]   PRO HLG 120/1714, N.S. Fisher to the Home Office, 18 July 1972; J.E. Hannigan to C.J. Pearce, 14 Feb. 1973.
[6]   Much of the following is based on Andrews's own account of the quest for city status, drawn up following the presentation of letters patent in 1977, and now held in Derby Council House. I am grateful to Philip O'Brien for making the material available to me.
[7]   Andrews MSS, A.P. Wilson to G.T. Andrews, 4 Feb. 1974; P.R.A. Fulton to Andrews, 24 March 1975; Sir Philip Moore to Andrews, 24 March 1975; A.J. Butler to Andrews, 28 May 1975; Andrews to Derby Borough Council, 5 June 1976; Ernest Preston to Andrews, 13 June, 20 Nov. 1975.

general support of trade and commerce, and only the Trades Union Council actively dissenting.[8]

By late November 1976 the Home Office had considered the various candidates, and 'after considering their respective merits', the Home Secretary, Merlyn Rees, put forward Derby for the grant of city status. Its success was explained on the grounds that 'it was the largest non-metropolitan district which is not already a city'. Croydon, Dudley, Sunderland and Wolverhampton were all ruled out because they satisfied the population criterion, but had recently been moved into metropolitan counties. Wolverhampton had also failed to convince the Home Office that it was especially distinctive within the West Midlands conurbation, while Sunderland, having been denied promotion because of local government reorganization, now fell foul of the new order: 'it is perhaps too soon after local government reorganisation, and the incorporation of the county borough into the metropolitan county of Tyne and Wear, to justify a favourable recommendation at this stage'. The proposal in favour of Derby went first to the Department of the Environment, and with the approval of the Secretary of State, was submitted to the Queen for formal ratification early in 1977. Derby's case was considered to be 'stronger than that of any of the other aspirants', although the Home Office recommendation smacked more of it being the least worse candidate than the outstanding favourite. In the words of the memorandum assessing the candidates:

> With a population of 218,000 it is now the largest non-metropolitan district which is not already a city. Its nearest rival in this sense is Luton with a population of only 164,000. The grant of city status to Derby should, therefore, cause little legitimate dissatisfaction amongst the other non-metropolitan aspirants. But Derby's merits are not wholly negative and a reasonable, if not overwhelming, case can be made for honouring it on the grounds of its antiquity and size – which reflects its industrial importance – and as (since 1927) the seat of a Bishopric. In themselves none of these points would be conclusive. Taken together, they amount to a case which appears to be stronger than that of any of the other aspirants.[9]

Proposals that the jubilee should be marked by the grant of a lord mayoralty were not taken further. Canterbury, Chester, Salford, Southampton and Swansea all applied, but none were considered to be 'based on any particularly outstanding claims', and since Southampton and Swansea were the last two towns to be granted city status they did not 'merit a further honour at this stage', and no grant was made. The Queen, not unexpectedly, accepted the various

---

[8]   PRO HO 286/126, Ernest Preston to Colin Thursby, 15 July 1976.

[9]   PRO HO 286/126, Merlyn Rees to Peter Shore, 26 Nov. 1976 (draft, the original is in PRO HLG 120/1714); Shore to Rees, 8 Dec. 1976; Shuffrey to Moore, 4 Jan. 1977; 'Annex' for the description of Derby.

recommendations,[10] and the grant of city status to Derby was announced on the day of the jubilee, 7 June 1977: Derby was to have city status 'to mark Her Majesty's Silver Jubilee', and the Queen would herself present the letters patent when she visited the new city on 28 July as part of her jubilee tour.[11]

The obvious loser in 1977 was Sunderland, which had previously been considered second in the pecking order behind Southampton. Now it had been overtaken by Derby, simply as a result of boundary changes.[12] The decision highlighted the arbitrary nature of the process when boundary changes could catapult individual towns to the head of the queue. Sunderland applied for promotion in 1982 as the Queen celebrated thirty years on the throne, but no cities were made on that occasion. Nor did it make any progress with a claim submitted in 1984.[13]

If Derby had benefited from local government reform, a number of existing cities found themselves faced with the potential loss of city status. In February 1973 a list was drawn up in the Home Office of 'existing cities'. In total 43 boroughs and one urban district outside of Greater London were considered to be entitled to the style 'city'. Of these, 28 were certainties: 'existing cities which will wholly or substantially comprise new districts and which will be the natural grantees of dignities enjoyed by the present authorities'. This list included all the eighteen cities whose mayors were Lord Mayors. Another four small cities (Ely, Ripon, Truro, Wells) were considered virtually certain to retain city status because they were to be governed by parish councils. This left eight cases (Canterbury, Durham, Lancaster, Lichfield, Rochester, St Albans, Salisbury, Winchester) where the successor authority was not expected to be a parish council, and the place itself would constitute only a proportion of the whole district: 'In these cases, if the new district does not apply for borough status then charter trustees will be established with the name "Charter Trustees of the City of [...]"'. No particular problem was expected, in such circumstances, to arise.[14]

---

[10]   PRO HO 286/126, Moore to Shuffrey, 29 Jan. 1977; A.W.P. to Home Secretary, 22 Nov. 1976.

[11]   Andrews MSS, Home Office to Borough Secretary, 31 May 1977; *Derby Evening Telegraph*, 8 June 1977; *The Times*, 29 July 1977. During the long silence between the application and the announcement even Gerald Andrews seems to have despaired of success, or at least this seems to be the implication behind his comments in a letter to Home Secretary written on 24 June 1977 in which he referred to the 'unexpected honour', and the 'surprise announcement' on 7 June: Andrews MSS.

[12]   Tyne and Wear Archives, CB/SU/2/78, f. 245.

[13]   I have found no evidence of an application in 1982 beyond an assertion to this end in literature produced by the new City at the time of its successful application in 1992. For 1984: PRO HLG 120/1714, Lord Bellwin to Roland Boyes, 8 May 1984. All we know is that the letter, sent to the Department of the Environment, was passed to the Home Office.

[14]   A copy of this memo is in PRO HLG 120/1714.

Even so, the Home Office was sufficiently alarmed by the potential impact of the legislation, that through the autumn of 1973 and spring 1974 it sent out letters stating that The Queen had agreed to the title and dignity of city being maintained beyond the date of local government reorganization, 1 April 1974.[15] In each case new letters patent were issued. Ripon became part of the county of north Yorkshire in 1974, with the city becoming a parish council. City status was re-granted, but following further difficulties in 1984 it received a charter confirming city status.[16] Truro would have lost city status under reorganization in 1974, but the outgoing city council applied for the title to be re-conferred. This was confirmed from the Home Office on 1 April 1974, and on 25 July 1974 Princess Anne visited Cornwall to present the new letters patent.[17]

Lichfield was one of the least clear-cut cases in 1974. The city council ceased to exist on 1 April and was replaced by the new Lichfield District Council, covering the responsibilities of the old city and the former Lichfield Rural District. The city was the only 'unparished' part of the new district. To handle the potential loss of city status 'charter trustees' were appointed, councillors elected to represent wards within the existing city area and constituting a body corporate of the city. The intention in Lichfield, as elsewhere, was to enable individual cities to maintain their status, or to have a separate body which could act as a city council even if it was no more than a parish council in practice. Lichfield's charter trustees were the fifteen district councillors elected from city wards. They were empowered to look after the civic and ceremonial property of the old city, and appoint the offices of mayor and sheriff. In 1980, following a request from the charter trustees, a new parish council for the city was established to replace them. The parish council is an autonomous body with thirty members (the largest membership of any such council in the country). It drew up a petition to the Queen, and city status was re-granted by letters patent in November 1980.[18]

By these various means the cities held on to their status. The exception was Rochester, Kent. Rochester has been a city since sometime in the seventh century. It was referred to as a city by Bede. In 1974 Rochester City Council, Chatham Borough Council and Strood Rural District Council were amalgamated to form a single new district council. Rochester's old city council petitioned for and received special letters patent to retain city status for Rochester, which became the City of Rochester within the District of Medway as of 1 April 1974. In this way it bypassed being protected by charter trustees.

---

[15]   PRO HLG 120/1714. Copies of the letters, signed by K.P Witney for the Home Office, can be found in this file. The majority are dated 1 April 1974, to coincide with the new regime. Information on Ely from Lee Gillett, 18 Jan. 2002.

[16]   http://www.ripon.org/.

[17]   W.J. Burley, City of Truro 1877-1977 (Truro, 1977), 63.

[18]   See http://www.lichfield.gov.uk/lcc-cc-background.html; PRO HLG 120/1714, E.N. Kent to D.P. Walley, 21, 25 July 1980.

Subsequently, the new Medway Council, which had swallowed Rochester and Chatham, applied for city status, and was refused, but the Home Office suggested that city status could be attained if the Rochester charter was expanded to include the whole district, provided that Rochester featured in the name. In 1982 a new charter was granted to the City of Rochester upon Medway, which replaced the special letters patent but wiped out the individual charter status of Rochester. Yet a further round of local government reorganization led to the inauguration on 1 April 1998 of Medway Borough Council, which included the City of Rochester upon Medway, and Gillingham, in a unitary authority. To preserve Rochester's city status, the Department of the Environment, Transport and the Regions suggested the appointment of charter trustees, a proposal the outgoing council chose not to adopt, effectively allowing city status to be lost. The result is that Rochester is no longer a city. Medway Borough Council entered both the 2000 and 2002 competitions without success, but local people concerned at the downgrading of their cathedral city have formed a City of Rochester society. Part of its remit is to try to rescue the lost status, and Medway Council is also now campaigning to the same end.[19]

Unfortunately for Rochester, charter trustees cannot be appointed retrospectively, and so there is no obvious way of reclaiming city status. By contrast, when on 31 March 1998 the City of Hereford amalgamated with various other district councils to become the County of Herefordshire District Council, charter trustees were appointed to take care of the city charters, plate and silver, and to carry out civic and mayoral functions. On 1 April 2000 the charter trustees were given parish council status, at which point city status was technically lost, but on 9 October letters patent were granted to Hereford reconferring city status, on the grounds that Hereford could show that it was traditionally referred to as a city in charters granted from 1189 onwards, by a Grant of Arms of 1648, and by letters patent of 1974.[20]

Some of these arguments must have seemed remarkably esoteric to towns which had never enjoyed the status of cities. From the late 1960s, accelerating after 1974, British towns and cities have suffered from significant de-industrialization. The reasons are both structural and spatial. Towns and cities contained more of the declining industrial sectors, and a disproportionate share of the older plants of these industries. Manufacturing was tending to move away from the larger centres towards suburban areas and small towns.[21] The implications for social structure, let alone tax revenue, were not lost on civic

---

[19]   *The Times*, 17 May 2002. I am grateful to Alan Moss for advice on the position of Rochester. PRO HLG 120/1714 contains further information on this complex issue.
[20]   http://www.hereford.gov.uk, 8 March 2002; Home Office Press Release 276/2000, 7 Sept. 2000.
[21]   S. Fothergill and G. Gudgin, *Unequal Growth: Urban and Regional Employment Change in the UK* (1982), Chapter 5.

leaders, who soon recognized that they needed to attract new economic activities. Since this was evidently not going to be in manufacturing industry, they had to become post-industrial service centres. To do this successfully required marketing, and from 1972 a number of places took advantage of a clause in the Local Government Act of that year, and its Scottish equivalent, to raise a small tax for any purpose for the benefit of its population. The money was predominantly used to promote inward investment.[22]

The use of these powers widened during the 1970s and brought local authorities into conflict with central government during the 1980s. However, in 1989 local authorities were given legal powers to raise money for spending on promotion.[23] Just as towns began to rethink their local priorities and economic policies, so they also began to consider the image they presented to the wider world. With this re-evaluation came a move away from the old concentration on annual handbooks, into brochures, information packs, videos, CDs, websites and other media forms. In 1977, 43 per cent of local authorities produced a guide, and around a quarter produced fact sheets and related information: by 1992 84 per cent were producing a guide, and three-quarters or more were churning out information sheets and similar marketing information. Clearly there was a cost, but this was absorbed in budgets designed to sell the place in a competitive market.[24]

City status was rapidly caught up in this re-branding process. Roy Hughes, MP for Newport East, supported by Paul Flynn of Newport West, spoke passionately in the House of Commons in December 1990 about what he regarded as the vital importance of having Newport promoted to city status 'in view of its growing economic, social and cultural importance in Wales'. Hughes had been MP for twenty-five years, and he emphasized inward investment in terms of diversifying the town's industrial base. At the same time he also noted how Newport was changing, and how public and commercial confidence was displayed in new commercial and administrative developments, including a Passport Office: 'Newport has long been established as the commercial and retail centre for the whole of Gwent and major new developments in this area are under way'. He added that city status 'would give a new dignity and status to Newport and to the whole county of Gwent and it would help to ensure future prosperity'. In these terms, promotion to city status, previously restricted since the Second World War mainly to large towns achieving a certain size and running the local services well, was here being converted into a way of 'promoting' the town to the

---

[22]   Stephen Ward, *Selling Places: The Marketing and Promotion of Towns and Cities, 1850-2000* (1998), 187-8; C. Philo and G. Kearns, eds., *Selling Places: the City as Cultural Capital, Past and Present* (Oxford, 1993).

[23]   A. Eisenschitz and J. Gough, *The Politics of Local Economic Policy: the problems and Possibilities of Local Initiative* (Basingstoke, 1993).

[24]   T. Hall, *Urban Geography* (2nd edn., 2001), 123.

international community. Hughes had noted that the Queen would celebrate forty years on the throne in 1992, and that 'on such occasions honours of the kind sought by Newport tend to be conferred'.[25]

City status as a form of civic boosterism was not new in the sense that we can trace its use back to Manchester in the 1850s, through Sunderland in 1932, but by the 1990s it was increasingly coming to be seen as a key tool in promoting a particular image of success, size, and general importance. Evidently sensing the way in which the wind was blowing, in July 1991 the Home Office decided to organize informal competitions for grants of city status and a lord mayoralty in conjunction with the Queen's fortieth anniversary the following year. It invited fourteen towns, which had recently sought the honour, to renew their applications, and it issued a general invitation to other towns interested in becoming cities. A total of twenty English towns entered the city status contest and nine sought a lord mayoralty (tables 2 and 3). Newport and St David's in Wales, and Armagh in Northern Ireland asked for their claims to be considered.

Table 2 English applicants for city status 1992

Blackburn	Guildford	Shrewsbury
Bolton	Ipswich	Southend
Brighton	Middlesbrough	Stockport
Chelmsford	Milton Keynes	Sunderland
Colchester	Northampton	Telford
Croydon	Preston	Wolverhampton
Dudley	Sandwell	

Source: *Hansard*, 11 Nov. 1991. Statement by the Home Secretary, Kenneth Baker.

No formal rules were issued: as R.O. Morris of the Home Office told the towns invited to apply, 'there is no formal procedure for seeking this Honour; a reply making as full a case as possible in whatever style you feel appropriate will suffice'. G.P. Key, chief executive of Sunderland Borough Council, immediately rang the Home Office asking for a meeting at which he could be briefed more fully about applying, but all he received in response was a telephone call offering him some general guidelines. Towns interested in claiming city status had to submit their claims by 1 October. Sunderland prepared an eight page application, without pictures, but with a statistical appendix, and attached a number of supporting documents about life in the

---

[25]   *Hansard*, 183 (1990-1), 329-31. Ironically Mr Hughes, despite having represented Newport in the Commons for twenty five years, was misinformed about Welsh cities. In his speech he claimed Cardiff, Swansea and St Davids were cities. St Davids was not a city in 1990, but Bangor was.

town. It also organised a letter-writing campaign from local MPs, and from MPs with local interests. The emphasis throughout was on the economic advantages to Sunderland of city status, perhaps best summarized in a letter from Edward Leigh, Parliamentary Under Secretary of State for Industry and Consumer Affairs to Kenneth Baker, the Home Secretary, written on 7 October 1991:

> As minister with special responsibilities for inner city initiatives in the North East, and Sponsor of the Tyne and Wear City Action Team (CAT) I was interested to learn that, together with other towns, Sunderland has recently been invited to submit a case to the Home Office to be granted City Status. There is no doubt that the town has had to face a severe challenge in tackling industrial decline in the traditional heavy manufacturing industries such as shipbuilding, but its efforts to regenerate the local economy have been impressive.... [it] now has the largest concentration of Japanese investment in England, centred upon Nissan.... If Sunderland were to achieve City Status it would be a very positive acknowledgement of the way it has risen to the challenge of industrial decline and a recognition of the achievements which have already been made.

Leigh was not alone; indeed, many of the other letters sent to the Home Secretary emphasized the same economic theme, including Lord Dormand of Easington, who wrote on 14 October 1991 to say that 'as with other places in the north-east Sunderland has had its difficult times and I am certain that city status would be an important boost to the morale of the people of the town on its way to recovery'. [26]

Once applications closed, Chelmsford was installed as the bookmakers' favourite at 4–1, with Brighton at 7–1, and Sunderland an outsider rated only ninth at 33–1. Although it had not told the applicants what qualifications were required, the Home Office worked to the assumption that 'a serious contender should, in England at least, have a population of over 200,000 ... be the acknowledged cultural, educational and commercial centre of the surrounding area, with a character and identity of its own', and have Royal and historical grounds. Population figures alone ruled out Blackburn, Brighton, Chelmsford, Colchester, Guildford, Ipswich, Middlesbrough, Milton Keynes, Northampton, Preston, Shrewsbury, Southend and Telford. Of these, Brighton was thought to have a good case for consideration despite its lack of numbers on the grounds of 'its identity, the range of its activities, and its historical and royal connections', and Chelmsford's case was also thought to have some merit.

---

[26]   This paragraph is based on files HON 91 0152/0017/001 and 008, which I read with permission in the Department of Constitutional Affairs, Victoria Street, London, on 22 Feb. 2005. Under the confidentiality rules in place until 31 Dec. 2004 these files would have been placed in the Public Record Office but not made available for public scrutiny until 1 Jan. 2023. I was permitted to see them under the terms of the Freedom of Information Act which came into force on 1 Jan. 2005.

Among those towns which satisfied the population minimum, Bolton and Stockport failed to convince the Home Office that they had an individual character separate from Manchester, and Croydon was once again condemned as being 'part of the London conurbation, rather than a place with a character and identity of its own'. In the west Midlands, Dudley was found to 'lack the individuality and character which would merit its elevation to city status' and had achieved the population minimum artificially as a result of 1974 local government reform, while Sandwell lacked 'character and identity' since it was simply a conglomeration of six loosely linked towns. Doubts were expressed about Wolverhampton's distinctiveness, but these were not sufficient to prevent it from being declared the runner up.[27]

Sunderland, with a population of 296,100 won, because 'although not the largest of the present applicants, none of those with a greater population has such a distinctive identity'. Its size, its history, its previous near misses including the time-lag since local government reorganization, and its 'clear identity' as 'the acknowledged centre for the surrounding area' all played in its favour, as well as its success 'in attracting new investment' following the loss of its traditional interests in coalmining and ship building.[28]

Sunderland learned of its success in February 1992. Buckingham Palace confirmed to the Home Office through the Queen's private secretary on 13 February that she accepted the recommendation regarding Sunderland. As a result, R.O. Morris of the Home Office passed on the good news the same day to Sunderland's Chief Executive: 'I write to confirm that The Queen has approved a recommendation by the Home Secretary that, to mark the 40th Anniversary of Her Accession to the Throne, Sunderland should become a city'. The announcement was released to the Press the following day, and covered by most of the newspapers on 15 February. 'I can hardly believe it', the mayor told the local press, 'the effect on the people of Sunderland will be immeasurable and the impact on the image of Sunderland throughout the world will be invaluable.' The *Sunderland Echo* claimed that it would mean a great deal for Sunderland in terms of 'prestige and status' but, harking back to earlier standards, it also wondered whether it would be necessary to nominate one of the new city's churches as a cathedral.

Sunderland South MP Chris Mullen expressed the hope that the new status 'will help put us on the map when it comes to competing for investment'.[29] The *Sunderland Echo* was quite sure that Sunderland's image would be improved: city status would mean 'a lot as far as prestige and status is

---

[27]   Department of Constitutional Affairs, HON 91 0152/0017/001/6, 6a. The reports on individual towns were drawn up by the Home Office after consultation with the Department of the Environment.

[28]   Ibid., *The Times*, 15 Feb. 1992.

[29]   *Sunderland Echo*, 14 Feb. 1992. Mullen displayed his political acumen here. He had not been one of the supporters of city status who wrote in to the Home Office.

concerned ... people tend to think of a city as more important than a town'. To capitalize on the award, it noted that 'a design team is already working on the new City of Sunderland logo', and within a month the mayor was pictured unveiling a new road sign on the A690 announcing 'City of Sunderland' – a clear indication of the way it was used to re-brand the image of the town.[30] Even the *Sun* accepted that what it called 'the former joke town of Sunderland' had just become 'wonderland and joined the big city league', while an editorial in the *Echo* on 17 February suggested that it was a massive fillip in terms of status and civic pride: 'now that the old town has graduated to city rank it can speak with a more authoritative voice and will be perceived at home and abroad as having greater stature'.[31]

It was more of a problem to discover precisely when Sunderland was to become a city, but in the end letters patent were issued on 23 March 1992, which became the formal promotion date. Hopes that the Queen would visit Sunderland to present them in person were dashed, but a civic delegation was invited to Buckingham Palace on 20 May for the formal handing over of the documents. The delegation, headed by the mayor, included the leaders of the three parties on the council, and the chief executive. The Queen visited Sunderland in May 1993 to unveil the city's new Coat of Arms. Celebrations connected with city status included a fireworks spectacular and a commemorative Royal Mail cover.[32]

Sunderland was quick to emphasize the boost which the town had received as a result of city status. It argued in 1999, seven years after its promotion, that 'city status has had a major positive impact on Sunderland.... It has boosted pride in the City and raised the image of Sunderland nationally.' The 1992 campaign cost £10,000, but politicians believed it had been money well spent because success helped to lift Sunderland out of the economic doldrums and to rebuild morale. Significant developments post-city status included the arrival of Nissan's car manufacturing plant, and the growth of a thriving service sector. The polytechnic became a university in 1992, and the National Glass Centre opened in 1998. Of course, some of this was simply brand imaging of developments which might have occurred anyway in the prosperous 1990s. The conversion of the polytechnic to a university, for example, was part of a national change in standing affecting towns across the country. Yet these and other developments pointed not directly to the grant of city status, but to the fact that 'in raising expectations and aspirations ... city status has played an important part, as a catalyst, in bringing about an impressive transformation in Sunderland'.[33] The *Independent* reported on 25 November 2000 that Sunderland had claimed the city status grant

30   Ibid., 23 March 1992.
31   Ibid., 17 Feb. 1992.
32   Department of Constitutional Affairs, HON 91 0152/0017/001.
33   Information supplied by Sunderland City Council, 1999.

'resulted in an extra 10,000 jobs being created'.[34] This message was not lost elsewhere.

The 1992 competition had been limited to English towns, but Newport and St David's in Wales, and Armagh in Northern Ireland were also proposed as candidates. Newport's case was rejected on the grounds that it could not show sufficient regional distinctiveness, but the position of St Davids and Armagh was more problematic. Both were thought to have some claims to consideration, St David's on 'historical and ecclesiastical grounds', and Armagh 'if all other things were equal'. Both were too small to have any chance in the 1992 competition, but the Home Office agreed to draw their cases to the attention of the Queen so that they could be considered in the context of events specific to Wales and Northern Ireland.[35] This was the background to the otherwise unexpected grants of city status to the two towns in 1994. Both grants were made at the request of the Queen, and both were 'in recognition of their important Christian heritage and their status as cities until the last century'.[36]

The background here was that both towns had a claim to city status as the seats of bishoprics, but in both cases the status had been lost. Armagh had argued its case since 1953, largely on the grounds that it had been the seat of a bishopric since it was founded by St Patrick in AD 440. The Home Office demanded proof that Armagh had enjoyed city status at any point in the intervening centuries, and then refused to accept that the case presented was watertight. After several years of negotiation, early in 1958 the Home Secretary told the town's MP that despite extensive research, 'Unlike other places which now use the title by ancient prescriptive right, the usage by Armagh does not seem to have been continuous in recent centuries. I do not think that any support for the claim can really be found'. Consequently, Armagh could be made a city only by royal prerogative which, in 1958, the Home Office was unwilling to recommend.[37]

Armagh simply continued to use the title, but St Davids, which considered itself to be Britain's smallest cathedral city, was less happy with using the title in an unauthorized manner. The Home Office accepted in 1969 that St Davids, St Asaph and Bangor 'may have ancient prescriptive rights to the title "city", but it has not been possible to confirm this'.[38] St Davids sought some form of confirmation and in 1991 the town council proposed that its case should be promoted in connection with the Queen's fortieth anniversary on the throne. The case for St Davids was based on precedent. Of the thirty ancient cathedral

---

34   http://www.independent.co.uk/news, 25 Nov. 2000.

35   Department of Constitutional Affairs, HON 91 0152/0017/001.

36   Personal Communication from the Home Office, 11 June 1999.

37   PRO HO 286/38, 39, R.A. Butler to C.W. Armstrong, 4 Feb. 1958. Armagh was called 'an inland city' in *Thoms Official Directory for 1890* (Dublin, 1890), 1191.

38   PRO HO 286/66, document entitled 'Swansea and City Status'.

cities in England and Wales, St Davids was one of only two (St Asaph being the other) which did not have city status. According to the town clerk, 'we feel it is wrong that we are a cathedral city but we are not allowed to call ourselves a city'. As we have seen, the case for St Davids was referred to Buckingham Palace rather than being handled as part of the competition.[39]

When Prince Charles visited Armagh in July 1994 he announced grants of city status to Armagh and to St Davids. As far as Armagh was concerned, it was now accepted that the town had been recognized as a city between 1226 and 'a century and a half ago', and that the title should be re-granted. The celebrations of the 1550th anniversary of St Patrick's founding of the bishopric was, ostensibly, the appropriate occasion for the announcement. Although the Prince did his best to sound convincing, and the chairman of the district council described himself as absolutely delighted, to most people in Armagh this was a hollow award, because they had always considered it to be a city. In the words of the *Armagh Observer*

> The news that Armagh is now a city may be looked upon by most Armachians as nothing new, yet this was the well guarded secret that the Prince of Wales brought with him on his recent visit to the Ecclesiastical Capital.... many Armagh people have held the opinion that Armagh was always a city, so it's unlikely that the Royal message was of much significance. It simply confirms that Armagh has been given back a title which had been wrongfully taken off it.

No celebrations or rejoicing followed the announcement.[40]

St Davids was rather more impressed with the news. Town clerk Mrs Jane Jenkins told the local press that 'It came out of the blue, but it is good news and I think everybody was thrilled'. According to the Bishop of St Davids, Rt Rev Ivor Rees, 'it was a wonderful surprise, totally unexpected. Everyone here is delighted.' The news was followed by a visit from the Queen, who attended a service in the cathedral on 1 June 1995, during which the letters patent were officially presented. 'It gives me great pleasure to present this charter to the ancient community of St Davids', the Queen was reported as saying, 'granting it the rights, status and appurtenances of a city'. According to the Dean 'we have always known we are a city but it is nice to have it confirmed officially'.[41]

The only loser on this occasion was St Asaph, also the see of a bishopric, and therefore potentially a city by ancient prescriptive right. Whatever St Asaph may have believed, searches for a charter or letters patent, undertaken during the 1970s, failed to reveal any supporting evidence, but more

---

39   *Western Telegraph*, 9, 16, 23 Oct. 1991, 19 Feb. 1992.
40   *Armagh Observer*, 14, 21 July 1994; *The Times*, 8 July 1994.
41   *Fishguard County Echo*, 13 Jan., 2 June 1995; *Western Telegraph*, 7 June 1995; *Western Mail*, 2 June 1995. Personal communication from the Dean of St Davids, Very Reverend J. Wyn Evans, 29 Sept. 1999.

importantly it does not seem to have put forward its case in 1991-2 and so was overlooked. When St Davids was promoted in 1994, St Asaph prepared a petition to the Queen requesting city status. This was not successful. The case for the town rested not on population (only 3,500) but on a petition which presented evidence of St Asaph having in the past been assumed to be a city. As such the case was unanswerable, because books and newspapers in the past had regularly referred to St Asaph as a city and its status was exactly the same as St Davids.[42] Yet despite entering the 2000 and 2002 competitions St Asaph remains a town – but calls itself a city on its website.

While Sunderland was revelling in its success, Chester was rather more modestly celebrating victory in the 1992 lord mayoralty competition. Uncertainty about the connection between city status and the lord mayoralty surrounded the grants to Swansea in 1969 and Derby in 1977. Swansea received an official letter in 1969 from the permanent secretary at the Home Office pointed out that 'in view of misunderstandings which have arisen in the past, the Secretary of State desires me to make it clear that the grant to the Town of the status of a City does not confer upon the Mayor the title of Lord Mayor; the grant of this privilege is an entirely separate matter'.[43] Swansea finally succeeded only in October 1981 when Prince Charles returned to south Wales during a tour of the province with Princess Diana in the wake of their marriage. During a gala, the Prince used the interval to make an announcement that the mayor would be elevated to the status of lord mayor.[44]

It was assumed in Derby in 1977 that the grant of city status would also mean that the mayor became lord mayor. The mayor 'expressed bewilderment at the fact that he and subsequent mayors of Derby will not automatically receive the title of Lord Mayor'. In part his surprise stemmed from the fact that 'Mayors of Derby have been entitled to wear the traditional Lord Mayor's robes of black and gold for many years, and this caused confusion at functions attended by other mayors and lord mayors in full regalia'.[45] Gerald Andrews told Home Secretary Merlyn Rees that there was 'a little bewilderment and confusion that the chief citizen has not been conferred with the title of Lord Mayor'. The Home Office replied that 'the title of Lord Mayor is an additional privilege granted, if at all, only after City status has been held for some considerable time. It is by no means an automatic concomitant of City status.'[46]

---

[42]   Details from the St Asaph bid documents of 2000, including papers prepared in advance.
[43]   Swansea City Council Minutes (1969), 595.
[44]   *The Times*, 29 Oct. 1981.
[45]   *Derby Evening Telegraph*, 8 June 1977.
[46]   Andrews MSS, Andrews to Merlyn Rees, 24 June 1977, and C. Thursby to Andrews, 10 Aug. 1977. Andrews should have consulted Ernest Preston, the borough secretary, who had been told by the Home Office that the grant of city status did not confer the title of lord mayor: PRO HO 286/126, R. Shuffrey to Preston, 31 May 1977.

The qualification relating to longevity was widely known, and cities did periodically apply for lord mayoralties, and their cases were put to the monarch for consideration. Occasionally they were successful: Canterbury's mayor was promoted to lord mayor in 1988.[47] In 1991 the Home Office decided to formalize the matter by running a parallel competition to the city status contest. As with city status, it invited applications from towns which had expressed an interest in the honour in recent years, and nine towns applied (table 3).

Table 3 Applicants for lord mayoralties 1992

Bath	Chester	Lincoln
Cambridge	Derby	St Albans
Carlisle	Lancaster	Southampton

Source: Department of Constitutional Affairs, HON 91 0152/0017/001.

As with city status, no formal criteria were laid down, but candidates needed to have a character and dignity of their own, and normally would have been a city for at least fifteen years. In the sense that a lord mayoralty represented a second – 'a double honour' – it was thought that it should be 'if anything … stronger than for a city'. Bath, Carlisle, and Lincoln were all cities by ancient prescriptive right, Chester was sixteenth-century creation, St Albans was a nineteenth-century city, and the other four candidates had all been promoted in the twentieth century. With no specific population qualification, drawing up a league table among this group was not easy, and most were disqualified on the straightforward grounds that they could offer nothing special to single them out from among the other candidates. Chester won because it had been a Royal borough since 1327, and because in 1992 its cathedral was celebrating the 900th anniversary of the founding of the original abbey. As the Queen had indicated in 1988 that she was not averse to Chester having a lord mayor, and as she was distributing the Maundy Money at the cathedral as part of the 900th anniversary celebrations in 1992, the case for Chester seemed unanswerable. Ten years on, Sue Proctor, who was the first lord mayor of Chester, recalled that 'there was great rejoicing and people were very excited. It had a remarkable impact.'[48] The runners up in 1992 were Carlisle, Cambridge and Southampton. Of these, Cambridge could consider itself the most unfortunate, since the Home Office admitted that it would

---

[47]   Canterbury Cathedral Archives, CC\A\AA65. The official correspondence gives no indication of why the grant was made.

[48]   Quoted in *Exeter Express and Echo*, 15 March 2002. Details of the grant are in Department of Constitutional Affairs, HON 91 0152/0017/001.

undoubtedly have been granted a lord mayoralty had it applied in 1962 when Oxford succeeded.[49]

Between the promotion to city status of Derby in 1977 and Sunderland in 1992, thinking about the image and standing of the city changed radically. Derby sought the status as a compensation for the downgrading of its council in 1974, but Sunderland had an altogether different agenda in 1992. Larger towns and cities such as Manchester and Sheffield had by this time come to recognize that de-industrialization was a permanent rather than a temporary state of affairs.[50] Marketing themselves was now seen as a way of re-invention, and that process involved promoting themselves as centres of business services such as finance, computer software, advertising and other professional, office-based, activities – it is surely no surprise that the supporting documentation for Sunderland's application in 1992 included a leaflet 'Sunderland Investor's Guide, *Next Generation Industries*'. In many cases, universities and hospitals have become part of this new image, together with a healthy retailing interest. This in turn was linked wherever possible to tourism, so hotels, conference centres and other service facilities had to complement these changes.[51]

Successful promotion of tourism required not only shops, but attractions, so post-industrial cities have usually followed their Victorian predecessors by investing in cultural capital such as museums, art galleries, theatres and concert halls,[52] sports stadia and leisure centres. The historic significance of the town has to be emphasized.[53] Older structures have to be imaginatively re-used, and the industrial heritage turned to good effect as a tourist attraction. Other documents in the Sunderland pack in 1992 included *A Visitor's Guide to Wearside*, and *Sunderland 1991 Holiday Guide*. To counteract nostalgia, new buildings of striking design and high quality finishing have been commissioned and built. Public art and night life are among other activities which are boosted in similar manner, including restaurants, night clubs and entertainments. Watersides (both former docks and canals) also have to be developed to clear away poor quality areas, but to bring in their place new forms of living and entertainment. While much of this is aimed at high income individuals in the new service areas, it comes together with the creation of numerous low income service jobs. Changing the town in this way was one thing, promoting it to the wider world another, and here Glasgow led the way in the mid-1980s with its own campaign, culminating in its year as European

[49]   Department of Constitutional Affairs, HON 91 0152/0017/001.

[50]   I. Taylor, K. Evans and P. Fraser, *A Tale of Two Cities: A Study in Manchester and Sheffield* (1996).

[51]   C.M. Law, *Urban Tourism: Attracting Visitors to Large Cities* (1993).

[52]   Ibid; F. Blanchini and M. Parkinson, eds., *Cultural Policy and Urban Regeneration: the West European Experience* (Manchester, 1993).

[53]   G.J. Ashworth and J.E. Tunbridge, *The Tourist-Historic City* (Chichester, 1990); Hall, *Urban Geography*, 127-8.

City of Culture in 1990.[54] Shaping the urban landscape has become more important than simply persuading outsiders that one place is better than another.[55] Promoting it as a city helps this process.

Competitions have become a major way of raising the profile of cities. Glasgow's successful exploitation of its year as European City of Culture helped to fuel interest in the competition for 2008, eventually won by Liverpool with a bid costing £2m, a sum expected to be more than reclaimed through tourism and regeneration.[56] Hosting major sporting events is also seen as a way of boosting income and image, hence competition for the Olympics and World Cup. Obviously such events affect only a handful of major cities, but the spin-offs have been considerable, and smaller places can learn lessons. The modern town is marketed as a place which is good for living, good for work, and the centre or capital of something – be it of a region, area, or culture. Most recently, towns have begun to see themselves in terms of European status. The invention of a core cities group, most of which aspire to be European cities, is part of this transformation. Much is made of opportunities, and a good deal of effort goes into playing down stereotypes and negative images – the modern city is sold as having thrown off its past, however downtrodden that may have been.[57] The images have to be positive.

This in turn leads to 'place management' techniques designed to provide the required image,[58] and city status has become tied into this branding process. In June 1998, Reading East MP Jane Griffiths introduced a debate in the House of Commons, as a result of which she was given leave to bring in a bill to regulate city-making. She complained that 'the process by which a place may be designated a city remains shrouded in mystery', and proposed that the criteria should be 'known to all', and that there should be 'a clear process ... by which any place could apply to the government to be judged against the criteria'. Ms Griffiths' bill was lost, but the fact that she was MP for Reading, a town thriving on new technologies, was an indication that she was fighting the cause of a place that could envisage its European image improving as a result of being a city. Nor is it insignificant that Ms Griffiths was seconded in the debate by Jenny Jones, one of the MPs for Wolverhampton, another would-be city which had been trying to achieve the status since at least 1953. Politicians were now responding to pressure from their constituencies to clarify the process of city-making as a way of helping aspirants to know what

[54] Ward, *Selling Places*, 191-2; M. Boyle, 'Civic boosterism in the politics of local economic development - 'institutional positions' and 'strategic orientations' in the consumption of hallmark events', *Environment and Planning A*, 29 (1997), 1975-1997.
[55] Helen Meller, *Towns, Plans and Society in Modern Britain* (1997), Chapter 8; P.J. Larkham, *Conservation and the City* (1996).
[56] *The Times*, 5 June 2003.
[57] J.R. Gold and S. Ward, eds., *Place Promotion: The Use of Publicity and Marketing to Sell Towns and Regions* (Chichester, 1994), Chapter 2.
[58] Ibid., Chapters 3, 6.

they had to achieve. *The Times* noted in 2000 that 'Cities are where people want to be, towns very much the poor relation'. It added, somewhat incongruously, 'Size matters'.[59]

While similar clarion calls had occasionally been sounded in the past, what was new in the 1990s was the branding of the town, and part of that imaging involved status. City status, however nebulous, was now part of the process, but public relations officers up and down the country were aware that, on past precedent, no further cities would be made if and until the Queen celebrated her Golden Jubilee in 2002. The government was already beginning to feel the heat, and in October 1998 Jenny Jones put a Parliamentary question to Home Secretary Jack Straw asking what future arrangements were being considered for grants of city status. In a written answer on 27 October, Straw informed the Commons that two competitions were being planned:

> Her Majesty had expressed the intention of marking both the Millennium and the 50th Anniversary of Her Accession to the Throne by grants of city status. Towns which have expressed an interest in this honour will be contacted in due course and invited to submit formal applications.[60]

The language was that of 1991–2, but the competition was to prove less than gentlemanly. Straw was opening up what would turn out to be nearly four years of political infighting in the struggle for city recognition, during the course of which the planned admission of two new candidates to the exclusive city club was expanded to eight, and the competition transferred out of the Home Office to the Lord Chancellor's Department. In the process, any remaining vestiges of the idea that this was an independent exercise, divorced from the political maelstrom, disappeared, and in the process the precedent established by Sunderland being awarded city status was added to the tools available for rebranding the town.

---

[59]   *The Times*, 19 Dec. 2000.
[60]   *Hansard*, vol. 313 (1997-8), 169-70; vol. 318, 57155, 27 Oct. 1998.

CHAPTER SEVEN

The Millennium Competition

The decision to make new cities in 2000 and 2002 as a result of competitions was not surprising in the light of the perceived success of the 1992 competition, but in the course of the 1990s the public relations world, and the whole concept of boosterism and civic promotion, had moved on. Sunderland had taken some pride in submitting in 1991 a bid which it called 'deliberately restrained in style. A simple eight-page document outlined the record of achievement and prospects for Sunderland's future.' Nothing would be so simple in 2000 and 2002 as the public relations departments of town halls across the United Kingdom swung into action in the wake of the Home Secretary's announcement in October 1998. What followed in a welter of glossy brochures, videos, CD Roms, websites and other materials – Warrington had a tee-shirt, a badge, a car sticker, and a CD recording of the local male voice choir singing 'The River of Life' – was nothing short of a campaign to raise profiles and boost images. It was these images which were seen as vital to a successful campaign, and which were funded because of the perceived, or imagined, rewards of achieving city status.[1]

Local authorities interested in applying for city status were asked to put their names forward to the Home Office by 1 February 1999. News soon began to filter out about conflict in the town halls. In April 1999 an article in *The Times* referred to 'an undeclared battle' between contestants hoping to succeed in the competition. Already, it suggested, the heavyweights were preparing for metaphorical military action, and it suggested that Blackburn, Brighton, Croydon, Stockport and Wolverhampton were the front runners.[2] This was all sparring because the competition was officially launched only on 28 May 1999 with a Home Office press release announcing a UK-wide contest. On the same day, letters were sent to those local authorities which had expressed an interest, inviting them to submit formal applications by 1 September. Applicants from England and Northern Ireland were asked to write directly to the Home Office. Those from Wales and Scotland were to submit their applications to the Welsh and Scottish Offices respectively.[3] There were no other rules. The Home Office returned to its well-known mantra by emphasizing that 'city status is not, and never has been a right that can be claimed by a town fulfilling certain conditions'. It added the usual disclaimer that 'the use of specific criteria could

---

[1]   Stephen V. Ward, *Selling Places: the Marketing and Promotion of Towns and Cities, 1850–2000* (1998), 200–02.

[2]   *The Times*, 5 April 1999.

[3]   *Local Government Chronicle*, 4 June 1999.

lead to a town claiming city status as of a right; which in turn might devalue the honour'. Consequently, formal applications 'may take whatever form is felt best to present the town's interest'.[4]

The competition closed on 1 September 1999, by which time thirty-nine applicants had come forward. Of this total, twenty-seven were English towns, four were from Scotland, six from Wales and two from Northern Ireland (table 4). Interest had multiplied since the Queen's fortieth anniversary. Two English towns dropped out of the race: Dudley and Sandwell. The decision in Sandwell was because 'the Members of the Council did not think it was appropriate',[5] while Dudley did not renew its application because it had heard that only four towns were seriously in the running: Wolverhampton, Brighton, Swindon and Milton Keynes.[6] Where it obtained this information is not known, but two months before the competition closed it had already identified the two English towns which would eventually succeed. It also knew rather more than the bookmakers William Hill, which installed Brighton and Hove as the favourite, but had Wolverhampton only as a 20 to 1 outsider.[7] Applicants presented their case in Westminster by various means, including the special train hired by Ipswich for the occasion.[8] When the competition closed, *The Times* listed what it considered to be the twelve leading contenders, adding to its original list Inverness, Middlesbrough, Milton Keynes, Newport, Paisley, Reading and Swindon.[9]

Four Scottish towns applied, Ayr, Inverness, Paisley and Stirling, but the position was confused. Scottish towns were excluded from the 1992 competition on the grounds that 'such honours are not awarded in Scotland'. As we have seen, only Dundee held city status by letters patent, but Aberdeen, Edinburgh and Glasgow are accepted as cities by long historic use. The Scottish Executive agreed that since none of the three have documentary evidence in the form of letters patent 'it is therefore impossible for them to prove conclusively that they are cities'. As such, they were entitled to enter the millennium competition, but it was not anticipated that they would do, because they enjoyed the status on similar principles to English cathedral towns with ancient prescriptive right.[10] Why Scottish towns were eligible to participate in

4   Personal Communication from Linda Henshaw, Home Office, 11 June 1999.
5   Personal Communication from Nigel Summers, Chief Executive, Sandwell Metropolitan Borough Council, 20 July 1999.
6   Telephone conversation, Chief Executive, Dudley Municipal Borough Council, 16 July 1999.
7   *Local Government Chronicle*, 10 Sept. 1999.
8   *East Anglian Daily Times*, 9 Aug. 1999.
9   *The Times*, 1 Sept. 1999.
10   Department of Constitutional Affairs, HON 91 0152/0017/001. David Nelson, Scottish Executive, to Councillor James Simpson, Dunfermline, 23 July 1999. I am grateful to Councillor Simpson for drawing my attention to the problems experienced by Dunfermline in respect of the millennium and Golden Jubilee competitions.

Table 4 Applicants for city status in the millennium competition

England

Blackburn*	Guildford*	Reading
Blackpool	Ipswich*	Shrewsbury*
Bolton*	Luton	Southend*
Brighton*	Maidstone	Southwark
Chelmsford*	Medway	Stockport*
Colchester*	Middlesbrough*	Swindon
Croydon	Milton Keynes*	Telford*
Doncaster	Northampton*	Warrington
Dover	Preston*	Wolverhampton*

Scotland

Ayr	Paisley	Stirling
Inverness		

Wales

Aberystwyth	Newport	St Asaph
Machynlleth	Newtown	Wrexham

Northern Ireland

Ballymena	Lisburn

*applied in 1992

the competition when they had been excluded in 1992 is not clear. In any case, this was little consolation to other Scottish towns such as Dunfermline. The burgh claims that in both public and private legislation, as well as in legal orders and agreements, in some cases going back as far as 1911, it has regularly been referred to as a city.[11] In 1924 it even awarded the Freedom of the City of Dunfermline to the Secretary of State for Scotland, who noted in a speech of acceptance that 'it will be one of my chief duties to safeguard and uphold all that pertains to the dignity and honour of this *city* and royal burgh.... Dunfermline from out the past and for many years has been fittingly

---

[11]   Councillor Simpson set out the documentary claims (with supportive material) in a letter to the Scottish Executive on 22 Nov. 1999.

designated a *city* as well as a royal burgh.'[12] That was in 1924, but in 1929 a major reform of local government in Scotland set up three types of burgh: four 'counties of cities', Aberdeen, Dundee, Edinburgh and Glasgow; twenty 'large burghs'; and 171 'small burghs'. This perpetuated the divide between those towns it acknowledged as cities and those it did not officially accept as such, a distinction subsequently maintained, for example, in the Local Government (Scotland) Act of 1973.

Once the millennium competition had been announced, Scottish towns had to decide whether to take part. The problem with which they were faced was that to enter the contest implied that they were not cities. Dunfermline enquired as to whether it should apply, but the message from the Scottish Executive was ambiguous. It was told that as it has no charter it could enter the competition, but the local authority was advised to consider 'whether Dunfermline's interests would be better served by continuing to use the designation without an extant royal charter, or by applying to be selected for the millennium grant along with other applicants from across the UK'.[13] Legally, there was a view that Dunfermline 'could simply reassert its city status and await a challenge. In view of the long history of the use of the city title prior to 1975 it is possible that no challenge would be made.'[14] Dunfermline decided not to apply, but the situation remained unsatisfactory because the Secretary of State for Scotland recognized that 'other towns, including Dunfermline, have in the past been described as "city and royal burgh" in local Acts of Parliament and other official documents but they are not separate local government areas and are not now, and never have been, described as cities in the legislation which constitutes local government areas'.[15]

This confusion was far from helpful. In August 2000, while results of the competition were still awaited, Dunfermline local councillor James Simpson learnt from the Home Office that 'there is, of course, nothing to stop a town referring to itself as a city, but the title would have no provenance'.[16] The Scottish Executive confirmed the position. On 7 August 2000 Callum Ingram of the Scotland Office told Robert McEwan of Dunfermline that 'there is no reason in principle to stop particular towns calling themselves cities if they wish to do so'. He added that: 'It follows from this that there does not exist a list of those towns accepted by the Scotland Office as entitled to use the word 'City', and further, there are no fixed criteria determining entitlement'. Historic Scotland agreed to amend its literature to cite Dunfermline as a city on these grounds.[17] However, the city status fact sheet which accompanied the

12   Simpson to the Scottish Executive, 8 Dec. 1999.
13   David Nelson, Scottish Executive, to James Simpson, 14 July 1999.
14   Legal opinion of J.R. Doherty, 15 Oct. 1999.
15   John Reid, Scotland Office, to James Simpson, 16 Dec. 1999.
16   Sylvia Brown, Home Office, to James Simpson, 1 Aug. 2000.
17   Pamela Craig, Historic Scotland, to James Simpson, 21 Sept. 2000.

Home Office's press release on 18 December 2000 announcing the winners of the millennium competition named only Aberdeen, Dundee, Edinburgh and Glasgow as cities in Scotland, thereby suggesting that the two departments of state were on different wavelengths, and causing additional annoyance in Scotland.

Once all the applications had been received in the autumn of 1999 it was the responsibility of the Home Office to decide on a winner. The task was slightly aided by the rules governing applications from Wales and Scotland. In each case the relevant Secretary of State was asked to assess the applications and put forward a single candidate from both provinces (six and four respectively), thus eliminating eight towns. In Scotland, the Secretary of State, Dr John Reid, visited all four of the bid towns. In Stirling he talked to some of the companies which had recently moved to the town from elsewhere in Scotland, the United Kingdom, Europe and the United States. He also visited schools and churches, and met community representatives and historians who helped to compile the bid. The university hosted a lunch at which he met a cross section of the local communities.[18] Reid visited Paisley on 16 August with the leader of the Scottish Assembly, the late Donald Dewar, when a party was held in the town.[19] Welsh Secretary Paul Murphy is known to have promoted the cases of both Wrexham and Newport, despite the guidelines.[20]

In the absence of rules, the competition took place in a vacuum.[21] Aspirant cities had no obvious way of developing their application in a manner which would distinguish them from any other town. Consequently, no two towns put in applications which were strictly comparable, because they had no template and no rules for guidance. They also worked with very different levels of resource: some obtained sponsorship from local businesses, while others diverted income from council tax receipts to the task. Perhaps as a result, some were very professional applications, and others rather less so. The Ayr video was admitted to be of an inferior quality because it was made by local teenagers rather than a professional company. Some applications seem to have been put together by a single individual, or by a group of local government officers. Others were a committee enterprise: Brighton and Hove, Swindon and Newport all established groups to press their case. In some of the applications (notably Middlesbrough's, which took the form of a newspaper) different sections were clearly written by different individuals or groups. Several towns, including Luton, ran successful awareness campaigns through the local press.

---

[18]   Personal Communication from Keith Yates, Chief Executive, Stirling Council, 26 Oct. 1999.

[19]   *Paisley City News*, Sept. 1999.

[20]   http://www.independent.co.uk/news, 25 Nov. 2000.

[21]   Most applicants were happy to provide me with a copy of their bid. A few, including Doncaster and Dover, failed to respond to letters and telephone calls, while Southend simply sent me a letter saying it had applied but offering no further information. Milton Keynes sent only its text. Much of what follows is based on my analysis of these documents.

Some emphasized the strength of support for the application within the town, often reproducing letters of encouragement. Wrexham included a separate booklet with supporters' letters, Northampton had a substantial appendix, and Milton Keynes devoted much of the application to showing evidence of local support. Finally, a few of the applications suggested a lack of forethought. Ayr's glossy brochure included a splendidly rural picture on the second page and a seaside scene on page three; while the first picture in the Newport bid offered rolling countryside populated by sheep with not a house in sight.

How much they all cost is not known. Colchester spent £8,000 on its campaign,[22] but other places put their applications together on a financial shoestring. The Clerk of Machynlleth Council wrote that:

> My Council, who work on a very small budget, did not go to a great deal of expense in putting its case forward – indeed, the actual expenditure amounted to the postage in sending the application to various Local Authorities, the National Assembly and to the Press.[23]

Newtown produced three sheets of print in the form of a petition, presumably at virtually no cost.

Summarizing thirty-nine separate applications is not easy – as the Home Office must also have found – but a few general points can be made. Most applicants (although not all) mentioned population size. If this had been the only criterion, Croydon would have won hands down. 'Croydon', its application announced in the opening paragraph, 'is the largest of the thirty-two London boroughs with a population of approximately 335,000 – a far greater number than many cities. It is the tenth largest town … in England.… In fact, Croydon is the largest town which does not have the title of City in the whole of Western Europe.' No other applicant could match such figures, but Brighton and Hove rather casually mentioned that with a population exceeding a quarter of a million they were larger than other south coast cities such as Portsmouth and Southampton. Wolverhampton also mentioned its quarter of a million population. Stockport claimed a population of almost 300,000, while Milton Keynes noted that its population exceeded 200,000 (206,000). Smaller towns chose to pass rather swiftly over population, some omitting the figures altogether. Several emphasized their relative position. Inverness noted that it was the largest town in the northern part of Scotland, and Newport that it was the third largest urban area in Wales after Cardiff and Swansea (and thus the largest not yet a city – a return to the position it had adopted in the early 1990s). Both Inverness and Newport also stressed the pace of recent growth as an indication of their dynamism. Paisley, with a population of 79,000, claimed to be the largest mere town in Scotland.

---

22   http://www.thisisessex.co.uk, 8 Jan. 2001.

23   Personal Communication from John Parsons, Clerk to the Council, Machynlleth, 16 Nov. 1999.

A second theme emphasized by many of the applicants was that of international and regional significance. Although regional status had been a criterion going back to the Home Office rules of 1907, modern marketing techniques ensured that many applicants would stress their position not just in terms of the area around them but also in European terms.[24] Bolton claimed to have worked hard to develop regional, national and international partnerships, and to have 'the flavour of a European city'. Colchester argued that it is a sub-regional commercial and retail centre, and the 'acknowledged cultural capital of Essex'. Guildford stressed its role as a diocesan centre with a cathedral, as a university town, a regional capital, and a town with significant European links. Warrington combined different aspects by noting that 33 per cent of the town's businesses traded with Europe and 24 per cent with the rest of the world. Northampton and Chelmsford stressed their natural regional importance as county towns, as did Ballymena in a County Antrim context. Inverness emphasized its role in northern Scotland, and Wrexham in North Wales, while Southwark played the London card by promoting itself as London's third city.

Several emphasized their regional role as a means of artificially boosting gross population numbers, including Blackpool (which boasted of being the sub-regional capital for the Fylde coast and thus the focus for 300,000 residents), Bolton (265,000 in eight separate townships), Ipswich (120,000 within the historic borough, but 150,000 in the town and a catchment area of over one-third of a million), Medway (250,000 people scattered through five towns, including the historic 'city' of Rochester), Shrewsbury (66,400 population, but the regional centre, it claimed, for 300,000 people) and Wolverhampton (where the borough included Wolverhampton, Wednesfield, Tettenhall and Bilston). Ayr, with a population of 48,000, argued that it was the focus of a region of 400,000 people. Inverness, with 65,000, suggested that it was a centre for 240,000 people throughout northern Scotland. Reading mentioned only its catchment area of 1.7 million people, not the town's population, while Telford offered an interesting spin on the issue by suggesting that city status would turn it into a regional centre.

A third theme was history and heritage, again reflecting part of the modern urban concern with conservation and tourism. As a proportion of individual applications this varied. Milton Keynes and Telford were not able to say a great deal about their past for obvious reasons, although Milton Keynes managed to work in a reference to flint tools from 6000BC. Middlesbrough, dating from only 1830, devoted little space to the subject. By contrast, Shrewsbury could offer little else apart from its history as a recommendation for city status, while Medway devoted ten pages to a detailed history of the area claiming city status. Both Stirling in Scotland and the smaller Welsh towns also emphasized their past. Almost all the applications offered a potted history and a list of important dates, although only Colchester was able to trace

---

[24]   Ward, *Selling Places*; John R. Gold and Stephen V. Ward, *Place Promotion: the Use of Publicity and Marketing to Sell Towns and Regions* (Chichester, 1994), 2.

its urban pedigree back to the Romans. Several applications stressed modern environmental concerns. Blackburn, Brighton, Ipswich and Swindon were among those which referred to sustainable development, while Ayr went further, with politically correct references to sustainability, connectivity and stakeholders. Milton Keynes mentioned its 'kerbside collection recycling scheme'. Applicants were clearly keen to stress their good record on conservation.[25]

A fourth theme which featured in many of the applications can loosely be described as economic significance, both of the town and of the expectations of city status. Economic success was emphasized by Guildford, Reading and Swindon, but it was not just southern England that took pride in stressing how successful the town was. In Scotland, Ayr, Inverness and Paisley all played up their economic importance, as did Newport in Wales.

A fifth theme running through the applications was that of community. This took several forms. One was an emphasis on areas such as the arts, leisure and entertainment, education, sport, and religion (either in terms of multi-ethnic activities, or because a particular town had an Anglican cathedral). The significance of community was also stressed in terms of the importance for local people of the town succeeding in its application. Some stressed how civic pride would be lifted. Telford was one example, while Preston wrote that 'this application for city status is about the people of Preston'. Brighton and Hove ran a campaign to raise awareness (the 100 faces campaign), and conceived of the city status campaign as both celebrating past achievements and providing a platform for tackling current problems.[26] Among other towns which opened campaigns to enable individuals to express their interest were Luton, Newport and Wrexham. Wolverhampton argued that the award would bring a greater sense of local community. Milton Keynes worked in a reference to the fact that its community web site was the largest and most used in the United Kingdom.

Finally, towns presented a range of different reasons why they were particularly suited to city status, which cannot really be classified in any particular way. Some provided a list of notable local people; others, including Northampton and Shrewsbury, listed Royal visits (which, as we shall see, turned out to be more important than might have been anticipated, although neither town was successful); while Maidstone included an account of the town at war, Lisburn stressed the role of the army since 1969, Blackpool asked to be thought of as the City of Fun, Ayr emphasized its tourist industry (although the video showed miles of empty beach), and Warrington presented itself (tee-shirt, badge and all) as the City for Peace, a result of its links with the troubles in Northern Ireland. Colchester, rather cannily, argued that it had in fact been the country's first 'city' as the Roman capital of Britain, founded almost 2,000 years ago, and that therefore it was simply asking for a

25   P.J. Larkham, *Conservation and the City* (1996).
26   I owe this information to Simon Fanshawe.

restoration of its historic rights given that it was the only Roman *coloniae* not currently a city.

These comments offer an inadequate flavour of the applications, which varied so much in shape, size, format, and content that any assessment will inevitably do rather less than adequate justice to individual entries. Much the same thought must inevitably have crossed the minds of the Home Office officials charged with sorting out the front runners from the also rans, and, ultimately, the winner or, as it eventually transpired, winners. Many of the applications were impressive. The cases for Chelmsford, Ipswich, Guildford and Northampton looked strong on the basis of their county position. The absence of a city in the adjoining counties of Suffolk and Essex looked to be a regional omission that the competition might help fill, although having three Essex towns (Chelmsford, Colchester and Southend) in the frame always looked like bad local politics. On regional grounds, Inverness offered the strongest Scottish case, while Wrexham (north) and Newport (south) looked the best hopes for Wales. Local competition always seemed likely to undermine some cases, as in Essex and also in the Thames Valley, where Reading and Swindon helped to rule each other out. Some applications did not seem to do full justice to the applicants, including Middlesbrough and Wolverhampton, while a few cases were relatively weak. Among these were Blackpool, Maidstone and Shrewsbury of the English towns, the smaller Welsh towns of Machynlleth, Newtown and St Asaph, and the Irish candidates Ballymena and Lisburn. None of these last five seemed plausible, although as we have already seen St Asaph was in the competition partly in the hope of following St Davids and having city status restored.

After being invited to enter a competition without rules, the thirty-nine would-be cities were then left to guess when the outcome might be known. From the outset the government refused to name a date when the new city would be announced.[27] Despite expectations that it would coincide with the millennium on 1 January 2000 the occasion came and went with no sign of a decision, and no indication from the Home Office of when, if at all, one would be made. Not surprisingly, there was rumbling in the town halls as January 2000 passed into February. On 4 February, Mike O'Brien, Parliamentary Under-Secretary of State at the Home Office, replied to a Parliamentary Question from David Stewart MSP, asking for 'a statement on progress in the award of city status'. O'Brien had nothing to offer: 'No date has yet been set for the announcement of the result'.[28] February passed into March, still with silence from the Home Office.

The first evidence that all was not well appeared on 6 March when a confidential document prepared in the Home Office was leaked to journalists in the House of Commons press gallery. The document, similar to one prepared in 1992, took the form of brief pen-portraits of a number of the

---

27   Home Office, Press Release 166/99, 28 May 1999.
28   *Hansard*, vol. 343, 108455, 4 Feb. 2000.

English applicants. It was immediately clear that despite the absence of rules the Home Office had applied an unofficial cut-off point for English towns at a population of 200,000, just as it had in 1992.[29] Those which passed this hurdle were then deconstructed in terms of their history, royal connections, and regional importance. The resulting conclusions did not make happy reading for most of the applicants. Blackburn with Darwen was 'considerably below the threshold for English towns', and although acknowledged as a regional centre it had 'no significant Royal or historical associations'. Blackpool was dismissed as 'only a medium-sized seaside town with no Royal associations and of fairly recent origin'. Bolton fared slightly better as 'a lively, thriving town and a focal point for the surrounding area, despite its proximity to Manchester', but it had few significant royal associations and had 'little history'. It is hard to see where the latter point came from, although the city status application included virtually no historical commentary (but there was rather more on the CD Rom). Chelmsford and Colchester were too small – the Roman heritage counted for nothing when Colchester was 'well below the 200,000 threshold'. Croydon was, as ever, condemned as having 'no particular identity of its own', being seen as one of London's outer suburbs. Similarly Southwark was 'very much part of London with little individual identity' – the same reason for its rejection in 1955. Dover was too small and unimportant. Doncaster was large enough (288,584) but not a regional centre. It lacked history and royal associations, and 'there has been recent controversy over councillors' expenses'. Most of the other towns were simply too small to qualify. Of those that did cross the threshold, Stockport, which had assiduously avoided mentioning Manchester in its application, was condemned as having 'little identity of its own … a suburb of Manchester'. Warrington, considered even though its population was just 198,000, lacked a clear focus apart from its connection with Northern Ireland following the 1993 IRA bomb in the town.

Some places were damned with faint praise. It was doubtful if Luton was 'a focal point for the region', and it had no significant royal connections or history. Reading had 'a long, although unexceptional, history'. Shrewsbury was 'very small' and Southend 'principally a seaside resort … overshadowed by its proximity to London'. Swindon not only lacked sufficient population and had little history, it had submitted a 'poorly constructed' application which gave 'the impression of a particularly materialistic town, rather than a rounded community'. Certainly it was a short application (only 11 pages), and it highlighted the fact that Swindon was 'one of the most successful economies in Britain', but there was reference also to 'a caring community' and 'a cultural centre'. Telford was 'not of great regional significance'.

The leaked report did not constitute a full survey of the applicants. It offered no information on the status of the Welsh, Scottish and Northern Ireland applicants, nor on a number of English towns. But there was sufficient

---

[29]   The document, entitled 'Applicants for the Millennium Grant of City Status', was neither signed nor dated.

information contained within it to make clear that the 200,000 population threshold still loomed large in Home Office thinking, and that it was attaching considerable significance to royal connections, regional importance, and historical importance – as it had in 1992. Richard Ford, Home Correspondent of *The Times,* drew on the report to suggest that Brighton and Hove, and Wolverhampton, were the English front runners and that no other towns were in contention.[30]

The report infuriated just about everyone apart from Brighton and Hove and Wolverhampton, and also Chelmsford's Tory MP Simon Burns, who was quoted as saying he believed that Chelmsford still had a chance because the leaked document had stressed the town's regional importance and local support for the bid, even though it fell below the 200,000 threshold.[31] Across the country the local press lined up to pour scorn on the Home Office's decision-making processes. Civic leaders in Ipswich and Colchester were quoted in the *East Anglian Daily Times* as condemning the decision as 'shambolic', 'scandalous', and 'farcical'.[32] Doncaster Councillor Colin Wedd was quoted in the South Yorkshire Press as claiming that 'I dare say whoever may have written this has not set foot in Doncaster'.[33] In Wales, Newtown's deputy mayor was reported to be 'disappointed', but Michael Williams of Machynlleth Town Council refused to accept that his town had been ruled out at this stage, which was fair enough given that the Welsh towns were not included in the report as leaked.[34] The *East Anglian Daily Times* called for the Home Secretary to institute a more transparent bidding process in the future, and – perhaps more tongue-in-cheek – to repay to councils and sponsors the sums of money spent on preparing bids which were never going to be taken seriously.[35]

The reaction to the leaked document was vociferous, and most of it had to be handled by Mike O'Brien, the Home Office minister who was overseeing the competition because Jack Straw, the Home Secretary, was compromised by representing Blackburn, an applicant town. Colchester MP Bob Russell tabled a question in the House of Commons to the Home Secretary asking 'when it was decided that towns competing for city status for the third millennium needed a population in excess of 200,000 to qualify'. O'Brien stonewalled in a Commons written answer on 10 March:

> No such decision has been made. Although population size is taken into account by my Right Honourable Friend the Home Secretary in submitting a recommendation to Her Majesty the Queen, the grant of city status is not a right that can be claimed

---

30   *The Times*, 8 March 2000.
31   http://www.thisisessex.co.uk, 8 March 2000.
32   *East Anglian Daily Times*, 8 March 2000.
33   http://www.doncasteronline.co.uk, 15 March 2000.
34   http://www.nwn.co.uk, 15 March 2000.
35   *East Anglian Daily Times*, 16 March 2000.

by a town fulfilling certain criteria, but an honour conferred by the Sovereign by Letters Patent.

He also confirmed once again that 'no date has been set for the announcement of the new city'.[36] Subsequently, in a face-saving exercise on behalf of the government, he wrote to MPs representing the towns which had applied, inviting them to make a further submission. Not surprisingly, this delayed the process of selecting a millennium city by several months.[37] But the Home Office continued to prevaricate. On 19 June O'Brien stalled further in a written reply to a question in the House of Commons, simply reiterating that 'no date has yet been set for the announcement of the new city'.[38]

For those towns which believed themselves still to be in the frame, the waiting went on, partly because Downing Street was having second thoughts. News leaked out that the Prime Minister had asked the Home Office to recommend four towns for promotion, of which it was thought one would be in Scotland.[39] Wrexham had previously called for new cities in Wales, Scotland, and Northern Ireland, as well as England, in recognition of the ongoing devolution issue. Clearly the 200,000 threshold could not apply outside of England if this was to happen.

For several more months there was silence. The Home Office carried nothing on its web site, and almost down to the announcement it was deflecting enquiries by arguing that since no date had ever been set it could not be accused of delay.[40] On 22 November The Times reported 'feuding between Cabinet Ministers' as the reason for 'delay' since it was now 'months after a decision might have been expected'. Already, however, the truth was suspected, since The Times reported that Brighton and Hove, and Wolverhampton would be promoted, along with Inverness, and that this was creating difficulties with Paul Murphy, the Welsh Secretary, who had endorsed the applications from Wrexham and Newport, both of which were likely to be unsuccessful.[41] On 26 November the BBC reported that an announcement might not even be possible before the end of 2000 as a result of internal feuding among government ministers. The Secretary of State for Wales was 'unhappy, and lobbying for a Welsh town to be included'. As a result, there had been an almighty row in Cabinet, which was taking time to resolve.[42]

It would, presumably, have been politically inconceivable to fail altogether to name the millennium city during the course of 2000, and on 17 December the media was alerted to an imminent announcement. The expectation was still that one city would be created, to be followed by a further creation at the

[36]   Hansard, vol. 345, 113847–8, 10 March 2000.
[37]   The Times, 22 Nov. 2000.
[38]   Hansard, vol. 352, 126575, 19 June 2000.
[39]   Personal Communication from Graham Dines of the East Anglian Daily Times.
[40]   Personal Communication, Sylvia Brown, Home Office, 6 Dec. 2000.
[41]   The Times, 22 Nov. 2000.
[42]   http://news.bbc.co.uk, 26 Nov. 2000.

Queen's Golden Jubilee in 2002.[43] The long-delayed information was finally given on the morning of 18 December in a written statement to the House of Commons by Mike O'Brien to a planted question from Liverpool Garston MP Maria Eagle.[44]

O'Brien announced that city status was to be conferred on Brighton and Hove, Wolverhampton and Inverness. The Queen had been advised by the prime minister that it would be politically expedient to make three grants in celebration of the millennium, and that these were the towns recommended for promotion. As ever, she had accepted her government's recommendation. Despite the Home Office's attachment to population figures in the past, and the leaked information about the 200,000 rule, it still repeated the usual mantra that 'City status is not, and never has been, a right which can be claimed by a town fulfilling certain conditions. The use of specific criteria could lead to a town claiming city status as of right, which in turn might devalue the honour.' Consequently, or so it was claimed, 'all applications were considered on their individual merits'.[45]

A subsequent press release from the Home Office included the comment that 'the quality of the thirty-nine applications received was very high and demonstrated the pride in their communities felt by local people in towns across the United Kingdom'. It went on to say that the thirty-six unsuccessful candidates would have a chance to renew their applications in a further competition to mark Her Majesty the Queen's Golden Jubilee, due in 2002, when four grants of city status (not the one grant announced in 1998) would be made, one for each country of the United Kingdom. In a tacit acknowledgement that all had not gone according to plan in the millennium competition, it was announced that new procedures would be published early in 2001 on how the 2002 competition would be run. Undeniably, however, the rules had already been altered. Although three grants of city status were made in 1897 at the time of Queen Victoria's Diamond Jubilee, subsequent grants had been made individually during the twentieth century with the exception of Armagh and St Davids in 1994. Furthermore, the original plan was for one grant in 2000 and another in 2002, not for a total of seven, and not in order to satisfy politically correct rules by making grants in each kingdom.

The local media was the first to break the story at lunchtime on 18 December 2000. In some areas it was jubilation, in others commiseration. Central East News, for example, ran a lunchtime story mainly to the effect that Northampton (the only applicant in its region) had failed in its bid while Brighton, Inverness and Wolverhampton had succeeded. But the city status story did not really catch fire. By the evening of 18 December it managed about 15 seconds halfway through the BBC's 10 p.m. news bulletin, and the time was split between congratulations for the winners and criticism from

Wales that none of their applicants had been rewarded. On 19 December *The Times* headlined its story of the event as 'New cities party after bitter battle', and opened its account by reflecting on the 'leaks, delays and ministerial wrangling' which had marred the competition. Even the proposed 2002 creations were reported as 'a last minute concession to the unhappy Welsh towns that have missed out this time', a reference to the Welsh Secretary's protest that two creations in England and one in Scotland 'would provoke a political backlash in Wales, where Labour is under pressure from Plaid Cymru'. It was also noted that the announcement was 'marred by accusations that the Government used the competition to boost Labour's chances of holding marginal seats'.[46]

The accusation of political chicanery reflected the fact that all three Brighton and Hove seats were marginals taken by Labour from the Tories in 1997, that there was a similar marginal in Wolverhampton, and Inverness had been a Labour gain from the Liberal Democrats in 1997. Simon Burns, one of Chelmsford's two Conservative MPs, was quoted in the *Independent* as saying that 'I am quite surprised that of all the towns that sought city status, the prime minister should recommend three with Labour marginal seats in them – three in Brighton and Hove, one in Inverness and one in Wolverhampton'.[47] Shadow Environment spokesman Archie Norman proposed that the whole business ought to be put in the hands of a commission in order to exclude politicians from an area 'that should be none of their business' – a sentiment older hands at the Home Office must have approved.[48]

Why were Brighton and Hove, Wolverhampton and Inverness successful, and what of the rest? Anyone reading the report leaked in March 2000 could hardly fail to see that Brighton and Hove and Wolverhampton were the front runners – and they had been the runners-up in 1992. Brighton, the March report noted, had previously been 'unsuccessful largely on account of the town's population falling below the 200,000 threshold', but now with the link to Hove following unitary status in 1998 it was around 250,000 and quite sufficient. The town 'occupies a central position in the surrounding area and has strong, although not recent, Royal connections'. It had also put together a convincing application, which reflected a local campaign to mobilize public support and opinion. A series of companies and organizations had helped to sponsor the campaign.[49]

Wolverhampton was never the bookmakers' favourite, despite the favourable review it received in the leaked report.[50] With a population of

46   *The Times*, 19 Dec. 2000.
47   http://www.independent.co.uk/news, 18 Dec. 2000.
48   *The Times*, 19 Dec. 2000.
49   PRO HO 286/126 listed Brighton as a strong runner in the 1977 race, disqualified by being too small. File HLG 120/1714 mentions claims to city status from Brighton in 1975 and 1983. An application in the 1930s was mentioned in the Millennium literature.
50   Somewhat surprisingly, given the publicity which surrounded the competition, bookmakers William Hill were caught out. By December 2000 they had as favourites

245,000 it satisfied the primary qualification, and it could also boast of being 'well-established commercially and educationally and is also a regional centre for leisure and entertainment'. But what had changed from its previous applications? In the past it had failed to convince the Home Office that it was a place of 'individual character', to use the phrase employed in 1953, while in 1966 it was seen as only part of a conurbation in the Black Country. Like Croydon in relation to London, it was considered incapable of establishing a profile as a regional centre in its own right.[51] Possibly the fact that Dudley, which applied in 1992, did not compete in 2000 helped, but Wolverhampton had more or less made its point in 1992. Previous applications had been rejected on the grounds that it was 'not sufficiently distinct from the rest of the West Midlands' but this had been questioned in 1992, and the Home Office accepted in 2000 that 'it retains and is proud of its own identity … [and] acts as a focus also for parts of Staffordshire and Shropshire'. Certainly the city status application was professionally produced, but it was by no means outstanding. Links with royalty were hardly mentioned, and its long history was passed over relatively briefly.

For Inverness we have no leaked report from the Home Office to provide us with guidance as to how its claims were viewed, but it was certainly not a bookmaker's favourite. It had first applied for city status as long ago as 1897, but it could never compete in an open market with English towns. We know that the recommendation of a Scottish candidate came from the Scottish Office, in consultation with the First Minister of the Scottish Assembly. We know also that the population threshold figure of 200,000 was applied only in the case of English towns. Since Paisley rather than Inverness was the largest of the Scottish applicants, we can assume that the final decision was taken on other grounds. If so, then Inverness's claim was presumably favoured perhaps because it had applied before, but more likely because it made a good case for itself as the regional capital of the Highlands. The case for Inverness was made in terms of history (given that it had been a royal burgh since the twelfth century), size (the largest town in the northern half of Scotland with a population of nearly 65,000 in 1999), regional role (serving 240,000 people in its hinterland, the focal point for a community the size of Belgium, and the shopping and cultural centre for the Highlands), as well as its national and European links. It certainly made the most convincing case of the four Scottish applicants for having a regional as opposed to a local role.

Not surprisingly, there was considerable rejoicing in those towns which had been raised to cities. The Wolverhampton *Express and Star* led its 18 December edition with the banner headline 'YES! We're a city', and quoted

---

Luton, which was in the news as a result of recently announced redundancies at the Vauxhall car plant, at even money, with Brighton and Hove second at 4/1, Guildford third at 11/2, and Inverness fourth at 14/1. Wolverhampton they put only among the also rans at 33/1: *East Anglian Daily Times*, 18 Dec. 2000.

51   PRO HO 286/11.

Dennis Turner (Labour MP, Wolverhampton South-East) as saying it represented the culmination of a campaign on his own part which started when he entered the Commons in 1987. In his view 'it will achieve exactly the right psychological atmosphere in Wolverhampton – the feel good factor, that something good has happened to the town…. It will bring the community together and … will be a boost for Wolverhampton's economy.' Jenny Jones (Labour MP, Wolverhampton South-West) told the paper that 'Wolverhampton deserves it. It will be a wonderful boost for the town and everybody in it', while Ken Purchase (Labour MP, Wolverhampton North-East) thought it 'will be a real tonic for the town'.[52]

The new city opened a roll of honour for proud Wulfrunians to offer their congratulations, and the mayor hit just the right note when he told the local press 'I hope it will attract a lot of inward investment into Wolverhampton, people would much rather invest in a city than a town'. Not surprisingly, some of the old confusions remained. The vice chairman of the Sports Advisory Council, Peter Holmes, was reported as asking 'will we have to choose one of our historic churches to be named as a cathedral, and will we have to apply to have a Lord Mayor?' A few embittered Conservatives claimed that Wolverhampton had been promoted to boost the government's chances of holding on to three Labour seats, a claim refuted by their own party leader in the borough.[53] The *Express and Star* also ran an eight-page supplement celebrating the promotion. Of course there were cynics. David Handley wrote to the paper on 19 December:

> I can't understand the amount of publicity behind Wolverhampton finally getting city status. Could someone explain to me what the people who live here stand to gain from it? I believe the only people who will be gaining are our councillors and council leaders who will be looking forward to their salaries going up at our expense. I couldn't have cared less about getting city status.

The public relations team saw things quite differently. This was an opportunity to re-brand Wolverhampton, and their first move was to order a new logo for the city.[54] Within months all the road signs had been upgraded.

The same lines of thinking were apparent in the other two new cities. Simon Fanshawe, the local broadcaster who masterminded the Brighton and Hove bid, talked about the enormous potential he anticipated from the award: 'It will transform us from a receding town into a place on the move turning imagination into reality'.[55] Brighton Pavilion Labour MP David Lepper spoke of how 'it will make it a more attractive location for businesses, bringing many jobs which are still much needed throughout the area'.[56] Bizarrely, royal

52   *Wolverhampton Express and Star*, 19 Dec. 2000.
53   Ibid.
54   Ibid., 21 Dec. 2000.
55   http://bbc.co.uk/news, 18 Dec. 2000
56   http://thisisbrightonandhove.co.uk, 19 Dec. 2000.

protocol deemed it unacceptable for the Queen herself to present the letters patent when she visited Brighton in March 2001, because the visit had been arranged before the grant of city status was announced. Consequently, the letters patent for the award of city status were issued on 31 January 2001 and presented to the mayor by the deputy lord lieutenant of East Sussex, Peter Field, at a ceremony in the town hall on 15 February.[57] Subsequently, the mayor threw a party for 850 people in the Corn Exchange, thus ensuring that the grant was seen as a community success, not simply something for the councillors to congratulate themselves about.[58]

Inverness, and Scottish politicians more generally, saw promotion in terms of civic boosterism. Dr John Reid, Scottish Secretary, expected the new city to receive a major economic hoist: 'I hope that its new status as a city will provide a welcome boost to its economy, identity and confidence'. He also hinted at why he had put forward Inverness's case: 'when I visited Inverness 18 months ago there was a real buzz about the millennium city competition and I am pleased that the efforts of all those involved have paid off.... I hope it will be a useful addition to the efforts of Inverness to attract investment and industry', and that 'it will increase the estimation of Inverness in the eyes of the people of the United Kingdom'.[59] Fergus Ewing, (Scottish National Party MSP, Inverness East), talked of the 'intangible' benefits which would 'help promote Inverness as a commercial centre as well as an international tourist attraction', and Inverness provost Bill Smith claimed it would 'give businesses in the town and indeed throughout the Highlands a tremendous marketing tool in attracting additional income to our fast-growing economy'.[60]

Not surprisingly, the candidates who failed to make the grade were less ecstatic about the outcome. In East Anglia, where four candidates were disappointed, it was time for brave faces from the local MPs. Bob Russell (Lib-Dem Colchester) made a pre-emptive strike when he recognized that failure was inevitable, telling the *East Anglian Daily Times* on the very morning of the announcement that 'it is deeply disappointing that the choice of millennium city could be decided on the basis of electoral advantage for the Labour Party'. He called for all thirty-nine applicants to be granted the honour: 'they have all made genuine bids backed by their communities'. Simon Burns (Conservative, Chelmsford West) also thought politics had a good deal to do with the final decision: 'cynically, the reason the honour will go to the south coast is that it has three Labour MPs with narrow majorities. If that is the case, it will be shameful.'[61]

On hearing the announcement, Reading business leaders warned that the town's failure to win city status 'could hit the Thames Valley's economic

---

[57]   Ibid, 3 Feb. 2001.
[58]   Ibid., 30 March 2001; ex inf. Simon Fanshawe.
[59]   Scotland Office, Press Release SSO307, 18 Dec. 2000.
[60]   http://news.bbc.co.uk/Scotland, 19 March 2000.
[61]   *East Anglian Daily Times*, 18 Dec. 2000.

standing in Europe', and offered their support to civic officers who were already preparing for the 2002 competition before the millennium winner had been announced. The mayor commented: 'I'm disappointed but not downhearted. Reading is such a buzzing town at the moment with so much going on and city status would have been the icing on the cake.' He added optimistically that 'with the continuing development and growth in the town it will only be a matter of time before Reading is awarded the city status it deserves'.[62] Swindon vowed to fight on, but the local press accepted that the town had done itself no favours. It criticized the 'cut-price bid' which had failed 'to make an impression with the people making the decision.... Our bid appeared to come from an elite few in the town.'[63]

In Lancashire there was deep disappointment in Blackburn and Bolton. The local press called for a positive response in Blackburn to ensure success in 2002, but it would need to be 'backed by a bigger and better attempt to sell itself as a city in what has become an increasingly crowded competition'. The press wanted greater emphasis on the town's strong economic growth, and the regeneration of the town centre, developments which were 'firm pointers to Blackburn being a town on the move and one with a future that merits city status'. They complained also about a selection process in which 'tiny Inverness with a population only a third of Blackburn' was favoured with city status.[64] Civic leaders in Bolton were depressed by the town's failure. Council leader Bob Howarth was quoted as saying that as the competition was all a lottery there seemed to be little point in proceeding, but industrialist Richard Hurst, chairman of Bolton's Vision for the Future Steering Group argued that the town needed to look at the successful bid formats used by Brighton and Wolverhampton to see what could be learnt. The debate continued subsequently in the town.[65]

Perhaps the greatest disappointment was in Wales where all six candidates failed. St Asaph vowed to fight on: 'we'll keep on trying until they recognize our importance'. Newtown thought it would try again. Newport was disappointed it had not succeeded first time but, like Aberystwyth, said it would try again in 2002. Former mayor of Aberystwyth, Sion Jobbins, added that 'I think the decision should be taken by the [Welsh] Assembly'. Machynlleth thought it had gained good publicity from the campaign, while Wrexham was disappointed but continued to believe it had a good case as a regional centre for north Wales.[66]

Ultimately this was a competition shot through with inconsistency, and a complex set of decision-making processes which seems to have defied rationality in numerous ways. Yet it was still possible to draw some fairly clear

62   *Reading Evening Post*, 19 Dec. 2000.
63   http://thisiswiltshire.co.uk, 19, 20 Dec. 2000.
64   http://thisislancashire.co.uk, 18–20 Dec. 2000.
65   Ibid., 19 Dec. 2000.
66   http://www.totalwales.com/news, 19 Dec. 2000.

conclusions. First, in England population was the deciding factor among those towns which established regional distinctiveness, although even those over 200,000 could be ruled out on other grounds. Croydon and Southwark failed to establish a case for being treated as separate from London, while Stockport fell by the wayside because it lacked distinctiveness from Manchester. Wolverhampton was specifically ruled in, because it was thought now to show real regional significance. On the grounds of population and regional importance, Brighton and Hove, and Wolverhampton were always eminently predictable front runners, particularly after the 200,000 threshold became public knowledge in March 2000. The application of this rule effectively debarred many of the competitors, several of whom would presumably not have wasted time, effort and money on an application had they known the drift of the Home Office's thinking. Indeed, the whole point of the competition seemed questionable given that the English winners had been the runners-up in 1992.

Second, besides population and regional role, towns had to jump through several other hoops of which they were not made aware in advance. A long history and significant connections with royalty were qualifying factors. A history was perhaps foreseeable, although this was of little benefit to Milton Keynes and Telford. Several towns pointed out that they had tried for city status before, as if to emphasize both their longevity, and their desire to win the race one day. Royal connections were slightly less predictable as a qualifying criterion, although economic success and community involvement were more predictable, and in any case these were points which all the towns highlighted. Swindon found itself damned as too materialistic, so there was clearly a fine line to be drawn between too little and too much. Even so, it is difficult to see how applicants could have gone in any other direction given that they were, in effect, asked to write a curriculum vitae for their town.

Third, for most of the duration of the competition the Home Office was working to the idea of promoting a single town, and as such it was presumably looking at a large English town with regional distinctiveness. Certainly, none of the Scottish, Welsh and Northern Ireland candidates were likely to have been regarded as contenders, at least until the competition moved beyond a single victor. But once the decision was taken to promote a Scottish town, the candidates from Wales and Northern Ireland were bound to be upset. After all, Newport, with a population of 137,000, is substantially greater than both Paisley, the largest of the Scottish applicants, and Inverness. We know from the Home Office announcement in December 2000 that the prime minister, Tony Blair, was personally responsible for advising the Queen that grants of city status should be made to more than one town. We can only assume that the decision was based on political considerations arising from devolution, or perhaps because there had been no promotions in Scotland since 1889, while Wales had three successes with Cardiff, Swansea and St Davids and Northern Ireland had been successful with Armagh.

Yet the result, whatever the reason for the final selection, was clearly a fudge, and political infighting apparently provoked a Home Office rethink, hence the announcement that four cities would be created in 2002, one for each of the four provinces, and that guidelines would be introduced. If population was to remain a key determinant, there would always be contention because the Scottish, Welsh and Northern Ireland communities argue that they cannot compete with their larger English neighbours; while the Blackburn press neatly inverted the argument following the December 2000 announcement by asking why Scottish towns should be promoted when larger English ones remained towns.[67]

Fourth, the Home Office gave little indication of being in control of the city status exercise. It is not unreasonable to argue that throughout the twentieth century the Home Office was more interested in preventing too many towns from becoming cities than in looking at whether city status would act as a positive incentive to development in the manner favoured, and regularly predicted, by the would-be cities. By announcing a competition without rules, and subsequently being seen to operate thresholds, it seemed to be acting without rationale, although inevitably there had to be some means of comparing the different applicants. But it was worse than that. In the absence of rules, applicants did not know how best to put together their case. They had to rely on hearsay and hints, and they were unhappy with this. Reading Labour MP Martin Salter was quoted as saying that the bidding process was flawed as there were 'no clear criteria to judge against'.[68] Furthermore, because it is a Crown prerogative they may never know why they succeeded or failed. Even when released, the official papers are likely to be carefully weeded.

The Home Office compounded the potential problems of judging the contest by refusing to establish either rules or guidelines. Just telling English towns that a minimum population of 200,000 was required would have simplified the position. But lessons were not learned. Along with the announcement in December 2000, the Home Office put out a fact sheet which declared, among other things, the old mantra that 'City status is not, and never has been, a right which can be claimed by a town fulfilling certain conditions. The use of specific criteria could lead to a town claiming city status as of right, which in turn might devalue the honour.' While this could be seen as reasonable, it is a matter for discussion as to whether claims by right would actually devalue the honour. It does not follow that towns which effectively had no hope of being elevated should have been encouraged to go ahead with applications. Similarly, the claim that 'all applications were considered on their individual merits', rather overlooks the fact that in England simply failing to have enough people was a disqualification.

It has yet to be made clear why the Home Office initially anticipated one promotion to city and then shifted its ground to a compromise position of two

67   http://thisislancashire.co.uk, 19 Dec. 2000.
68   *The Times*, 19 Dec. 2000.

English towns and one Scottish town. Home Office minister Mike O'Brien was widely quoted in the press as extolling the virtues of all the applications, so why did they not all succeed? After all, merely because they are the seats of bishops, relatively small and unimportant places such as Hereford, Ripon and Lincoln, enjoy a status which thriving industrial and commercial centres believe would benefit them in the international marketplace, hence their promotional efforts. Sunderland has always maintained of its 1992 promotion that it was beneficial for numerous reasons, and Newport went so far as to quote the claims from Wearside in its application.

Despite the many inconsistencies in the process of finding a millennium city or, as it transpired, cities, the competition passed off without much debate. Few of the towns which failed were keen to complain too loudly because a further opportunity for promotion was already on the horizon, with the promised Golden Jubilee competition in 2002. As a political exercise it was a success for the government, since at the 2001 election it won all three seats in Wolverhampton, two in Brighton and one in Hove, and Inverness. There was still, of course, dissatisfaction in Wales, where Nick Bourne, leader of the Welsh Conservatives suggested that Paul Murphy had 'failed to live up to his title',[69] but the general sense was that this was a town hall matter with benefits which it would take years rather than months to assess. Dennis Turner, one of the Wolverhampton MPs, writing in April 2001, noted that there was a feel-good factor in the new city, but that 'in these very early days there is a difficulty in identifying any concrete examples of positive outcomes in terms of business or employment advantages'.[70] And, without feedback from Whitehall, the failed applicants had no grounds for introspective self-examination, or even complaint: all they could do was prepare for the next round.

[69]   http://www.aberystwyth.co.uk, 13 Nov. 2001.
[70]   Personal Communication, 4 April 2001.

CHAPTER EIGHT

The Golden Jubilee Competition, 2002

The Home Secretary announced in 1998 that a new city would be created to coincide with the Queen's Golden Jubilee in 2002. For obvious reasons this was a less certain occasion than the millennium. Fortunately, the Queen's good health ensured that having seen Derby raised to city status on the occasion of her Silver Jubilee, and Sunderland to celebrate forty years on the throne, the planned further opportunity for civic honours occurred in 2002. However, between 1998 and 2000 the plans were changed, largely as a result of the Cabinet infighting over the millennium promotions. On 23 November 2000, in a written Parliamentary answer, the prime minister set out plans for celebrating the Golden Jubilee. Civic honours would include grants of city status and a lord mayoralty.[1] The full extent of the civic honours programme became clear on 18 December 2000, when it was announced that the Queen had agreed that there should be city status grants to suitably qualified towns in each of England, Scotland, Wales and Northern Ireland. In practice even this plan was amended and five towns, rather than the anticipated four, were raised to city status in 2002. A lord mayoralty competition was also announced for the Golden Jubilee.

Clearly, this concession to devolution seriously disadvantaged English towns. On the basis of the millennium competition, the six unsuccessful towns in Wales, three in Scotland and two in Northern Ireland, would now be competing for three grants of city status. At the same time twenty-five or more English towns were likely to be competing for a single promotion.[2] At least the government was a little more open about what it was looking for, promising to set out guidelines, to be published sometime during the first half of 2001. Aspirant cities simply had to bide their time, and begin planning their applications. Meantime, the government had other things on its mind, notably an election.

The general election was held on 7 June 2001, and Tony Blair's Labour party was returned to power. In the wake of this success the prime minister pushed through a series of significant alterations in the powers and responsibilities of different departments within Whitehall. The Constitutional Unit was relocated in the Lord Chancellor's department, thus removing powers over city status grants from the hands of the Home Office where they had lain since the nineteenth century. It has subsequently become the Department of Constitutional Affairs. Perhaps inevitably, as a result of these upheavals, the timetable for the Golden Jubilee competition slipped. The promised guidelines were published only on 25 July.

---

[1]   *Hansard*, vol. 357, 140120, 23 Nov. 2000.
[2]   *The Times*, 19 Dec. 2000.

The Constitutional Unit may have moved departments, but it remained wary of too much commitment. It accepted that the acrimony surrounding the 2000 competition needed to be avoided in future. Consequently, it set out guidelines for would-be applicants to follow. They were specifically 'not criteria', but 'merely suggestions as to what a town might include in an application'. Three main factors were stressed: first, notable features, including significance regionally or nationally; second, historical (including royal) features; and third, 'a forward-looking attitude'. The latter criteria doubtless reflected one of the themes the Queen had herself emphasized in relation to the Golden Jubilee, that it should be about looking forward as well as back. 'Suggested indicators', designed to show aspirant cities how they could adopt a 'forward-looking attitude', included evidence that a whole community was working together towards a socially inclusive and sustainable future, that a town was expanding or even recovering from past difficulties as well as being open to new ideas and technology, and that it was responsive to its citizens' wishes.

To counter claims about the millennium competition, it was laid down that 'population size will only be considered, as a possible measure of a town's significance within its region, if applicants in contention are otherwise evenly matched'. Expressed in a different way, the first two criteria laid down in 1907 had been reversed. Towns also needed to show themselves to be centres of industry, commerce, religion or the arts, to have definitive boundaries, major civic buildings and good transport links. They were to have a real community, a sense of place and be some distance from other towns. Historical features could include ancient monuments, museums or evidence of local interest in history or significant connections with royalty, either historic or recent. Aspirant cities were given until 12 October to submit their claims, and *The Times* immediately installed Reading (its preferred candidate in 2000), Newport, Stirling and Ballymena as favourites.[3]

Towns which had been unsuccessful in 2000 were invited to submit a new application, or to allow their previous application to stand, or to submit additional material in support of their case. Most candidates preferred to submit a new application, which they prepared during the summer of 2001. Sporadic interest in the competition was shown by the media. Swindon, one of the front runners, was featured on BBC's *Newsnight* programme on 24 July, and two days later Simon Jenkins wrote a provocative piece in *The Times* suggesting that the whole procedure bore little relationship to the needs of a present-day society.[4] By the time of the closing date for applications on 12 October, attention had shifted across the Atlantic as a result of the attack on the World Trade Centre in New York on 11 September, and there was little interest in the national press as to which towns had applied, or the manner of

---

3   Ibid., 26 July 2001; Lord Chancellor's department, Constitutional Unit, Press Release 273/01, 25 July 2001.
4   *The Times*, 26 July 2001.

their applications. The first national newspaper to give any coverage of the competition was the *Sunday Express*, which carried a lukewarm account of the competition on 21 October, expressing mainly sceptical views reflecting what was considered to be the government's political manipulation of the Millennium competition. Theresa May, shadow secretary of state for the regions, was quoted as saying:

> This is not the first time this Labour Government has run such a competition, and based on the experience of the last one – to mark the millennium – we have concerns. The cynical might point out that the winners contained a large number of Labour marginal Parliamentary seats. It would be very disappointing to other towns if good claims were invalidated by the Labour Government purely because they did not have marginal Labour seats within their boundaries. This calls into question once again the extent to which public awards are open to political abuse.

The article also suggested that success in the competition did not necessarily bring rewards. While Norman Davies, leader of Wolverhampton council, believed that city status had been 'a great boost to the self confidence not only of the citizens but also the business community', local leaders in Inverness and Brighton and Hove were less clear as to the advantages of promotion.[5]

An announcement of which towns had entered the competition was given in a written House of Commons answer on 22 October by Rosie Winterton of the Lord Chancellor's department, to a question from Bob Russell, MP for Colchester. That in turn was followed by a press release later in the day.[6] Since millennium applicants were allowed simply to have their earlier application taken into account, it is no surprise that all but one of the unsuccessful candidates were back in the contest. Southwark did not renew its application, and Telford resubmitted its claims only as a formality. According to council leader Phil Davis, this was not the right time to promote city status as Telford was seeking borough status. City status, he added, required a campaign that would take resources better used elsewhere. The main effort was to achieve borough status, and a more focused campaign for city status might follow at a future date.[7] In total twenty-five English, six Welsh, four Scottish and six Northern Irish towns applied (table 5). The Constitutional Unit announced that consultation would take place with the secretaries of state for transport, local government and the regions. As for a result, Rosie Winterton told Bob Russell that 'the Lord Chancellor hopes to announce the results in the early months of next year'.

---

5   *Sunday Express*, 21 Oct. 2001.

6   *Hansard*, vol. 373, 8454–5, 22 Oct 2001; Lord Chancellor's Department, Press Release, 22 Oct. 2001.

7   http://www.shropshirestar.com/news, 24 Oct. 2001.

Table 5 Golden Jubilee competition contenders 2002

England	Wales	Scotland	Northern Ireland
Blackburn and Darwen	Aberystwyth	Ayr	Ballymena
Blackpool	Machynlleth	Dumfries*	Carrickfergus*
Bolton	Newport	Paisley	Craigavon*
Chelmsford	Newtown	Stirling	Coleraine*
Colchester	St Asaph		Lisburn
Croydon	Wrexham		Newry*
Doncaster			
Dover			
Greenwich*			
Guildford			
Ipswich			
Luton			
Maidstone			
Medway			
Middlesbrough			
Milton Keynes			
Northampton			
Preston			
Reading			
Shrewsbury			
Southend			
Stockport			
Swindon			
Warrington			
Wirrall*			

* denotes newcomer since 2000

Source: Lord Chancellor's Department, Press Release, 22 Oct. 2001.

Within the town hall, interest was rekindled by the new competition, particularly perhaps because there were now some guidelines to follow. Once again local councils had to decide how to respond, and in the process they provided another collection of glossy brochures, CD Roms, videos, websites, and even (in the case of Lisburn) a DVD.[8] The great majority of English applications were desktop assessments in the town hall, perhaps reflecting the costs incurred by more extensive campaigns in 2000. Design quality varied

---

[8]   I was able to see all the 2002 applications, except for those of Guildford, Maidstone, St Asaph and Southend, all of which failed to respond to numerous requests. In what follows the material is taken from these applications except where stated otherwise.

considerably. Northampton did not include any pictures, and Dover simply submitted a two-and-a-half page letter pointing to a few of its strengths. Only Blackpool and Northampton attempted slavishly to follow the Lord Chancellor's department's guidelines: most other towns preferred to address the issues raised from their own particular angle. Many applications were little more than puffs for local government achievement, although quite a number, including Colchester and Preston, included quotations from local residents as well as from businessmen and community leaders. Doncaster claimed that 'the whole community has come together in a spirit of pride and enthusiasm to prepare this bid for City Status', by which it meant business and educational interests, as well as the local media.[9] On the other hand, the decision to call its campaign 'every mayor needs a city' was curious if not confusing. Ipswich claimed that 10,500 of 12,000 respondents in a radio phone-in favoured its case, although by an unfortunate coincidence it surely weakened its cause by claiming similar status to neighbouring Colchester as the oldest English town.

If possible, the applications were rather more sombre than for the millennium. Blackpool no longer sold itself as a city of fun, preferring the slightly more serious image of a tourist centre for which city status would act as a 'tool for regeneration ... by sending a clear signal of belief in growth and renewal'. The guidelines encouraged Blackburn with Darwen to emphasize how city status 'would be a fitting recognition of the shared sacrifices and efforts of our residents to work together over a sustained period and against the odds to improve their lot, whilst embracing the needs of those less able to help themselves'. Much was also made of the fact that the competition coincided with the 150th anniversary of the town's incorporation.[10] Milton Keynes happily admitted that its 2001 application was lower key than for the millennium because the original application had summed up the achievements of the would-be city.[11] Bolton prepared a glossy brochure detailing cultural, historical and architectural reasons why it should receive the honour.[12] Its reason for returning to the competition after the disappointment of 2000 was, according to the assistant director of central services, Des Grogan, because 'we have spoken to other towns which have become cities in the past and they say there has been a marked increase in civic pride.... Cities tend to be more attractive to large companies.'[13] As a result, Bolton worked hard on finding notable features and a forward-looking attitude. As it believed it had been ruled out in 2000 for lack of royal connections, a good deal of effort went into locating a direct descendant of the Queen in William de Radcliffe, past owner of the historic Smithills Hall. His other descendants included Diana, Princess of Wales, but, rather more sinisterly, Lord Lucan. The application listed all recent royal visits.

Among other towns, the Thames Valley rivals, Reading and Swindon, were back in the race. Reading's impressive application featured a strong pictorial presentation along with a CD Rom and website. Under the title 'Living Reading', the CD Rom, which was produced by the borough council in conjunction with local business, emphasized the strength of community feeling which lay behind the application. Swindon, stung by criticism of its millennium application, prepared a completely new bid, 'one that celebrates all the hard work and commitment local people have made to secure the town's continued success'.[14] It still stressed the economic success story, but claimed that the bid was about 'the town, the people and their achievements.... If there was ever a time Swindon deserved the mantle of city status it is now.' Stress was laid on community, education, culture, and how the town was moving forward, although it could claim little by way of history, heritage or royal connections. Unfortunately, all this hard work and self-promotion was rather spoiled when the local branch of Friends of the Earth opposed the bid on the grounds that 'the borough should see the town in reality and that amenities such as a first-class library, a real town square and a better museum/art gallery need to be in place before time and resources are spent on obtaining the name city'. The group had previously opposed the 2000 bid because the focus on physical growth and economic development had shown little concern with sustainable development.[15] As early as 15 May the local newspaper had acknowledged that there were deficiencies in Swindon's hopes of city status, including the need for a centre for the arts and a decent library – classic requirements of a modern city in promotional terms – and the need for evidence to show that Swindon had a properly developed policy towards urban conservation.[16]

Both Croydon, in relation to London, and Stockport to Manchester, had to consider how to address the criticism expressed in 2000 of their lack of distinctiveness. Croydon addressed the issue head on, claiming that 'our aspiration to become a city is not a plea for separation from London. Rather it is a way of reinforcing our contribution to the wider metropolitan community of which we are pleased and privileged to be a part.' A dedicated website emphasized Croydon's history, identity and pioneering activity.[17] In Stockport, Liberal Democrat council leader Fred Ridley sought to deny that it was simply an appendage of Manchester and argued that it was distinct in its own right: 'If Salford, ridiculed as Manchester's back yard, could be a city, he claimed

---

[14]   http://www.swindon.gov.uk, 14 Nov. 2001.
[15]   http://thisiswiltshire.co.uk/swindon, 31 Aug., 6 Sept. 2001.
[16]   Ibid., 15 May 2001.
[17]   http://www.croydon.gov.uk/croydoncity, 14 Nov. 2001.

Stockport could claim greater glory'.[18] Stockport did not prepare a completely new application, preferring simply to supplement its earlier submission. While the additional material included a good deal about what Stockport had been doing since 2000, the proximity of Manchester was again ignored. Other towns which submitted addenda to their millennium applications included Chelmsford, Ipswich, and Shrewsbury and Atcham.[19] The latter emphasized how 'the new material focuses on how Shrewsbury embraces the future and includes views of local residents and people associated with the town about some of the things that set us apart from other market and county towns'.[20]

Towns which had not applied for the millennium competition were also invited to apply, which brought in seven new contenders – two in England, four in Northern Ireland, and one in Scotland. Greenwich and Wirral were the English newcomers. Greenwich declared itself to be 'a distinctive urban quarter of London' and, somewhat improbably, 'to London what Versailles is to Paris', and stressed in its application the borough's royal and maritime connections.[21] Wirral's bid was somewhat tongue-in-cheek, opening with the claim that 'it is undeniable that the peninsula of Wirral does not conform to any traditional view of a city', so that the application was likely to be 'greeted with surprise'. The main reason for applying was that city status would be a major stimulus to efforts being made 'to market the area and attract investment'.[22] No other application made quite such a clear statement in the direction of civic boosterism.

When the Golden Jubilee competition was announced in July 2001, a Scotland Office press release quoted the Scottish Secretary, Helen Liddell, as urging Scottish towns to 'think big' since this was 'a golden opportunity for a Scottish town to gain the prestige, confidence and identity that city status brings. The awarding of city status is a great honour, and I hope that towns throughout Scotland will "think big" and put themselves forward.' Ayr, Paisley and Stirling reapplied, and Dumfries joined the queue. All produced new applications, although Stirling used the same format and cover as at the millennium, and much of the same material, if in a different order. It also produced a CD Rom. The others produced large glossy booklets evidently designed to catch the eye of the Minister for Scotland, particularly Dumfries's application, undoubtedly the widest of any at 33 centimetres. Paisley also organized a 'City Day' on 24 September 2001, and sought support for its bid from local people via an internet site.[23]

All six Welsh towns unsuccessful in 2000 reapplied in 2002, and as on the earlier occasion their applications were generally less glamorous than those

18　http://www.guardian.co.uk, 26 July 2001.

19　*East Anglian Daily Times*, 26 July 2001. Whether an individual town had submitted a new application, or simply added supplementary information, is usually clear from within the bid document.

20　www.shrewsbury.gov.uk/citystatus, 30 Oct. 2001.

21　www.greenwich.gov.uk/council/strategicplanning/citybid, 31 Oct. 2001.

22　www.wirral.gov.uk, 6 Nov. 2001.

23　www2.renfrewshire.gov.uk/welcome/city, 8 Nov. 2001.

produced in England. Four of them (Aberystwyth, Machynlleth, Newtown and St Asaph) allowed their earlier applications to stand, although Machynlleth added a covering note of no great substance. Councillor Gaynor Pugh, mayor of Machynlleth, told Radio Wales listeners that the town had 'a tremendous amount going for it and Machynlleth had a right to city status after all they had achieved'. All the Welsh cities, she added, are in the south, 'and we want one in mid Wales'. She was presumably unaware that Bangor, in the north west, is a city.[24] St Asaph also vowed to fight on after losing out in 2000,[25] and launched its new bid in the cathedral on 11 September 2001. Once again it stressed that with its long church heritage the surprise was that it was not recognized as a city.[26] Newport and Wrexham submitted new applications. Newport's was prepared by a city status bid committee, which took advice from Sunderland. The bid emphasized its history, its strategic importance in south Wales (as well as being the largest non-city in the principality), its future prospects, and the involvement of the community in the application, which included petitions and celebratory events such as the launch of the bid in November 2001.[27] Wrexham's mayor, Councillor Sandy Mewies, personally delivered the town's bid to Welsh Secretary Paul Murphy at the National Assembly. Wrexham based its claims on having become a regional capital for its area and a modern industrial centre with a concentration of international companies and local enterprises based on various industrial parks.[28] The council backed the claim in order 'to project the area as one of high quality, growth and opportunity'.[29] On the other hand, there was obvious confusion in Wales about city status since Clywd South MP Martyn Jones thought Wrexham's case good on the grounds that there were only two cities in Wales, both in the south – presumably he was unaware of Bangor, in the north-west, and St Davids in the south-west.[30]

Only in Northern Ireland was there a serious shake-up in applications for the Golden Jubilee. Here (with the best odds, given that only Lisburn and Ballymena applied in 2000), four newcomers entered the competition: Carrickfergus, Coleraine, Craigavon and Newry. Town leaders in Ulster were happy to admit that they were taking advantage of the new rules. In the words of a spokesman for Newry Council 'it didn't indicate the last time that there would be a specific city chosen from Northern Ireland, so we thought we would have a better chance this time around'.[31] All the applicants produced extensive documentation, with Coleraine, Craigavon and Newry including CD Roms in their submissions, and Lisburn producing a DVD. Coleraine's presentation had rather too much grass in its opening sequences to suggest it is

---

[24]   *Powys County Times*, 26 July 2001.
[25]   *Free Denbighshire Press*, 20 Dec. 2000, 8 Aug. 2001.
[26]   www.staspah.co.uk/city, 3 Jan. 2002.
[27]   *South Wales Argus*, 13 Nov. 2001.
[28]   http://www.eveningleader.co.uk, 9 Oct. 2001.
[29]   www.wrexham.gov.uk/citystatus, 2 Nov 2001.
[30]   http://www.eveningleader.co.uk, 26 July 2001.
[31]   *Sunday Express*, 21 Oct. 2001.

a thriving town verging on a city. Craigavon's CD Rom presented the images from its application set to music, but the application itself looked to be little more than a desktop exercise with no evidence of any community involvement. Lisburn's application, printed on A3 paper, was by far the largest and, with a sizeable print size, most eye-catching of all the applications. Neither Lisburn nor Newry showed much sign of community involvement in the production of their applications, although Lisburn's website promised that its campaign, entitled 'Lisburn, a City for Everyone', really would be a community project.[32] Carrickfergus produced a great deal of information about itself, but it was not really formed into an application as such.

The prime minister, in his Commons written answer of 23 November 2000, also announced a competition for a lord mayoralty (or, since Scotland was now included, a lord provostship). He described the title as 'an exceptional distinction conferred on the Mayors of a few – normally long-established and important – cities', granted 'usually on occasions of particular Royal significance'. The rules of the competition were announced simultaneously with the city status competition on 25 July 2001, and there were no specific criteria, although cities which expressed an interest in the competition were 'provided with guidance on the factors that will be taken into account'. The key factors were that no claim would be entertained from a city of less than ten years' standing – it had been fifteen in 1992 – thereby apparently ruling out Armagh, Brighton and Hove, Inverness, St Davids, Sunderland and Wolverhampton. Other factors to be taken into account included 'a character and dignity of its own', and 'a quasi-metropolitan position within its region or sub-region'. As with city status, applicants from England submitted their claims to the Lord Chancellor's department, and those from Northern Ireland, Scotland and Wales to the Northern Ireland Office, the Scotland Office and the Wales Office respectively. Applications were allowed to take 'whatever form is felt best to present the town's case'.[33]

Together with the list of city status applicants, candidates for the lord mayoralty/lord provostship competition were announced in October 2001. In total there were fifteen (table 6). Given that it had been agreed at the beginning of the competition that applications from cities of less than ten years' standing were unlikely to succeed, the appearance in the list of Wolverhampton, St Davids and perhaps even Sunderland represented extreme optimism. Salford, always rejected out of hand by the Home Office, perhaps thought its chances would be improved now that the Lord Chancellor's department was in control. Bath, Carlisle, Chichester, Exeter, Lincoln and Worcester, represented cities by ancient prescriptive right, Gloucester was a sixteenth-century city, St Albans and Truro were nineteenth-century cities, and the other six have all become cities since 1926.

32   www.lisburn.gov.uk/city, 2 Nov. 2001.
33   Lord Chancellor's department, Press Release 273/01, 25 July 2001.

Table 6 Golden Jubilee lord mayoralty competition applicants 2002

Bath	Gloucester	Southampton
Cambridge	Lancaster	Sunderland
Carlisle	Lincoln	Truro
Chichester	St Albans	Wolverhampton
Derby	St Davids	Worcester
Exeter	Salford	

Source: Lord Chancellor's Department, Press Release, 21 Oct. 2001.

As at the Millennium Competition, the Lord Chancellor's department made no commitment as to when announcements could be expected regarding the successful candidates for city status and the lord mayoralty. Through the winter of 2001–2, growing concern was expressed about a competition in which English towns were clearly disadvantaged. Bob Russell (Liberal-Democrat, Colchester) asked in the Commons on 23 January 2002 whether a date for the announcement had been set – it had not – and whether more than one English town could be promoted – it was not anticipated.[34] Reading used a classic marketing ploy to raise its profile, seizing on an upbeat report in *The Times*, which its council officers helped to compile, to suggest that its bid was fully supported in the wider community.[35] Colchester was damaged by a critical report on the responsiveness of the borough council to local needs. Labour leader Tim Young even stated publicly that his group was not supporting the bid.[36] Otherwise, the competitions were allowed to hibernate while other Golden Jubilee planning and events received a greater share of media interest.

The results of the competition were announced on 14 March 2002 in a written answer to the House of Lords from the Lord Chancellor, Lord Irvine of Lairg, and a concurrent press release. The successful towns were Preston in England, Newport in Wales, Stirling in Scotland, and – the major surprise – Lisburn and Newry in Northern Ireland. The surprise had less to do with the towns named for promotion, than the fact that two candidates were successful. According to Irvine, 'the standard of all the applications was impressive and some were outstanding'. He gave no indication of how the final decisions had been reached, beyond adding that the decision to promote two towns in Northern Ireland was exceptional and was as a result of a recommendation

---

[34]   *Hansard*, vol. 378, 28752–3, 23 Jan. 2002; *East Anglian Daily Times*, 25 Jan. 2002.
[35]   *The Times*, 19 Feb. 2002; Stephen V. Ward, *Selling Places: the Marketing and Promotion of Towns and Cities, 1850–2000* (1998), 202.
[36]   *East Anglian Daily Times*, 13 Feb. 2002.

from the Secretary of State for Northern Ireland.[37] Exeter won the competition for a lord mayor.[38] The announcements failed to make the front page of any of the following day's broadsheets.

Among the applicant towns there were celebrations and commiserations. The successful towns were all convinced that they were worthy of their new-found status. The Preston challenge team immediately claimed that becoming England's newest city would 'raise its national and international profile', and the mayor, Councillor Alan Hackett, was quoted as saying 'we're absolutely delighted. This is a wonderful achievement and richly deserved ... it really puts Preston on the international map and will help to attract further investment and jobs.' Ian Hall, Labour leader of the borough council, told the *Preston Citizen* that 'The people of Preston can celebrate this success and look forward to an exciting future – with the multi-million pound city centre redevelopment scheme and regeneration projects all now taking shape'. All the leading local politicians joined in with suitable comments, and Mark Hendrick, the new city's Labour MP added that 'I am absolutely delighted that Preston has been selected for city status.... It is an excellent town, with excellent people, diverse industry, a brilliant university, excellent architecture and fully deserves to be a city.'[39] By contrast with the confusion at the millennium, the city status grants were announced early enough for the Queen to present the letters patent in person to the successful candidates. She visited Preston and presented the charter on 5 August 2002, the final day of her jubilee tour.[40]

No one seemed particularly surprised at the choice of Stirling in Scotland, which had been a clear favourite among the bookmakers, although Paisley was considered the most unfortunate of its rivals to miss out.[41] Tom Brookes, Stirling's provost, told the press that 'Stirling was the town that always thought it was a city – now the whole of Britain knows it is a city'. He added that he expected the new status to bring economic spin-offs. Roman Catholic Archbishop Keith O'Brien, who happened to be visiting Stirling on the day of the announcement, took the opportunity of offering his congratulations. Scottish Secretary Helen Liddell said that Stirling's royal history had enabled it to stand out among the other candidates.[42] The only uncertainty seemed to concern the size of the new Scottish city, the *Daily Telegraph* and the *Independent* claiming it had a population of 'only 29,000', and the *Guardian*

---

[37]   The secretary of state was Dr John Reid, who was previously secretary of state for Scotland. At the time of the millennium competition he had successfully argued the case for a Scottish city.

[38]   *Hansard* Written Answers, 14 March 2002, col WA 93. Press Release at www.lcd.gov.uk/constitution/city, 14 March 2002.

[39]   http://thisislancashire.co.uk/Preston, 15 March 2002.

[40]   *The Times*, 6 Aug. 2002; http://thisislancashire.co.uk/Preston, 5 Aug. 2002.

[41]   www.dailyrecord.co.uk, 14 March 2002.

[42]   Ibid., 15 March 2002; Scottish Catholic Media Office, Press Release, 14 March 2002.

giving a figure of 83,000. The BBC put the figure at 41,000.[43] When the Queen visited Stirling on 24 May thousands of people lined the streets in steady rain to see her arrive at the municipal chambers where she presented the letters patent.[44]

Paul Murphy, the Secretary of State for Wales who had been so disappointed with the results of the millennium competition, told the press that in his view Newport had all the qualities needed for a modern city.[45] The press was not so sure. The *Independent* called Newport 'unprepossessing' with 'undistinguished' architecture, and the *Daily Telegraph* noted that it had 'the highest violent crime rate in Britain'.[46] Newport's claims had not been considered strong enough in either 1977 or 1992, and it is not clear what had altered to push it up the pecking order. The Queen presented the letters patent on 13 June.[47]

Yet it was obvious to political commentators that behind the rhetoric lay real political considerations which were difficult to deny. The major concern raised in England was as to whether a town which did not have Labour MPs could, under the present government, ever be raised to city status. Simon Burns, Conservative MP for Chelmsford, claimed that the Labour government was determined to use city status to either curry favour in Labour marginals (such as Stirling), or to encourage the Labour faithful (as in Preston), and that this showed a pattern which had commenced at the millennium. In Wales the question was raised as to why Newport was successful, when the southern part of the country already had three cities (Cardiff, Swansea and St Davids) but the north could boast only Bangor. Martin Jones (Labour MP for Clywd South) was quoted as saying that Wrexham was the victim of a 'north-south divide',[48] and an unnamed but 'furious' member of the Welsh Assembly called on the Welsh Secretary to justify his decision.[49] St Asaph noted wearily that it had lost out 'in favour of yet another town in South Wales' but vowed to 'continue to use the title "City" and ... continue to lobby for the recognition it deserves'.[50]

The main concerns were expressed about Northern Ireland. The decision to create two cities in the province was seen as deliberately political, an appeasement to the sectarian divide within the community, given that Lisburn was a unionist stronghold and Newry was nationalist dominated. Little credence was given to John Reid's claim that he had recommended both towns

---

[43]   *Daily Telegraph*, 15 March 2002; *Independent*, 15 March 2002; www.bbc.co.uk/news/scotland, 15 March 2002.

[44]   http://www.travelscotland.co.uk, 30 March 2002; http://www.instirling.com/stirling/news.htm

[45]   The Wales Office, Press Release, 14 March 2002.

[46]   *Daily Telegraph*, 15 March 2002, *Independent*, 15 March 2002.

[47]   http://www.royal.gov.uk, 13 June 2002.

[48]   *Daily Telegraph*, 15 March 2002.

[49]   www.bbc.co.uk/news, 14 March 2002.

[50]   www.stasaph.co.uk, 25 May 2002.

because he had been unable to decide between the relative merits of the two.[51] Local politicians claimed that the decision was a case of expediency, and that Lisburn was little more than a suburb of Belfast. Samuel Gardiner, mayor of Craigavon, complained that 'we have a Secretary of State who is still making divisions while the people of Northern Ireland are trying to work together'. Newry republicans were uneasy about the town's success, given the link between city status and the Crown. Even Sinn Fein had opposed the bid on these grounds,[52] although Seamus Mallon, the local Sinn Fein MP was gracious enough to note that this was 'a great day for Newry'. Robert Coulter, a former mayor of Ballymena, was said to be 'mystified' by the decision, given that the north-east of the province was not rewarded.[53] The Queen presented the letters patent to the two successful candidates during her tour of Northern Ireland on 14 May 2002.[54]

Among the unsuccessful English towns there was much soul searching. East Anglia's four unsuccessful candidates were bitterly disappointed. Bob Russell, Liberal Democrat MP for Colchester, noted that 'it is clear this government's criteria when awarding city status is whether the town is represented in parliament by Labour'. Others were more circumspect. Chelmsford's chief executive limited himself to commenting that 'our hard work in partnership with the community in making the application has not paid off', and Ipswich's chief executive James Hehir commented 'we are all naturally disappointed that Ipswich's claims have been overlooked as we believe strongly that we would have been worthy winners'. Colchester's Conservative MP Bernard Jenkin thought the time had come to call a halt: 'the two bids have cost around £20,000. Local people are concerned about public services, such as litter in the street and the lack of affordable housing in Colchester.'[55] Reading's political leaders were said to be 'shocked and downcast' when they heard that Preston had won the competition, and Reading West MP Martin Salter was quoted as being 'extremely disappointed'.[56] In neighbouring Swindon the lack of unanimity over the campaign was reflected in a newspaper report that 'the decision was a bitter blow to a few people in the town', adding that the majority thought it 'an irrelevant time wasting and expensive distraction', especially as local residents had not been involved in the campaign.[57] There was disappointment in Blackburn and Bolton, although in both cases civic leaders said it would not distract them from their work of regenerating their towns.[58] Croydon put on a brave face by claiming the verdict was 'not a setback ... essentially this week's verdict changes nothing' because

51   *The Times*, 15 March 2002.
52   *Independent*, 15 March 2002.
53   www.bbc.co.uk/northernireland, 14 March 2002; *The Times*, 15 March 2002.
54   www.bbc.co.uk/northernireland, 15 May 2002.
55   www.eadt.co.uk, 15 March 2002.
56   *Reading Evening Post*, 14 March 2002.
57   www.swindonlink.com/news2002, 14 March 2002.
58   www.thisislancashire.co.uk, 14 March 2002.

the town was 'a city in all but name'.[59] Wirral said that its bid had captured the imagination of the public, and that it would be trying again.[60] Perhaps wisely, it resisted any temptation to suggest when it would be trying again.

Exeter was awarded a lord mayoralty, which the city's business leaders immediately hailed as an important boost to its image and status in the United Kingdom and beyond. Ian McGregor, the chairman of Exeter Chamber of Commerce and the Sowton Business Forum, said: 'I think it is recognition of the city's place. We are the regional capital and now it is officially recognized. I think we should shout about it and celebrate it.' The lord lieutenant of Devon, Eric Dancer, told the press he was 'absolutely delighted and it is a very fitting approval for one of the country's oldest cities'. Everyone took the view that the decision reflected a belief that Exeter was the regional capital of the south west. Councillor Granville Baldwin, the mayor of Exeter, became the first lord mayor, and the Queen presented the letters patent in Exeter on 1 May during her Golden Jubilee tour. Councillor Baldwin admitted to being 'very excited. It is a great honour for the city. I am very proud of Exeter.'[61] His successor in office, Councillor Val Dixon, became the first person to be installed as lord mayor of Exeter, although the city then began to have worries as to whether the change in status should be accompanied by a change in role.[62] Carlisle had been the runner up in 1992 when Exeter had not even entered the competition.

The Golden Jubilee competition was in many ways rather disappointing in the light of events in 2000. Doubtless this was because it came so hard on the heels of the previous competition, and its newsworthiness was lost in the wider publicity which surrounded the jubilee celebrations. The decisions were taken rather more efficiently and effectively than in 2000, with no major leaks, and by making the announcements on 14 March it was possible to ensure that the Queen could present the various letters patent during her Golden Jubilee tour. The Lord Chancellor's department kept to its word on population: Preston, with 135,000 people, was far from being the largest of the applicants, and was only 16,000 larger than it had been in 1953 when it was turned down for a coronation honour on the grounds of size. On the other hand, the Lord Chancellor's department was not quite so loyal to its earlier guidelines in respect to heritage and royal connections. In its application Preston made little mention of either its history or royal connections; indeed, it was far from clear that it could show any of the latter beyond a visit by the Queen in 1955.[63] In this sense perhaps the most obvious casualty of the competition was the idea of city status being a gift of the Crown, even though the Queen presented the letters patent in person. The political aspects of the campaign were demonstrated not only by the party loyalties of the successful candidates, but

59   Croydon Council, Press Release PR 439, 14 March 2002.
60   www.thisiswirral.co.uk, 14 March 2002.
61   *Exeter Express and Echo*, 15 March 2002.
62   *The Exeter Citizen*, Summer 2002; *Exeter Express and Echo*, 27 Sept. 2002.
63   *Daily Mail*, 15 March 2002.

also by the decision to create two cities in Northern Ireland. While a small town such as St Asaph could claim that the campaign had been 'hugely beneficial in terms of publicity',[64] and a front runner such as Reading could conceive of its campaign as part of a wider public relations exercise, it was still the case that many towns had applied three times since 1991, at considerable expense, without success and without any feedback on their applications. Milton Keynes could and does continue to claim it is a city, and other places could also declare that the decision made no difference to them. Yet the energy and effort which went into the competitions of 2000 and 2002 suggest that failure to gain city status continues to rankle in many town halls, and to upset public relations staff charged with the task of urban promotion.

[64]   www.stasaph.co.uk, 26 June 2002.

Conclusion

On 15 March 2002 the Press Association put out a report headed 'Ministers Accused of "Political Fix" over New Cities'. It quoted a claim made in the House of Commons by Simon Burns (Chelmsford West's Conservative MP) that the government is 'engaged in a cynical political fix' to give city status at the Queen's Golden Jubilee only to towns in Labour strongholds. The Ides of March truly had come for city status. Here was a title which had for centuries been closely associated with the Crown as the font of all constitutional honours, which the government stood accused of manipulating for party political purposes – or so the Conservatives were prepared to argue. The Roman *civitas* had become the political plaything of the new millennium, ostensibly linked to a royal event, but in reality turned into nothing more than a party political weapon. How had this happened and, just as importantly, why is city status in the form of a brief charter so important in today's world?

Cities have traditionally been places of importance in the United Kingdom. The link existed at the Conquest, and was recorded in the pages of Domesday Book. Subsequently, the link was formalized by Henry VIII: when he gave city status to towns he created sees of new Anglican dioceses, thus confirming the idea of a substantive connection. This was continued in the nineteenth century when, after 300 years of inactivity, the Anglican church began to create new dioceses. Now, however, the initiative lay with the Anglican church which, by nominating a particular place as the see of a diocese, effectively pre-judged the city status issue. Since the church chose its new cathedral towns largely on the basis of architectural considerations rather than 'importance', the connexion to city status soon started to seem inappropriate. Large towns such as Birmingham would apparently never be promoted, while market centres like St Albans qualified without reservation. It made no sense, and the decision in 1888 to break the link between city status and cathedrals had two effects: first, it meant that future cathedral towns had no automatic right to city status; and second, it allowed the monarch – in reality, the government – to grant the title to particular important towns whether they had cathedrals or not. This was a return to the Roman idea of *civitas*.

In the late Victorian years *civitas* was in effect conferred upon the great industrial towns of the age. City status represented the blessing of a state anxious to approve of efforts by rewarding civic achievement. After the First World War, with the Home Office anxiously attempting to apply unacknowledged criteria in order to keep a lid on the pan, the title increasingly came to be seen not so much as a reward for greatness attained as a means of distinguishing the real *civitas* from the would-be great towns. Hence the insistence that population alone was not a sufficient qualification, although the slow down in urban growth after 1911 made this particular rule almost impossible to operate. Regional standing, even international links, increasingly came to be viewed as important for qualifying a town to be promoted, while for their part towns sought city status to 'promote' their own position in the wider arena from which they felt excluded. Unfortunately, or perhaps simply as a result of the unwillingness of the Home Office to provide benchmarks against which a town could measure its standing, the whole business of promotion became a mess. By the 1960s it even proved possible for a determined MP to succeed in pressing the case for Southampton against all existing precedents, plus a few more or less invented for the term of the local government commission, in order to win an election.

Subsequently, city status has been linked to royal and national events, but in the context of the post-industrial town, the queue for honours has been lengthening since the early 1990s. With public relations officers and marketing agencies developing ever more sophisticated techniques to promote towns they have looked for any handle that would seem relevant, including city status. This new world of competition was exposed to full public glare – although the public proved relatively uninterested – in the context of the millennium and Golden Jubilee competitions, during which politicians became increasingly involved in this supposedly non-political contest, to the extent that final decisions in 2000 seem to have been taken in 10 Downing Street.

In 1992 it was just about possible to argue that politics was not a factor in city status. With a Conservative government in power, it was Sunderland – which returned two Labour MPs to Parliament – which was promoted. It was in no way a marginal which the Tories could hope to exploit for political purposes; indeed it has continued rock-solid Labour. The Home Office was so pleased with its earlier competition that it repeated the experiment for the millennium and Golden Jubilee, but the outcome of these contests was such that it was no longer easy to deny a link with electoral politics; indeed, it is undeniable that political considerations have undoubtedly caught up with royal occasions. Simon Burns' assessment of the electoral implications of these competitions was hard to refute, and the decision to create cities in each of the four provinces in 2002 represented a clear sop to devolutionary politics. When it was then decided to create two cities in Northern Ireland, for what looked to have been predominantly political reasons, any idea that neutrality could be observed in constitutional matters was difficult to maintain with much credence. Since the powers of granting city status have been removed from the Home Office but given to the Lord Chancellor's department, future grants will surely remain parts of government largesse: Jane Griffiths' abortive attempt in 1998 to introduce city status legislation is unlikely to be repeated with government support.

Patronage is in some respects the key to understanding city status since the 1880s. After Wakefield, the Home Office changed the rules to break the link with Anglicanism, but because it wanted to retain control over city status it refused to be drawn into laying down criteria for would-be cities to match up to, and instead sought to ensure that only suitable candidates were admitted to this very exclusive club. Salford epitomized the new way of doing things. On population grounds it had a claim (at least in comparison to several other towns), but the Home Office civil servants were appalled that a place they regarded as lacking any of the other qualifications for promotion should be let through on the whim of the minister. Their revenge, if that is the correct word, is to have consistently and persistently refused to countenance Salford's case for a lord mayoralty. Generally, Salford apart, political interests were kept at bay, and the purity of the process maintained, but the promotion of Southampton showed the ever-present danger that the process could be subverted for party political ends. There is a telling phrase in the Southampton file at one point in 1963 when Home Secretary Henry Brooke assured chief whip Martin Redmayne that 'the whole matter has been handled at ministerial level throughout'. The decision to press the Southampton case, to put it another way, was recognized to be a political decision taken by the politicians, who had effectively removed the final say from their (necessarily neutral) civil servants.

When politicians are involved there is bound to be an element of concern about election results or potential election results, and the implications of this were apparent in 1964. Until then politicians were content to accept that although they had a role to play in promoting applications, the process itself was above politics. When this principle collapsed, as it did in the midst of local government boundary reviews, it was hauled back by strengthening the link with royal events, which had operated intermittently since Queen Victoria's Diamond Jubilee. This more or less worked until the millennium, although the case for Swansea in 1969 was undoubtedly helped by Labour fears as to the strength of Welsh nationalism. The millennium competition was neither a royal nor a political event, and the autumn Cabinet battles of 2000 produced a Golden Jubilee competition in 2002 which in many respects was avowedly political. At least the award of a lord mayoralty to Exeter maintained the principle established with Chester in 1992 of ensuring that such grants went to long-established cities. Whether or not it is significant that Exeter is a Labour stronghold, and had not entered the previous competition in 1992, is open to discussion.

What of the future? There is no obvious occasion for further grants of city status, at least until either the Queen reaches her Diamond Jubilee in 2012 or, in the event of her death, there is a coronation and, if so, perhaps another investiture to provide an opportunity for promotion of a Welsh town. No other plans have been drawn up. Bob Spink (Conservative, Castle Point) asked in the House of Commons on 22 July 2002 how many new cities were expected to be created in the next three years. The reply was that 'the usual occasions for awards of city status to be made' are royal anniversaries, and that in the absence of any such occasions imminently 'Her Majesty has not yet expressed a wish to create any more new cities and no awards are foreseen in the near future'.[1] A bland answer was perhaps all Spink could anticipate, but it leaves

---

[1]   *Hansard*, vol. 389, part 183, 22 July 2002.

open a number of city status issues. If city status is simply a title conveying no real privileges, why not accept the advice proffered by Sunderland and promote all the places which believe they would benefit from promotion? As it stands, Whitehall seems obsessed with limiting the number of new creations, while willingly finding ways (primarily charter trustees) of protecting the interests of long-established but often tiny cities. It was almost surreal that Hereford's readmission to city status was announced on 7 September 2000, at a point when numerous larger and more important would-be cities were on tenterhooks awaiting the result of the millennium competition.

Also undecided are questions of usage. The position is most complicated in Scotland where, according to Dunfermline local councillor James Simpson, the Scotland Office has told him that 'any place with two houses and a garage could call itself a city'.[2] Dunfermline, Elgin and Perth are not, according to the Home Office's official list, recognized as cities, but because of the attitude taken by the Scotland Office all three continue to refer to themselves as such.[3] In England Milton Keynes, and in Wales St Asaph (which would seem to have just as strong a claim as St Davids) continue to refer to themselves on their websites as cities, with or without the appropriate letters patent, while the City of Rochester website has the blessing of the Home Office to use the title even though Medway Council has been told that the title has been irretrievably lost.[4] Councillor Simpson's advice to Rochester is that far from worrying about how to retrieve its lost city status 'all they had to do was change the signposts as you enter the town'. In this climate of cynicism, competitions for city status costing thousands of pounds of council tax payers' money, and involving numerous officials, seem increasingly redundant. Ken Purchase, MP for Wolverhampton North East, was naturally pleased at the success enjoyed by his constituency in the millennium competition, but he admitted that 'obfuscation is the watchword', and suggested that a more open and transparent system of qualifying for promotion would be in everyone's interests.[5] Yet, Milton Keynes and St Asaph apart, no other towns unsuccessful in 2002 have broken ranks: they all claim only borough or council status on their websites.

City status was for centuries connected directly to Anglican diocesan standing. It made sense in the nineteenth century to break the link when it no longer seemed relevant, but during the course of more than a century since Wakefield was the last diocesan town to receive automatic promotion, the business of creating cities has gradually fallen into disrepute even as the number of applicants has risen. As Newcastle's mayor appreciated when the

---

2   Councillor Simpson was quoted on the BBC's Radio Kent website, on 1 Aug. 2002.

3   http://visit.elginscotland.org, http://perthshire-scotland.co.uk/perth2, http://www.dunfermlineonline.net/forum.

4   Personal Communication from Alan Moss, 6 March 2004.

5   Personal Communication from Ken Purchase, 19 March 2001.

town was promoted in 1882, city status carried advantages: 'it will be a pleasure to every one of us to see the commerce of this city advancing at a very rapid rate'. More than a century later Colin Anderson, council leader of Newcastle's near neighbour Sunderland, encouraged entrants in the millennium and Golden Jubilee competitions on the grounds that city status had made a considerable difference on Wearside. In the 1980s the area had been devastated by the loss of coal mining and shipbuilding, but

> the city has boomed since 1992 and we have really made a big play on the fact that we are not a town any more. We advertise the city in America, explaining what the place is like and that the Queen decided it should be given higher status. Investment has rocketed since then and unemployment has nose-dived.... City status gave us recognition. Somebody from outside the area placed a big tick next to our name and that made our people more proud.[6]

It was this kind of sentiment which led in 2002 to forty-one towns putting a great deal of effort into their applications for a status which would, ostensibly, do no more than bring them a piece of paper (or technically parchment, in the form of letters patent), and allow them to change their letterheads and alter the road signs. The fact is that the intangible benefits are perceived to outweigh the tangible ones, simply because everyone in the United Kingdom and abroad accepts that a city is more important than a town, and that therefore promotion of the city is easier than of the town.

Consequently, the time has surely come to decide what the qualifications are, to abandon the patronizing system which gives considerable and unattributable influence to the Department of Constitutional Affairs, and to accept that if city status is a valuable asset we should be looking to make more cities, not to 'fend off' – a phrase much loved in the Home Office – applicants simply to maintain government rights of patronage over a title that, if it means anything in the twenty-first century, should surely be encouraged rather than denied. As Jane Griffiths, MP for Reading, has written, 'it is a nonsense that there are no criteria or that they are secret'.[7] In the new Labour world of open, transparent, government, surely the time has come to decide what a city actually is?

[6]   http://thisislancashire.co.uk, 'People power will fuel bid to be city', 25 Sept. 2001.
[7]   Personal Communication from Jane Griffiths, 6 Sept. 2002.

United Kingdom Cities in 2002

England

Bath
Birmingham
Brighton & Hove
Bradford
Bristol
Cambridge
Carlisle
Canterbury
Chester
Chichester
Coventry
Derby
Durham

Ely
Exeter
Gloucester
Hereford
Hull
Lancaster
Leeds
Leicester
Lichfield
Lincoln
Liverpool
London
Manchester

Newcastle-upon-Tyne
Norwich
Nottingham
Oxford
Peterborough
Plymouth
Portsmouth
Preston
Ripon
Rochester-on-Medway*
St Albans
Salford
Salisbury

Sheffield
Southampton
Stoke-on-Trent
Sunderland
Truro
Wakefield
Wells
Westminster
Winchester
Worcester
Wolverhampton
York

Scotland

Aberdeen
Dundee

Edinburgh
Glasgow

Inverness
Stirling

Wales

Bangor
Cardiff

Newport
St Davids

Swansea

Northern Ireland

Armagh
Belfast

Lisburn
Londonderry

Newry

Source: Home Office list, 1999, with subsequent additions.

* Rochester is included although technically it lost the status at local government reorganization in 1996. See Chapter 6.

Bibliography and references

Primary Sources

Bradford City Archives
  78D80/1-2, 4, BBC/1/1/27, BB/1/14, BBC 1/56/2

British Library
  Additional MSS, 44,346

Cambridgeshire Record Office
  R101/47

Canterbury Cathedral Archives
  CC/A/AA65

Cornwall Record Office
  B/TRU/99/3

Department of Constitution Affairs, London
  Honours Files

Derby Council House
  Andrews MSS

Hertfordshire Record Office
  Off Acc 1162/889, 632

Lambeth Palace Library
  Tait Papers 96

Lancaster City Museum
  LM73.50/1

Leicestershire Record Office
  CM1/23, 22DE57/97, 219, 310, DE 1973/20/194

Lincolnshire Archives Office
  BB, 2/A/30, AO BB, Boston Letter Books, 25, 1943-4

Manchester City Archives
  M116/6/3

National Archives of Scotland
   Dunfermline, Dundee, Inverness files

North Yorkshire Record Office, North Allerton
   DC/RIC II 1/1/6

Nottinghamshire Archive Office
   CA.TC 10/57/74/116, 131

Public Record Office, the National Archives
   HO 45; HO 286; HLG 43/1195; LCO 2/2013, 6/1391, 2325; CO 1032;
   PC 1/13

Public Record Office of Northern Ireland (PRONI)
   Belfast Corporation, Town Minute Books

Royal Archives, Windsor Castle
   RA PS/GV/PS22361; PS/GVI/PS 1909

Sheffield Archives
   CA 530(22); CA 666/5

Southampton City Archives
   SC/TC, box 220/1

Tyne and Wear Archives, Newcastle upon Tyne
   209/271; CB/SU/2/78

West Yorkshire Archives, Wakefield
   WW1/9

Printed Primary Sources

Acts of Parliament
   6&7 William IV c.77.
   28 & 29 Victoria c.cxxvi (1865).
   41 & 42 Victoria c. xxx 1878.
Arnold, Thomas *Principles of Church Reform* (4th edn. 1833).
Belfast and Ulster Directory for 1890 (Belfast, 1890).
Birmingham, City of: City Council Minutes 1888-9.
Blackner, John, *History of Nottingham* (1816).
Burnet, Gilbert, *The History of the Reformation of the Church of England* (1679).
Cambridge, City of: Council Minutes, 1951.

Church Quarterly Review (October, 1876).

Hansard.

Hull City Council Minutes (1897).

Jacob's *Law Dictionary* (10th edition, 1782).

Newcastle City Minutes 1881-2.

Nottingham, Borough of: Reports to Council, 1896-7.

Plymouth City Charters

Portsmouth Town Council Minutes (1911).

Rymer's *Foedera*, XIV.

Stevenson, W.H. ed. *Calendar of the Records of the Corporation of Gloucester* (Gloucester, 1893).

Swansea City Council Minutes (1969)

Welch, C.E. ed. *Plymouth City Charters, 1439-1935* (Plymouth, Corporation of Plymouth, 1962).

Wordsworth, Christopher, *On a Proposed Subdivision of Dioceses* (1860).

Yearbook of the Church of England (1883).

Newspapers

Armagh Observer

Belfast News-Letter

Birmingham Daily Post

Birmingham Weekly Mercury

Bradford Daily Telegraph

Bradford Observer

Cambridge Independent Press and Chronicle

Cork Evening Echo

Cork Weekly News

Royal Cornish Gazette

Coventry Evening Telegraph

Daily Chronicle

Daily Telegraph

Derby Evening Telegraph

Derby Mercury

Exeter Express and Echo

Fishguard County Echo

Guardian

The Herts Advertiser

The Daily Mail Hull Packet and East Yorkshire and Lincolnshire Courier

Lancaster Observer and Morecambe Chronicle

Leeds Mercury

Leicester Mercury

Liverpool Daily Post

Manchester Guardian

Morning Post,
Municipal Review
Newcastle Daily Journal
Northern Whig
Nottingham Daily Express
Nottingham Daily Guardian
Nottingham Journal
Nottingham Evening Post
Portsmouth Times
Ripon and Richmond Gazette
Salford City Reporter and Salford Chronicle
The Reporter for the Borough of Salford and Salford Chronicle
Sheffield Daily Telegraph
South Wales Echo
Staffordshire Sentinel
Sunderland Echo
Surrey Times and County Express
The Times
Wakefield Express
Western Mail
The Western Morning News and Mercury
Western Telegraph
Wolverhampton Express and Star

Secondary Sources

Ashworth, G.J. and Tunbridge, J.E., *The Tourist-Historic City* (Chichester, 1990).

Beckett, John (ed.), *A Centenary History of Nottingham* (Manchester, 1997).

—, 'City Status in the Nineteenth Century: Southwell and Nottingham, 1884-97', *Transactions of the Thoroton Society*, 103 (1999), 149-58.

—, 'City Status in the United Kingdom', *History Today*, 51 (11), (November 2001), 18-19.

—, 'The City of Boston [Lincolnshire]?', *Lincolnshire Past and Present*, 47 (2002), 18.

—, 'City Status for Swansea', *Welsh History Review*, 21/3 (June 2003), 129-47.

—, 'Edward Trollope, the Archbishop's Palace, and the Founding of the Diocese of Southwell in 1884', in Beckett, John (ed.), *Nottinghamshire Past* (Nottingham, 2003), 137-54.

Beckett, John and Windsor, David, 'Truro: Diocese and City', *Cornish Studies*, 11 (2003), 220-27.

Beresford, M.W., 'A Tale of Two Centenaries: Leeds City Charter and City Square, 1893', *University of Leeds Review*, 36 (1993/4), 331-46.

Best, Geoffrey, *Temporal Pillars* (1964).

Bianchini, F. and Parkinson, M. (eds.), *Cultural Policy and Urban Regeneration: the West European Experience* (Manchester, 1993).

Borsay, P., *The English Urban Renaissance: Culture and Society in the Provincial Town, 1660-1770* (Cambridge, 1989).

Boyle, M., 'Civic boosterism in the politics of local economic development – "institutional positions" and "strategic orientations" in the consumption of hallmark events', *Environment and Planning A*, 29 (1997), 1975-97.

Briggs, Asa, *History of Birmingham* II (Oxford, 1952).

—, *Victorian Cities* (1968 edn.).

Brown, H.M., '*A Century for Cornwall*': *the Diocese of Truro 1877-1977* (Truro, 1976).

—, *The Story of Truro Cathedral* (Redruth, 1977).

Burley, W.J., *City of Truro 1877-1977* (Truro, 1977).

Burns, A., *The Diocesan Revival in the Church of England, c.1800-1870* (Oxford, 1999).

Callaghan, J., *Time and Chance* (1987).

Cannadine, D., 'Civic Ritual and the Colchester Oyster Feast', *Past and Present*, 94 (1982), 107-30.

—, D, *The Decline and Fall of the British Aristocracy* (Yale, 1990).

Carter, H. and Lewis, C.R. (eds.), *An Urban Geography of England and Wales in the Nineteenth Century* (1990).

Chadwick, Owen, 'The Victorian Diocese of St Albans', in Robert Runcie (ed.), *Cathedral and City: St Albans Ancient and Modern* (1977), 71-82.

The Church of England Yearbook 1996 (112th edn., 1996).

Clark, P. (ed.), *The Cambridge Urban History of Britain, II, 1450-1840* (Cambridge, 2000).

Clay, P.S. and Richards, J.H., *City of Nottingham: Official Record of the Celebration of the Diamond Jubilee of Her Majesty Queen Victoria* (Nottingham, 1898).

Croll, A., *Civilizing the Urban: Popular Culture and Civic Space in Merthyr, c.1870-1914* (Cardiff, 2000).

Cunningham, Colin, *Victorian and Edwardian Town Halls* (1981).

Daunton, M. (ed.), *The Cambridge Urban History of Britain, III 1840-1950* (Cambridge, 2000).

Davies, John, *A History of Wales* (1993).

Dennis, R., *English Industrial Cities in the Nineteenth Century* (1984).

Devine, T.M. and Jackson, G. (eds.), *Glasgow, Volume I: Beginnings to 1830* (Manchester, 1995).

Dodds, G.L., *A History of Sunderland* (1995).

Dyos, H.J. and Wolff, S., *The Victorian City: Images and Reality* (2 vols 1977-8).

Eisenschitz, A. and Gough, J., *The Politics of Local Economic Policy: the Problems and Possibilities of Local Initiative* (Basingstoke, 1993).

Elton, Arthur, 'Becoming a City: Leeds, 1893', *Publications of the Thoresby Society*, 2nd ser., III (1993).

Escott, T.H.S., *Social Transformation of the Victorian Age* (1897).

Evans, N., 'Region, Nation and Globe: Roles, Representations and Urban Space in Cardiff, 1839-1928', in Fahrmeir, A. and Rembold, E. (eds.), *Representation of British Cities* (Berlin, 2003), 108-29.

Fahrmeir, A. and Rembold, E. (eds.), *Representation of British Cities* (Berlin, 2003).

Fothergill, S. and Gudgin, G., *Unequal Growth: Urban and Regional Employment Change in the UK* (1982).

Fraser, D., *Power and Authority in the Victorian City* (Oxford, 1979).

Fraser, Hamish, 'Municipal socialism and social policy', in R.J. Morris and Richard Rodger, *The Victorian City* (1993).

Fraser, W. Hamish and Maver, Irene (eds.), *Glasgow, Volume II: 1830-1912* (Manchester, 1996).

Fraser, S.M.F., 'Leicester and Smallpox: the Leicester Method', *Medical History*, 24 (1980), 315-32.

Freeman, E.A., 'City and Borough', *Macmillans Magazine*, 60 (1889).

Gold, J.R. and Ward, Stephen V. (eds.), *Place Promotion: the Use of Publicity and Marketing to Sell Towns and Regions* (Chichester, 1994).

Gunn, Simon, 'Ritual and Civic Culture in the English Industrial City, c.1835-1914', in R.J. Morris and Trainor, R.H. (eds.), *Urban Governance: Britain and Beyond since 1750* (Aldershot, 2000).

Hall, T., *Urban Geography* (2nd edn., 2001).

Hennock, E.P., *Fit and Proper Persons* (1973).

Hunt, William, *The English Church: from its foundation to the Norman Conquest (597-1066)* (New York, 1899).

Jagger, Peter J., 'The Formation of the Diocese of Newcastle', in W.S.F. Pickering, *A Social History of the Diocese of Newcastle, 1882-1982* (Stocksfield, 1981), 24-52.

Keith-Lucas, B. and Richards, P.G., *A History of Local Government in the Twentieth Century* (1978).

Larkham, P.J., *Conservation and the City* (1996).

Larkham P.J. and Lilley, K.D., 'Plans, Planners and City Images: Place Promotion and Civic Boosterism in British Reconstruction Planning', *Urban History*, 30 (2003), 183-205.

Law, C.M., *Urban Tourism: Attracting Visitors to Large Cities* (London, 1993).

Lipman, V.D., *Local Government Areas, 1834-1945* (Oxford, 1949).

Maitland, F.W., *Township and Borough* (Cambridge, 1898).

Meller, Helen, *Towns, Plans and Society in Modern Britain* (1997).

Morgan, K.O., *Callaghan: a Life* (Oxford, 1999).

Morris, R.J., 'Structure, Culture and Society in British Towns', in Daunton, M. (ed.), *The Cambridge Urban History of Britain, III 1840-1950* (Cambridge, 2000).

Morrish, P.S., 'County and Urban Dioceses', *Journal of Ecclesiastical History*, XXVI (1975), 279-300.

—, P.S., 'The Struggle to Create an Anglican Diocese of Birmingham', *Journal of Ecclesiastical History*, XXXI (1980), 59-88.

—, 'Leeds and the Dismemberment of the Diocese of Ripon', *Proceedings of the Thoresby Society*, 2nd ser., 4 (1994), 62-97.

—, 'The Creation of the Anglican Diocese of Liverpool', *Northern History*, XXXII (1996), 173-94.

—, 'Parish-Church Cathedrals, 1836-1921: Some Problems and their Solution', *Journal of Ecclesiastical History* 49 (1998), 438-9.

Mumford, Lewis, *The City in History* (1961).

Murie, Ian, 'Inter-war Town Hall Design', (B.Arch thesis, University of Nottingham 1980).

Nicolson, H., *King George V: His Life and Reign* (1952).

Ogle, H., *Royal Letters Addressed to Oxford* (1892).

Overton, John Henry and Wordsworth, Elizabeth, *Christopher Wordsworth, Bishop of Lincoln, 1807-1885* (1888).

Palliser, D.M. (ed.), *The Cambridge Urban History of Britain, I, 600-1450* (Cambridge, 2000).

Philo, C. and Kearns, K. (eds.), *Selling Places: the City as Cultural Capital, Past and Present* (Oxford, 1993).

Pirenne, Henri, *Medieval Cities* (1925).

Redford, A., *The History of Local Government in Manchester, vol II, Borough and City* (1940).

Rees, William, *Cardiff: A History of the City* (Cardiff, 1962).

Reynolds, S., *Ideas and Solidarities in the Medieval Laity* (Aldershot, 1995).

Ridding, Laura, *George Ridding: Schoolmaster and Bishop* (1908).

Scarisbrick, J.J., *Henry VIII* (1968).

Service, A., *Edwardian Architecture* (1977).

Stobart, J., 'Identity, Competition and Place Promotion in the Five Towns', *Urban History*, 30 (2003), 163-82.

Taylor, A.J., 'Victorian Leeds', in D. Fraser, (ed.), *A History of Modern Leeds* (Manchester, 1980).

Taylor, I., Evans, K. and Fraser, P., *A Tale of Two Cities: A Study in Manchester and Sheffield* (1996).

Theakston, K., *The Civil Service Since 1945* (Oxford, 1995).

Tittler, Robert, *Architecture and Power: The Town Hall and the English Urban Community, c.1500-1640* (Oxford, 1991).

Verhulst, Adriaan, *The Rise of Cities in North-West Europe* (Cambridge, 1999).

VCH *Cambridgeshire*, III (City of Cambridge) (1959).

VCH *Gloucestershire*, IV (1988).

VCH *Oxfordshire*, IV (1979).

VCH *Staffordshire*, VIII (1963).

VCH, *Warwickshire*, VIII (1969).

Ward, Stephen, *Selling Places: The Marketing and Promotion of Towns and Cities, 1850-2000* (1998).

The numerous websites have not been listed separately since many are ephemeral, but reference is given in the text.

Index